Henry Huth, Joseph Lilly, George Daniel

A Collection of 79 Black-Letter Ballads and Broadsides

Henry Huth, Joseph Lilly, George Daniel

A Collection of 79 Black-Letter Ballads and Broadsides

ISBN/EAN: 9783744695596

Printed in Europe, USA, Canada, Australia, Japan

Cover: Foto ©Thomas Meinert / pixelio.de

More available books at **www.hansebooks.com**

A

COLLECTION OF SEVENTY-NINE

Black = Letter Ballads and

Broadsides,

PRINTED IN THE REIGN OF QUEEN ELIZABETH,

BETWEEN THE YEARS 1559

AND 1597.

ACCOMPANIED WITH AN INTRODUCTION AND

ILLUSTRATIVE NOTES.

LONDON:

JOSEPH LILLY, 17 AND 18, NEW STREET,

AND 5a, GARRICK STREET, COVENT GARDEN.

1867.

PREFACE.

"I LOVE a ballad in print," are the words put by Shakefpeare into the mouth of one of his characters, and from his evident fondnefs for them we muft infer that he is conveying his own feelings through the mouth of the fpeaker. Another great writer of our own days, Sir Walter Scott, had an equal predilection for this fpecies of literature, and has availed himfelf of them in the fafcinating productions of his pen.

The Collections of Phillips, Percy, Evans, Ritfon, Pinkerton, Jamiefon and others, are a convincing proof of the favour with which they have been received by the public.

It may be confidently afferted that the prefent collection is not lefs interefting, and is certainly much more curious, than any that have preceded it, illuftrating as it does the language, opinions, manners, ufages, the feelings and paffing events of the greater part of the reign of Queen Elizabeth.

Thefe ballads, all of the higheft intereft and curiofity, hitherto unknown and prefumed to be unique, are reprinted without the flighteft alteration from the celebrated Collection formerly in the library of Mr. George Daniel, of Canonbury Square, at the fale of whofe library it was purchafed by the publifher for Henry Huth, Efq., to whom his beft thanks are due for his kindnefs and liberality in permitting the prefent publication.

The Introduction and Notes are fupplied by two gentlemen profoundly verfed in early Englifh literature.

Joseph Lilly.

INTRODUCTION.

I T is remarkable how foon after its invention the art of printing became an inftrument of popular amufement and inftruction,—an active agent in the development of the mind of the people. This character, however, arofe in fome degree out of the neceffity which called the art itfelf into exiftence, and which would naturally extend itfelf rapidly in proportion as it was indulged. The works which the firft experimenters in printing fought to produce were prints and fmall books intended for religious teaching, which had been previoufly drawn and written by the hand, and which were thus neceffarily fold at higher prices than the majority of the clafs for whom they were intended could afford to pay. The great want, therefore, to be fupplied, was the means of producing an indefinite number of copies of a book in the fame time and at the fame coft which had formerly been employed in producing one, and thus reducing the coft of each individual copy to a very fmall fraction of the whole. In moft countries, for fome length of time after the introduction of printing, the full advantage of the art was imperfectly appreciated, perhaps for want of an agency by which a great number of copies of a book could be rapidly and widely circulated ; and the firſt books were bulky, no doubt expenſive, and calculated for anything but what we ſhould call popular reading. It was in France that the art of printing firſt aſſumed a more popular character. There already exiſted in that country during the laſt twenty years of the fifteenth century, which muſt, therefore, have originated within very few years of the invention of the art, an extenſive literature of a very popular character, conſiſting chiefly of farces and drolleries in a dramatic ſhape, poetical tracts on various ſubjects, tales in verſe and proſe, ſatires on contemporary manners and ſentiments, almanacks and facetiæ, many of the later degenerating into ſimple coarſe obſcenities, ſo early did the objectionable uſes of printing accompany this more than uſeful art. All theſe appeared in the form of ſmall pamphlets, of a few, often not more than three or four, leaves each. They appear to have been ſold by itinerant bookſellers, who hawked them about the country, and were called technically *biſouarts*, and who ſtill preſerve in France another of their old names, that of *colporteurs*.

This literature ſpread from France into Italy and Spain at an early period. It was introduced into England at the beginning of the ſixteenth century, no doubt from France, becauſe nearly all the Engliſh ſamples of it we know are tranſlations or adaptations from the language of that country. Our literary antiquaries call them *chapbooks*. They were a claſs of books expoſed by their nature to ſpeedy deſtruction, but a ſufficient number of them are preſerved, though in unique or very rare copies, to leave no doubt that they were very numerous, even at an early period.

There was another clafs of literature, we may perhaps fay ftill more popular, which appears to have flourifhed moft in England, and which we ufually call *broadfides*. The Germans call them *fliegende Blätter*, and the French *feuilles volantes*, both comparatively modern terms, and the laft perhaps tranflated from the other. Thefe broadfides became far more popular in England than in other countries, and during a long period they have been the ufual mode of publifhing popular ballads. They were the form employed with us for royal proclamations and fimilar documents from a very early period in the hiftory of printing. Setting thefe afide, the broadfide appears to have been employed firft for printing papal indulgences, feveral examples of which, dating from 1513 to 1527, will be found in the collection of broadfides preferved in the library of the Society of Antiquaries, of which a valuable catalogue, compiled by Mr. Robert Lemon, has been recently publifhed. In this collection, which is, for the earlieft period, the richeft and moft valuable in exiftence, we find no example before the middle of the fixteenth century of what we now underftand more fpe-cially by the name of ballad,—of that peculiar clafs of popular literature which belonged to the long period of tranfition in our country between mediæval fociety and the fociety of our own times. We foon find the printed broadfide em-ployed in the various circumftances of temporary agitation, whether political or focial. In fact, the prefs was deftined very foon to become the

moſt powerful agent in all ſocial agitation. On
the 11th of June, 1540, late in the reign of
Henry VIII., Thomas Lord Cromwell, that
king's miniſter and counſellor in all his acts of
hoſtility againſt the Church of Rome, fell into
diſgrace, and was committed to the Tower. To
the papal party it was of courſe a ſubject of
exultation, which was diſplayed in a ballad, pub-
liſhed no doubt ſoon after his impriſonment, at
all events before his execution on the 28th of
July following. The Proteſtant party took up
the cauſe of their protector, and the reſult was a
rather bitter warfare carried on by means of
poetical broadſides, eight of which are contained
in the collection of the Society of Antiquaries.
The original ballad againſt Cromwell is printed
in Percy's " Reliques." Cromwell's aſſailants
offended the king, who was perſonally identified
with the acts for which they cenſured Cromwell,
and it is curious that the writer of moſt of the
ballads in defence of the fallen miniſter was
Thomas Smith, who deſcribes himſelf as " ſer-
vaunt to the kynges royall majeſtye ; and clerke
of the queenes graces counſell, though moſt un-
worthy." Three or four known broadſides of a
ſimilar character belong to the cloſing years of
the reign of Henry VIII. When we enter the
reign of his ſon and ſucceſſor, Edward VI., we
find rhyming broadſides of the ſame character.
Firſt in date of thoſe preſerved in the collection
of the Society of Antiquaries are two ballads for
and againſt Biſhop Gardner, printed probably in
1548, when that prelate was committed to the
Tower. We now fall in with the names of
printers who were ſubſequently remarkable for

the number of ballads which iſſued from their preſſes. John Waley, who lived in Foſter Lane in London, printed "A Newe Balade made by Nicholas Balthorp, which ſuffered in Calys the 20 daie of Marche, M.D.L.," which means March, 1551. In the year following, another of the great printers of ballad literature, Richard Lant, introduces us to a new controverſy in theſe poetical broadſides. It was provoked by a young man in literature who afterwards roſe to conſiderable celebrity, Thomas Churchyard, who wrote a ſhort metrical ſatire on contemporary ſociety entitled "Davy Dycars Dreame." Churchyard found an opponent in a man who ſigned himſelf T. Camel, and whoſe printer was Henry Sutton, another well-known printer of ballads, who dwelt in St. Paul's Churchyard. In the collection of the Society of Antiquaries there are no leſs than thirteen broadſide poems belonging to this controverſy, thoſe by Churchyard and his friends printed by Lant, and thoſe of his aſſailant by Sutton, and all within the year 1552. The number of broadſides of this deſcription belonging to Edward's reign is very ſmall, but among them is the earlieſt example of which we have any knowledge of the true ballad literature, though it is not written in what was afterwards conſidered as ſpecially ballad verſe. John Waley printed, as it is preſumed, in the reign of Edward VI., a broadſide in verſe, entitled, "A new mery balad of a maid that wold mary wyth a ſervyng man," the author of which informs us that his name was Thomas Emley. Two or three poetical broadſides printed in the reign of Queen Mary are all more or leſs of a political character.

One only, which is afcribed by conjecture to Mary's reign, and which is entitled, " A new ballet entituled howe to wyve well," is a veritable ballad, and is written in ballad metre. The author was Lewis Evans, and it was printed by Owen Rogers, " at the Spread Egle, betwyxte both the Saynct Bartholomews." It is probable, however, that it belongs to the beginning of the reign of Elizabeth, rather than to that of her predeceffor.

We are thus only able to point out one literary ballad printed in England previous to the middle of the fixteenth century, and that belonging to fo late a period as the reign of the Sixth Edward, and we can hardly imagine that this clafs of literature was very common at that period. We know that it was circulated in a very perifhable form, and we fhould not expect to find now any very large remains of it from fo early a date, yet ftill we ought to find more frequent allufions to it. We are unable to fay exactly when the literature of the ballad firft came into exiftence, but it appears to have become fuddenly very popular. It was a new branch of commerce, and which, as is often the cafe, created a new want. The Stationers' Company was incorporated in the year 1556, and its regifters begin in the following year. When we look at thefe, we are aftonifhed at the great number of ballads which, from the firft opening, were licenfed for publication, and yet, of them all, there is only a rare example here and there of which we have any trace beyond the entry of the title in thefe regifters. But it would feem that this multiplicity of broadfide ballads was then only beginning, for at the commencement of the Stationers' Regifters we find only one or two printers of ballads, and it is a year or two later when they become more numerous. During the firft ten years of the reign of Queen Elizabeth, the names of about forty printers from whofe preffes ballads were iffued appear in the regifters of the Stationers' Company, and other names of ballad-printers are met with which are not to be found in the regifters.

It is chiefly to this moft interefting period of the hiftory of our ballad literature that we owe the ballads printed in the prefent volume. The greater number of them range from 1560 to 1570, and only a very fmall number pafs the year 1572. They have no doubt been originally collected by fome man of pofition who lived at that time and took a lively intereft in all that was paffing around him, and were moft likely preferved among his family papers. Mr. Payne Collier, in 1840, edited for the Percy Society twenty-five ballads of the fame character, and belonging to the fame period, which are known to have belonged to the fame collection. Altogether they form, no doubt, the moft extraordinary and valuable collection of early Englifh ballads now known to exift. They are the more interefting, becaufe they have not been collected by one whofe tafte ran upon any particular clafs of fuch productions, but they prefent a variety which embraces the whole field of broadfide literature; and it will be worth our while, in our prefent confideration of them, to treat them in detail in this point of view. In the firft place, they naturally feparate into two great divifions, thofe of a purely literary character, and thofe which

are more or lefs political or relate to contemporary events or feelings.

To the former of thefe divifions belong fentimental and love poetry, romances and ftories,
and facetiæ. A part of the latter clafs was taken
or imitated from the French popular literature ;
they were the fabliaux of an earlier period.
Many of them were fatires upon the failings of
the other fex, which then formed a favourite
theme. Of thefe we have examples in the prefent volume, in the ballad of " The Pinnyng of
the Bafket," (p. 105), in " A mery Balade, how
a wife entreated her hufband to haue her owne
wyll," (p. 129), and in " A very proper dittie, to
the tune of Lightie Loue," (p. 113). Some are
loofe and indelicate ftories, fuch as that of the
Brewer and Cooper, (p. 60), a true reprefen-
tative of the ancient fabliaux, which appears to
have been very popular, as two or three editions
of it have been traced. Others, again, are more
or lefs openly obfcene, of which there is one example only in the prefent volume, the ballad of
" Mother Watkins Ale," (p. 251). This, alfo,
appears to have been extremely popular, for it is
not unfrequently alluded to in the lighter literature of the Elizabethan age, though no traces of
its exiftence had been difcovered until the prefent
collection came to light. Perhaps we may confider as belonging to this clafs the dittie "Shewing what vnkindnes befell by a kiffe," (p. 214),
and the verfes entitled, " Adewe, Sweete Harte,"
(p. 222). This defcription of literature appears
to have been fufficiently abundant in Elizabeth's,
as it was indeed in the ages which followed:
Among the " Old Ballads" is one by a preacher

named Thomas Brice, who is known as the author of some other publications, and died before 1570, " Againſt filthy writing, and ſuch like delighting." This ballad appears to have been directed againſt two of the licentious writers of the day, who had written ballads in defence of their productions, and it commences with the lines,—

> What meane the rimes that run thus large in every ſhop
>   to ſell,
> With wanton ſound and filthie ſenſe?   Me thinke it grees
>   not well.
> We are not Ethnickes, we forſoth at leaſt profeſſe not ſo;
> Why range we then to Ethnickes trade?   Come back,
>   where will ye go?
> Tel me, is Chriſt or Cupide lord?   Doth God or Venus
>   reigne?

In the preſent collection, we have another ſatirical ballad on the contemporary literature, or at leaſt on the poets, which has for its title the following rather clumſy lines (p. 205),—

> To ſuch as write in metres, I write
>   Of ſmall matters an exhortation,
> By readyng of which men may delite
>   In ſuch as be worthy commendation.
> My verſe alſo it hath relation
>   To ſuch as print, that they doe it well,—
>   The better they ſhall their metres ſell.

The writer of this ballad, who ſeems to think that it was the duty of the printer to look to the goodneſs of what came from his preſs, profeſſes to imitate the example of Horace, who proteſts againſt the inferior poets among the Romans, ſuch as Lucilius for example, and there were plenty of ſuch wretched rhymeſters in the days of Elizabeth,—

> Wherfore let vs not open a gate,
>   Eyther the printer, or they which write
> To fuch as they be, knowyng their ftate.

And he fingles out efpecially for his criticifm the writers on love,—

> Your balades of loue, not worth a beane,
>   A number there be, although not all;
> Some be pithie, fome weake, fome leane,
>   Some doe runne as round as a ball;—
>   Some verfes haue fuch a pleafant fall,
> That pleafure it is for any man,
>   Whether his knowledge be great or fmall,
> So that of a verfe fome fkyll he can.

Of thefe love ballads there is no great number in our collection, and many of them to which we can give a date, as well, indeed, as of all the purely literary divifion, belong to rather a later period than moft of the hiftorical and political ballads, fo that they were perhaps collected by another and younger member of the family, who afterwards mixed them with the others. To this clafs of amorous and fentimental ballads belong, "A Newe Ballade of a Louer extollinge his Ladye," (p. 24), a fheet of poems of this defcription preferved in manufcript (pp. 190-194), and "A prettie newe Ballad, intytuled,—

> "The Crowe fits vpon the wall,
>   Pleafe one and pleafe all."

The writer of the latter, who is unufually large and liberal in his fentiments, recommends his reader to pay his homage to the whole fex and not to confine himfelf to an individual.

There are three ballads in this collection which belong to the clafs of novels and romance. One has for its fubject the well-known ftory of

Patient Griſſel (Grifeldis), which has been a favourite with Engliſh poets ſince the days of Chaucer, and appears here in its earlieſt ballad form, under the title of "A moſt pleaſant Ballad of Patient Griſſell," (p. 17). The other two are, the ballad of "The Marchants Daughter of Briſtow," (p. 66), which was no leſs popular than Patient Griſſel, and that of "The Faire Widow of Watling-Street, and her 3 daughters," both of them in two parts. Theſe are both the earlieſt editions known, belonging to a period approaching near to the cloſe of the ſixteenth century, when this claſs of ballad hiſtories was coming into great popularity.

The political and hiſtorical ballads in the preſent collection poſſeſs an extraordinary intereſt, for they belong to one of the moſt momentous periods of our national hiſtory. Little more than a generation had paſſed ſince the overthrow of feudaliſm. Henry VIII. had broken the power of the papacy in England, and his ſon, Edward VI., ſeemed to have eſtabliſhed Proteſtantiſm; but, on the death of the latter, the older religion, in the perſon of Mary, reſumed its ſway during more than five years, under its leaſt pleaſing attribute, that of perſecution. Mary alſo was juſt dead, and her ſiſter Elizabeth had ſtepped into her place with a cautiouſneſs which, although the proteſtant party looked upon her as their friend, almoſt left room to doubt which party ſhe intended to eſpouſe. The cloud, which was already burſting over Weſtern Europe, added greatly to people's doubts and fears, and they were filled with anxiety, not only to be made acquainted with the prefent, but to get even a flight glimpfe into the probabilities of the future. The publication of news, whether true or falfe,—and the latter was, perhaps, the moft faleable, becaufe it was the moft extraordinary,—became thus a profitable trade. For thefe reafons the political ballads and broadfide literature are now very important evidence not only of the popular feelings of the time, but of the means employed to influence thofe feelings. In the fuperftition of thofe days, every unknown or unufual natural phenomenon was looked upon as a warning from heaven of focial and political difafter, and was, therefore, watched with the moft intenfe intereft.

Among thefe figns, none created greater apprehenfion than monftrous births, which we find continually recorded even by the hiftorians and more ferious writers of the day. The year 1562, the fourth of Elizabeth's reign, is recorded by the Englifh chroniclers, fuch as Hollinfhed and Stowe, as efpecially fertile in monfters. The prefent collection contains nearly a dozen broadfides defcriptive of thefe prodigies, generally accompanied with a picture. No lefs than five of them belong to the year juft mentioned, 1562. The firft (p. 27) is a "true reporte" of a child born at Great Horkefley, near Colchefter, having neither legs nor arms; the defcription of the child is prefaced by verfes fetting forth the myfterious defign of thefe monfters. The next (p. 45) is an account of a monftrous pig with a dolphin's head, born at Charing Crofs a few days fubfequently, fimilarly accompanied with verfes moralizing upon the phenomenon. Another pig, farrowed at Hampftead, near London, in the October of that year, is described in a third broadside, "imprinted" by Alexander Lacy (p. 112). A fourth broadside (p. 186), also belonging to the year 1562, as we learn from the entry in the Stationers' Registers, describes another monstrous pig, and is accompanied with a poetical "exhortacion or warnynge to all men, for amendment of lyfe." And another of the same year (p. 201), entirely in ballad verse, represents a monstrous child born at Chichester. Another monstrous child, born at Freshwater, in the Isle of Wight, in 1564, is described and explained in a moral or religious light, in a ballad by John Barker (p. 63). The year 1566 produced twins joined together at the stomach, described in a ballad by one John Mellys of Norwich (p. 217), and a child with ruffs round the neck, born at Mitcham in Surrey (p. 243). In 1568, we have a monstrous child born at Maidstone, in Kent (p. 194), having "first the mouth slitted on the right side, like a libarde's (leopard's) mouth, terrible to beholde," which the author of the ballad explains as a rebuke to the kingdom for its wickedness, and as a sign of God's displeasure,—

> This monstrous shape to thee, England,
> Playn shewes thy monstrous vice,
> If thou ech part wylt vnderstand,
> And take thereby aduice.

And finally we have a description of a "marueilous straunge fishe," caught between Calais and Dover, in June, 1569 (p. 145).

People lived in that condition which naturally arises out of the breaking up of one great social system, and the transition towards another, the character of which is as yet unknown. Men were confcious that the whole frame of fociety was disjointed and corrupt, and looked forward anxioufly to the coming reform. Latterly the revolution had taken a ftrongly religious character, and the feeling of difcontent partook alfo of a religious fhade, and one clafs of the popular ballads, of which there are fome good examples in the prefent collection, formed a powerful agent in fowing and cherifhing the feeds of that puritanifm which was to exercife fo great an influence on the deftinies of our country in the next generation. None of thefe ballads, indeed, are more curious than thofe which attempt to picture the vices and corruptions of the times during the earlier, and, perhaps we may fay, lefs fettled part of the reign of Queen Elizabeth. One of the earlieft of thefe, belonging to the year 1561 is entitled, "A balade declaryng how neybourhed (neighbourlinefs), loue, and trew dealyng, is gone" (p. 134). The author, John Barker, complains of the illcondition of the world generally,—

> How ftraunge it is to men of age,
>   The which they fe before their face,
> This world to be in fuch outrage,
>   It was neuer fene in fo bad cafe.
> Neibourhed nor loue is none,
> Trew dealyng now is fled and gone.

These two lines form the burthen of the fong, if one can call it a fong. John Barker complains that flattery and deceit were then the means of fuccefs; that wickednefs prevailed everywhere; that covetoufnefs was the great principle of men's actions; that the landlords acted unjuftly towards their tenants; and that every man was the enemy of his neighbour. Another ballad, publifhed in the fame year, bearing the name of a better known writer, John Heywood, is entitled, "A Ballad againft Slander and Detraction" (p. 9). Another ballad of this clafs, which appears from the Stationers' Regifters to have been publifhed in 1566 or 1567, is directed againft the crime of bribery, and, the text being taken from Scripture, is entitled, "A proper new Balad of the bryber Gehefie" (p. 42). Another ballad, printed in November, 1566 (p. 101), is directed againft the licentioufnefs of the age; as is alfo one publifhed a few years later, under the title, "Of the horrible and wofull deftruction of Sodome and Gomorra" (p. 125). With thefe may be claffed "A new Ballad againft Unthrifts" (p. 153), which is aimed againft the then numerous clafs of fpendthrifts and rioters, who, the writer tells us, fpent their money in the tavern, or threw it away at dice, until they fell into ftill worfe practices, and finifhed with Tyburn and the gallows,—

> Then fome at Newgate doo take fhip,
> Sailing ful faft vp Holborne Hil;
> And at Tiborn their anckers piche,
> Ful fore indeed againft their wil. .

Another ballad, "The xxv. orders of Fooles" (p. 88), which, according to the Stationers' Regifters, belongs to the year 1569, is more playfully fatirical. It had long been the fafhion to reprefent mankind, as then exifting, in the garb of fools, and claffifying thefe according to their various weakneffes and peculiarities. The Ship of Fools, of Sebaftian Brandt, is well known, and it was popular here in an Englifh verfion as well as in its original form in Germany; and our own Sir Thomas More wrote in praife of Folly. The writer of the ballad divides the fools of this world into twenty-five orders. Some fools, according to his view, look upon wifdom with difdain; fome preach to others virtues which they do not practife themfelves; others fpend all in their youth, and make no provifion for their old age; others again delight in difcord and ftrife; and fo on to the end of the lift. One of the moft curious broadfides in the whole collection is the ballad which pictures the various orders in the ftate, arranged under the heads of the prieft, the king, the harlot, the lawyer, and the clown, each boafting of the power he holds over the others (p. 98). The prieft alleges that he prays for the other four; the king that he defends and protects them; the harlot, introduced in a manner which would feem to fhow a low ftate of morals at that period, fays, " I vanquefh you fower;" the lawyer, " I helpe yov iiij. to yovr right;" the clown, " I feede yov fower;" and death comes in and proclaims his errand, " I kill yov all." This fubject is found, treated a little differently, in the French popular literature of that age, from which the idea was taken by the Englifh ballad-writer, who has, no doubt, modified it a little to make it accord with the difference of Englifh fentiments. It is to be remarked that we have here alfo (p. 173) one of the moft curious and earlieft of the Englifh reprefentations of that well-known allegory, the Dance of Death, a very popular fubject during Elizabeth's reign.

The earlieſt dated ballad in this collection is of the year 1559 (the firſt of the reign of Queen Elizabeth), and is entitled, "The Wonders of England" (p. 94). It is a brief retroſpective review of Engliſh hiſtory ſince 1553, when God, as a puniſhment for the ſins with which the land abounded, took away from us the good King Edward. The people had ſince ſuffered from mental darkneſs and perſecution, until God relented and ſent us Elizabeth, and,—

> Straightway the people out dyd cry—
> Prayſed be God, and God ſaue thee,
> Quene of England!

It may be remarked that this ballad is one of the poetical productions of the printer from whoſe preſs it iſſued, John Awdeley, who ſeems to have ſought frequently to exhibit his talents as a ballad-writer. There is another ballad of a ſatirical character, which belongs apparently to the earlier part of the reign of Queen Elizabeth, which deſcribes the defects of contemporary ſociety by their contraries. It has for title, "Other (i. e. *either*) thus it is, or thus it ſhoulde bee" (p. 247), and ends with a prayer that Elizabeth might rule her ſubjects well, and that they might prove true in their obedience. We have a ballad breathing a ſimilar vein of ſatire (p. 208), which unfortunately bears no direct evidence of date, though it is believed to be very early. This ballad declares that the goſpel was then read in its original purity throughout Chriſtendom; that all people led their lives "after Chriſte's rule;" all neighbours lived lovingly together as though they were kinsfolk; the earth had become like heaven, and the people

in it like angels ; the prifons were empty; and
all things went on fo flourifhingly, that it was
believed that doomfday was near at hand ; but
the writer adds, rather waggifhly, "O wounders
good tydynges, yf al fayinges be tru !"

The religious and moral poems are hardly fo
numerous in the following collection as might be
expected.   A poet named Chriftopher Wilfon is
the author of a ballad written in 1566 (p. 166),
in which an acroftic, containing his name, runs
through the initial letters of the lines from beginning to end.   In another ballad, printed in
1568 (p. 138), the well-known writer Elderton has
expounded the fayings of the ancient philofo-
phers in verfe.   A third poet, John Symon, has
given a metrical commemoration of Scripture
worthies, under the title of "A pleafant pofie,
or fweete nofegay of fragrant fmellyng flowers,
gathered in the garden of heauenly pleafure"
(p. 5).   This belongs to the year 1572.   The
ballads againft popery are more numerous, and
every incident which could be made the ground
of an attack upon the Romifh party appears to
have been feized upon with eagernefs.   We have
here "A Balade of a Preift that lofte his nofe"
(p. 141), to which the writer adds, as a rhyme,
"for fayinge of maffe, as I fuppofe."   It is a
very fatirical defcription of the mifhap of a
prieft, ftated to have been the vicar of Lee,
who had been waylaid, it would appear, on his
return from mafs, robbed, and his nofe cut off.
A broadfide, probably of a later date than the.
laft, gives an engraving, accompanied with
verfes, of two friars of the order of Capuchins
(p. 156).   The pope's bull, hung againft the

Bifhop of London's palace-gate, in 1571, is the fubject of two ballads in this collection (pp. 33, 224). We have alfo a rather earneft proteft againft the mafs, in a ballad printed in 1566 (p. 171); and a rather good ballad, belonging apparently to a rather early period of the queen's reign, and publifhed under the fimple title of a "A newe Ballade" (p. 30), was intended to warn her againft the hoftile defigns of the fpiritualty, meaning thereby the Romifh party, by the examples of fuch of her predeceffors as had fallen victims to the unfcrupulous ambition of the clergy. The ftrong feelings of the proteftant party in England at this time led to a fpirit of exaggerated loyalty and devotion which not unfrequently difplays itfelf in thefe ballads. A curious ballad by Elderton, entitled, "Prepare ye to the Plowe" (p. 174), and to be fung to the rather fingular tune of "Pepper is blacke," reprefents the queen as holding the plough, and exhorts her fubjects to be always ready to help her,—

The queene holdes the plowe, to continew good feede;
Truftie fubiectes, be readie to helpe, if fhe neede.

This loyalty, which led Elizabeth's fubjects to employ the extreme of flattery, is fhown in a ballad by a not unknown writer of that age, named Bernard Garter, entitled, "A ftrife betwene Appelles and Pigmalion" (p. 151), who feigns a conteft between thofe two artifts for fuperiority, the refult of which was a ftatue, by the latter, of a woman of fuch furpaffing beauty as had never been feen before, and dame nature took it away, gave life to it, and reftored it to earth in the perfon of Queen Elizabeth. The pious Englifhman of that day imagined, in his devotion, that no beauty could furpafs that of the great champion of Proteftantifm.

Thefe earlier years of the reign of Elizabeth formed, indeed, a period of anxiety and uncertainty among all claffes. Elizabeth and her minifters knew that the catholic party, not only at home but on the Continent, were confpiring againft her, and that not only her religion, but her throne, and even her life, were in danger. People's doubts were not leffened by occafional difplays of exultation on the part of fome of the lefs difcreet of the catholic party, who could not conceal their hopes of fuccefs; and by the knowledge that a very great part of the population of the country was ready to join to whichever fortune fhould feem to promife fuccefs. People were, by no means, affured of the fate of Proteftantifm, until the rebellion of the Dukes of Northumberland and Weftmoreland, in the autumn of 1569, which difplayed the real weaknefs of the other party. The alarm which this rifing created, not only among the people, but in Elizabeth and her court, was very great; but it did not laft long: before the end of the year the rebellion was crufhed, and the two earls were fugitives. This fuccefs evidently drew forth a great number of broadfide ballads, the titles of many of which are entered in the Stationers' Regifters, and a few of which are preferved. No lefs than five of thefe are in the prefent collection, the earlieft of which is a metrical prayer for divine protection againft the rebels (p. 121); the others all relate to the period which followed the fuppreffion of the rebellion. The firft ballad in the prefent volume commemorates the execution of a prieft named Plumtree, who had taken poffeffion of the church of St. Nicholas, in Durham, and of the flight of the leaders of the rebellion. Another, entitled "The Plagues of Northomberland" (p. 56), is alfo fomething like a fong of triumph over the defeat of the rebels; and a third (p. 231), having for its title the diftich,—

Joyfull Newes for true Subiectes to God and the Crowne,
The Rebelles are cooled, their Bragges be put downe,—

is written in the fame fpirit, but in a more fcornful tone. Laftly, we have "A Newe Ballade, intituled, Agaynft Rebellious and falfe rumours" (p. 239), bearing the date 1570, and publifhed no doubt early in the year. Before thefe curious pieces were made known by the difcovery of the collection now printed, only two or three contemporary ballads on the northern rebellion of 1569 were known to exift. Two, publifhed by Bifhop Percy in his Reliques, from his folio manufcript, are border ballads, compofed by minftrels who feem to have fympathized more or lefs with the two Earls and their followers, and they are of an entirely different character from thofe here printed. Among the "Old Ballads" printed by Mr. Payne Collier, which had originally formed part of the prefent collection, there is alfo a ballad on this rebellion, written by Thomas Prefton, and entitled,—

A lamentation from Rome how the Pope doth bewayle,
That rebelles in England can not prevayle.

And there is one in the collection of broadfides

in the library of the Society of Antiquaries, alfo
exulting over the defeat of the rebellion, and entitled, " Newes from Northumberland." Thefe
are, we believe, all the popular ballads now
known to exift relating to this important event;
and they are very curious as illuftrating the popular feelings which it excited.

The other hiftorical ballads in this collection
are chiefly of a lefs degree of importance, becaufe
they relate generally to events of no great intereft at the prefent day, with two efpecial excep-
tions. Thefe are two Scottifh ballads, both by
Sempill, a known Scottifh poet. The fubject of
the firft is the maffacre of the Proteftants in Paris
on St. Bartholomew's Day, 1572, and it is entitled, "Ane new Ballet fet out be ane fugitiue
Scottifman that fled out of Paris at this lait murther" (p. 37). The Scots, who were of courfe
by their form of religion more clofely allied
in feeling with the French Proteftants than
the Englifh, were greatly affected by thefe fan-
guinary perfecutions in France, and, under the
terror they created, the Scottifh government then
in power fought to draw ftill clofer its relations
with Queen Elizabeth. Such is the fpirit of the
prefent ballad. It preffes upon Elizabeth the
prudence of united and vigorous meafures of
defence,—

Now, wyfe Quene Elizabeth, luik to yourfelf,
  Difpite them, and wryte thame ane bill of defyance,
The Papiftis and Spanjards hes partit jour pelf,
  As newly and trewly was tald me thir tythance.
Beleue thay to land heir, and get vs for nocht;
Will je do as we do, it fal be deir bocht.

The other of thefe Scottifh ballads (p. 49) is entitled, " Ane Complaint vpon Fortoun," and was publifhed early in 1581, on Morton's fall, but before he was brought to trial and executed.

Of the Englifh hiftorical ballads, or broadfides, which remain to be mentioned, one (p. 236) is a poem by " Ber. Gar." (Bernard Garter), entitled " A dittie in the worthie praife of an high and mightie Prince," who appears from the context to have been Thomas Howard Earl of Norfolk, but the occafion on which it was written is not explained. There are three ballads on the deaths of eminent perfons, who were, firft, " my Ladie Marques" (p. 14), (perhaps the Marchionefs of Southampton), which was entered in the Sta- tioners' Regifters in 1569; fecond, " the Ladie Maioreffe" of London (p. 178); the third, " the Earl of Huntingdon," which bears the date of 1596. A ballad named " Saparton's Alarum" (p. 118), bears the name of John Saparton as its author, and appears, from another ballad on the fame individual entered in the Stationers' books, to belong to about the year 1569; its meaning is not very clear. We have " A famous dittie" on a fomewhat memorable vifit of the queen to the city on the 12th of November, 1584 (p. 182); and " A mournfull dittie" (p. 197) on a fudden mortality which took place among the judges and others at the Lincoln Affizes of 1590. There are two ballads on another accident which happened in the provinces, the burning of the town of Beccles, in Suffolk, in 1586 (pp. 78, 81); they were both printed by Robert Ro- binfon in London for Nicholas Colman of Nor- wich, fo that even at this time ballad-printers appear to have been only to be found in London.

Laſtly, we have a ballad entitled "Franklin's Farewell to the World" (p. 85). James Franklin was the apothecary who ſupplied the poiſons uſed in the Overbury murders, and was condemned and executed on the 9th of December, 1615. Another ballad, on the ſame ſubject, is preſerved in the collection of the Society of Antiquaries. This ballad muſt have been added to our collection long after the original collector had departed from the ſcene of his labours.

With the maſs of ballad literature here revealed to us, we may naturally be curious to learn ſomething of the ballad-writers, but we can collect little beyond a few obſcure names, and others which are merely hinted to us by their initials. Among them, however, are the names of one or two writers who are better known in the ſmaller literature of the Elizabethan period. Such is Thomas Churchyard, whoſe name is found attached to one of the ballads ſeparated from the preſent collection, and printed by Mr. Collier. Such alſo are William Elderton, and Thomas Deloney. The firſt of theſe was celebrated for his tippling propenſities, as well as for his rhymes, and is ſaid to have drunk himſelf to death, ſome time before 1592. His ſpecial characteriſtic is commemorated in a contemporary epitaph, recorded by Camden, and tranſlated by Oldys, as follows :—

Hic ſitus eſt ſitiens, atque ebrius Eldertonus,
   Quid dico hic ſitus eſt ? hic potius ſitis eſt.

   Dead drunk here Elderton doth lie ;
   Dead as he is, he ſtill is dry ;
   So of him it may well be ſaid,
   Here he, but not his thirſt, is laid.

He was the author of three ballads in the prefent volume (pp. 16, 140, 178), and of two of
thofe edited by Mr. Collier. One of the latter
was printed on the 22nd of March, 1559, which,
in our reckoning, means 1560. Deloney was a
profeffed ballad-writer on all paffing events.
His only production in the prefent volume is
one of the poems on the burning of the town of
Beccles, in 1586 (p. 84); one in Mr. Collier's
volume, printed in the fame year, has for its fubject the execution of the confpirators in the celebrated Babington Confpiracy. Deloney ufually
figns only with his initials, T. D. John Heywood, who alfo is a well-known writer of the
middle of the fixteenth century, was a firm
Roman Catholic, and went into voluntary exile
on the death of Mary, dying at Mechlin, in Bra-
bant, in 1565. If he be the author of the
" Ballad againft Slander and Detraction" (p. 9),
to which the name of Haywood is attached, it
muft have been intended as a proteft againft per-
fonal abufe to which fome of the Catholics,
perhaps himfelf, had been fubjected. Richard
Tarlton, another well-known minor Elizabethan
writer, is the author of one of the moft fprightly
ballads in the prefent collection (p. 259); as well
as of one in Mr. Collier's collection, to which
his name is given in full. John Awdeley, the
printer, appears not unfrequently to have written
his own ballads. Two of them occur in our prefent volume, the firft (p. 97) printed in 1559,
the fecond (p. 123) in 1569; and there is a third
in Collier's volume, fuppofed to belong to about
the fame date as the former. A few alfo of the
other names of authors attached to thefe ballads

are known by fome other contributions to the literature of the age. John Barker, who wrote three of our ballads (pp. 59, 66, and 138), one of them printed in 1564, and another entered in the Stationers' Regifters in 1569-70, is alfo known as the author of a ballad " Of the horrible and wofull deftruction of Jerufalem," printed by Colwell about 1568. The initials "T. Gr." attached to one of our ballads (p. 94) probably ftand for Thomas Greepe, who was the author of a poem on the exploits of Sir Francis Drake, printed in 1587. Leonard Gibfon, whofe name occurs here as the writer of a ballad on the lightnefs of the ladies (p. 117), was the author of a little book called " The Tower of Truftinefle," in verfe and profe, printed in 1555; and there is a fong called "L. Gibfon's Tantara" in the " Handefull of Pleafant Delites," 1584. The individual defigned under the abbreviated form Ber. Gar. (pp. 153, 239), and in one cafe merely by the initials, B. G. (p. 150), was Bernard Garter, who wrote the " Tragical Hiftory of Two Englifh Lovers," printed in a fmall volume in 1565, and " A New Yeares Gifte," printed in quarto in 1579, and fome of whofe verfes are prefixed to " Pafquine in a Traunce," 1584. John Philip, whofe name is attached to one of our ballads printed in 1570 (p. 182), and to whom probably belong the initials I. P. attached to the lines added to the account of the Wonderful Swine (p. 190), is known by feveral poetical works ftill extant, of which perhaps the moft curious is " A rare and ftrange hiftoricall Novell of Cleomenes and Sophonifba," printed in 1577. John Mellys, of Norwich, the author of a ballad on two monftrous children, printed in 1566 (p. 220), was perhaps the fame perfon, for he bears the fame name, as the compiler of " A briefe Inftruction how to keepe Bookes of Accompts," which bears the date 1588. The other names and initials found in our collection of ballads appear to be entirely unknown. When we compare them with the few other ballads of this period now known, which prefent us with many new names, we cannot but be furprifed at the great number of individuals who muft have found employment in writing ballads at this very early period in the hiftory of ballad literature.

CONTENTS.

ANCIENT BALLADS AND

BROADSIDES.

A Ballad intituled, A newe Well a daye,
As playne, maiſter papiſt, as Donſtable waye.

Well a daye, well a daye, well a daye, woe is mee,
Syr Thomas Plomtrie is hanged on a tree.

AMONGE manye newes reported of late
As touchinge the rebelles their
wicked eſtate,
Yet Syr Thomas Plomtrie their
preacher, they ſaie,
Hath made the North countrie to crie well a
daye.
Well a daye, well a daye, well a daye, woe is me,
Syr Thomas Plomtrie is hanged on a tree.

And now manie fathers and mothers be theare,
Are put to their trialles with terrible feare,
Not all the gaye croſſes nor goddes they adore
Will make them as merie as they haue ben
before ;
Well a daye, well a daye, &c.

B

The widowes be woful whofe hufbandes be taken,
 The childerne lament them that are fo forfaken,
The church men thei chaunted the morowe maffe
  bell,
 Their pardons be graunted, they hang verie wel.
  Well a daye, well a daye, &c.

It is knowne they bee fled that were the beginers,
 It is time they were ded, poore forofull finners ;
For all there great hafte they are hedged at a ftaye,
 With weeping and waylinge to fing well a daye ;
  Well a daye, well a daye, &c.

Yet fome hold opynion, all is well with the higheft ;
 They are in good faftie wher freedome is niefte ;
Northumberland need not be doutefull, fome faye,
 And Weftmorlande is not yet brought to the
  bay ;
  Well a daye, well a daye, &c.

No more is not Norton, nor a nomber befide,
 But all in good feafon they maye hap to be fpide ;
It is well they be wandred whether no man can fay,
 But it will be remembered, they crie well a daie ;
  Well a daye, well a daye, &c.

Where be the fyne fellowes that caried the croffes ?
 Where be the deuifers of idoles and affes ?
Wher be the gaie banners were wont to be borne ?
 Where is the deuocion of gentyll John Shorne ?
  Well a daye, well a daye, &c.

Saint Pall and Saint Peter haue laid them a-bord,
 And faie it is feetter to cleaue to Gods worde,

Their beades and their bables are beſt to be burnd,
  And Moiſes tables towardes them to be turnde ;
    Well a daye, well a daye, &c.

And well a daye wandreth ſtill to and froe,
  Bewailinge the wonders of rumors that goe ;
Yet ſaie the ſtiffe-necked, let be as be maye,
  Though ſome be ſore checked, yet ſome ſkape
    awaie ;
    Well a daye, well a daye, &c.

And ſuch ſome be ſowers of ſeedes of ſedicion,
  And ſaie the Popes pardon ſhall giue them re-
    miſſion,
That kepe themſelues ſecrete, and preeuilie ſaie,
  It is no greate matter for this, well a daye ;
    Well a daye, well a daye, &c.

You ſhall haue more newes er Candelmas come,
  Their be matters diffuſe, yet lookte for of ſome ;
Looke on, and looke ſtill, as ye longe to here newes,
  I thinke Tower Hill will make ye all muſe ;
    Well a daye, well a daye, &c.

If they that leaue tumblynge begin to wax climing,
  For all your momblinge and merie paſtimeing
Ye will then beleeue, I am ſure as I ſaie,
  That matter will meeue a newe well a daye ;
    Well a daye, well a daye, &c.

But as ye be faithleſſe of God and his lawe,
  So till ye ſee hedles the traitors in ſtrawe,
You wil be ſtill whiſperinge of this and of that,
  Well a daye, woe is me, you remember it not ;
    Well a daie, well a daie, &c

Leaue of your lyinge, and fall to trewe reafon,
 Leaue of your fonde fpieng, and marke euery
  feafon ;
Againft God and your countrie to taulke o
 rebelling   .
 Not Syr Thomas Plumtrie can bide by the
  telling ;
  Well a daye, well a daye, &c.

And fuch as feduce the people with blyndnes,
 And byd them to truft the Pope and his
  kyndnes,
Make worke for the tynker, as prouerbes doth
 faie,
 By fuch popifhe patching ftill comes well a
  daye ;
  Well a daye, well a daie, &c.

And fhe that is rightfull your Queene to fubdu
 ye,
 Althoughe you be fpitfull, hath gyuen no cauf
  to ye ;
But if ye will vexe her, to trie her hole force,
 Let him that comes next her take heed of he
  horfe ;
  Well a daie, well a daie, &c.

Shee is the lieftennante of him that is ftowteft,
 Shee is defender of all the deuowteft ;
It is not the Pope, nor all the Pope may,
 Can make her aftonyed, or finge well a daie ;
  Well a daie, well a daie, &c.

God profper her highnes, and fend her his peac
 To gouerne good people with grace and increafe

And ſend the deſeruers, that ſeeke the wronge
   way,
   At Tyborne ſome caruers, to ſinge well a daie;
   Well a daie, well a daie, &c.

      Finis.   W. E.

¶ Imprinted at London in Fleeſtrete beneath the
   Conduit, at the ſigne of S. John Euan-
      geliſt, by Thomas Colwell.

*A pleaſant Poeſie, or ſweete Noſegay of frag-
rant ſmellyng Flowers gathered in the Garden
of heauenly Pleaſure, the holy and bleſſed Bible;
to the tune of the Black Almayne.*

STOCK of flowers, bedewed with
    ſhowers,
     In a garden now there ſprings;
    With mirth and glee, vpon a tree,
  A byrd there ſits and ſings;
So pleaſant is her voyce,
It doth my hart reioyce :
   She ſets her tunes and noates ſo meete,
   That vnto me it ſeemes ſo ſweete,
That all the flowers, that euer could be,
Was neuer ſo ſwete as this to me ;
   The lyke before I dyd neuer ſe.

⁋ The Bible it is, that garden i-wys,
　　Which God preferue alwayes :
Lykewyfe Gods worde it is that byrde,
　　That now fo much I prayfe.
Alfo thofe goodly flowers,
So well bedewed with fhowers,
　　I wyll now go about to gather,
　　And put them in a pofy together ;
I wyll not put them in no cheft,
But bynd them vp as I thinke beft,
　　And kepe them alway next my breft.

⁋ The fyrft I fynd, to pleafe my mind,
　　Abell be had to name ;
Enoch alwayes is worthy of prayfe,
　　Likewyfe of worthy fame.
Looke you what Mofes wrytes,
And in Genefis there refites,
　　How God tooke hym the ftory fayth,
　　That he fhould neuer taft of death :
And alfo Noe, that righteous man,
A curious worke dyd take in hand,
　　To make the arke we vnderftand.

⁋ Good Abraham, that faithfull man,
　　In God dyd truft alway :
He dyd not feare, nor once difpayre
　　His onely fon to flay ;
Ifacke was no weede,
Nor Jacob in very deede :
　　Jofeph was a flower of price,
　　God dyd hym faue from cruell deuice ;
Alfo Mofes eke we fynd,
And Aaron lykewyfe vp we bynd,
　　Jofua is not out of mynd.

❡ The Judges alfo, both leſſe and mo,
  They were of worthy fame :
To ſpeake of all, my tyme is ſmal,
  To rehearce them all by name.
The prophet Samuell,
Our God dyd loue him well :
  Dauid was a flower ſo ſweete,
  To make hym kyng God thought it meete,
For great Golias he hath ſlayne ;
And Sallomon after him dyd raygne,
  Which vnto wyſedome dyd attayne.

❡ When Achab dyd floryſh, the rauens did
      noriſh
  Elia, a man of God ;
Kynge Joſias and Eſdras
  We finde, and pacient Job.
They feared our God of might,
And ſerued him day and night :
  No ioy nor payne could them procure,
  But alwayes by hym to endure :
Eſay lykewyſe and Jeremy,
They preached alway earneſtly,
  And dyd their duty faithfully.

❡ And Daniell deſtroyed Bell,
  The Babilonians God :
The dragon alſo he brought to wo,
  Without either ſword or rod.
To rehearce the Prophets all,
By their names them for to call,
  Although they be of worthy fame,
  It is to long them for to name :
We may not Tobyas leaue behynd,
Yet was he almoſt out of mind,
  But few ſuch flowers now can we fynd.

❡ Full wel we know, no flowers can blow,
    But boyſterous ſtormes muſt fynd :
For that is no flower, that euery ſhowre
    Doth driue away with wynd.
For all theſe goodly flowers
Had many ſtormy ſhowers,
    ˙ Before that they could blow or bud,
    Or bring forth ſeede to doe any good :
They dyd abyde both cold and blaſt,
Yet allwayes dyd they ſtand ſtedfaſt,
    Tyll all the ſtormes were gone and paſt.

❡ Now at this time, for our gracious Queene,
    Let vs geue harty prayes :
God may her defend, from enemies hand,
    At this time and alwayes ;
And ſend her proſperous raygne,
With vs for to remayne,
    For to defend Gods word ſo pure,
    And euer with it for to endure :
    That ſhe may be to vs a bower,
To kepe vs alway when it doth ſhowre ;
    I pray God ſaue that princly flower !

                ❡ Finis.   John Symon.

            ❡ Imprinted at London by Richard
            Johnes, dwellyng in the upper end
                    of Fleet Lane, 1572.

A Ballad againſt Slander and Detraction.

❡ Gar call him downe, gar call him downe, gar call him
    downe downe a :
❡ God ſend the faction, of all detraction, calld downe and
    caſt away.

LMYGHTY God
   Dooth ſhake his rod
     Of iuſtiſe, and all thoſe,
   That vniuſtly,
Detractyfly,
   Detract their freends or foes.

He telthe eche one,
Thou ſhalt iudge none ;
   And if thou iudge unbiden,
Thyſelf, ſaith he,
Shall iudged be ;
   This leſſon is not hiden.

To this now ſturd,
This is concord,
   Whiche wilthe vs in eche dout ;
To deem the beſt,
That may be geſt,
   Till time the trueth try out.

Knowing by this,
That think amiſſe
   Againſt no man we may ;

Muche more muſt we
Ill langage flee,
   And call it downe downe a ;
     Gar call him downe, &c.

❧ With ſwoord or ſkaine
To ſee babes ſlaine,
   Abhorth to look upon ;
Attend to me,
And ye ſhall ſee
   Murder and ſlaunder one.

Like as a knife
By reuing life,
   So ſlaunder fame hath ſlain ;
And bothe ones doone,
Bothe alike ſoone
   May be vndoon again.

Then what more ill
With knife to kill,
   Or with the tung to ſting :
With knife or tung
Strike olde or yung,
   Bothe in effect one thing.

Theſe woords are ſhort,
But they import
   Sentence at length to way :
Of all whiche ſence,
To flee offence,
   Call ſlaunder downe I ſay ;
     Gar call him downe, &c.

⁌ When vice is fought,
Al vice is nought,
  But fome vice wors then fome :
And eche man fees
Sundry degrees
  In eche vice felf dooth come.

Now fins the leaft,
We fhould deteft
  Vice or degree in vice :
If in the mofte
We fhowe our bofte,
  That fhoweth vs mofte unwice.

If I in thee
Suche faults ones fee,
  As no man ells doth knowe ;
To thee alone,
And other none,
  Thefe faults I ought to fhowe.

Then of intent
If I inuent
  Fauls tales, and them difplay :
That is mofte vile,
Whiche to exile,
  God calleth this down, downe a.
    Gar call him downe, &c.

⁌ Some count no charge
To talke at large
  Suche il as they doo heare ;
But Gods account
Dooth not amount
  To take fuche talkers heere.

Of woork il wrought,
When it is fought,
 In telling foorth the fame,
Though it be true,
The talke may brew
 Drink of damnable blame.

To frame excufe,
Of tungs mifufe,
 We haue no maner mene ;
So that by this,
No way ther is
 Il talles to cary clene.

Whiche makes me call
Vpon you all,
 As calling cal you may ;
Tales falfe or true,
Me to enfue,
 To call them downe, down a.
  Gar call him downe, &c.

❡ Chrifte crieth out ftil,
Say good for il,
 But we fay harme for harme ;
Yea ill for good
Ill tungs doo brood,
 Wrath is in them fo warme.

Slander to fere
And to forbere,
 This text ftands well in place ;
Wo by the tung,
Wherby is fprung
 Slander in any cace !

To fleke this fier
Of flanders yre,
   Repentance muft deuife
To fet all hands,
To quenche the brands
   With water of our eies.

Whiche brand then blowe
To make loue glowe,
   That loue by grace may ftay,
And by refort
Of good report,
   Call flander downe I fay.
     Gar call him down, &c.

FINIS,   q^d Haywood.

Imprinted at
London, at the long Shop
adioining vnto Saint
Mildreds Churche
in the Pultrie, by
John Allde.

A proper new Balad in praife of my

Ladie Marques,

whofe Death is bewailed to the Tune of New lufty gallant.

LADIES, I thinke you maruell that
   I writ no mery report to you,
And what is the caufe I court it not
   So merye as I was wont to dooe;
Alas! I let you vnderftand,
   It is no newes for me to fhow;
The faireft flower of my garland
   Was caught from court a great while agoe.

For, vnder the roufe of fweete Saint Paull,
   There lyeth my Ladie buryed in claye,
Where I make memory for her foule
   With weepinge eyes once euerye daye;
All other fightes I haue forgot,
   That euer in court I ioyed to fee,
And that is the caufe I court it not,
   So mery as I was wont to be.

And though that fhee be dead and gone,
   Whofe courting need not to be tolde,
And natures mould of flefhe and bone,
   Whofe lyke now liues not to beholde,
Me thinkes I fee her walke in blacke,
   In euery corner where I goe,
To looke if anie bodie do lacke
   A frend to helpe them of theyr woe.

Mee thinkes I fee her forowfull teares,
    To princelye ftate approching nye;
Mee thinkes I fee her tremblinge feares,
    Lefte anie her fuites fhulde hit awrie;
Mee thinkes fhe fhuld be ftill in place,
    A pitifull fpeaker to a Queene,
Bewailinge every poore mans cafe,
    As many a time fhee hath ben feene.

Mee thinkes I fee her modefte mood,
    Her comlie clothing plainlie clad,
Her face fo fweete, her cheere fo good,
    The courtlie countenance that fhee had;
But, chefe of all, mee thinkes I fee
    Her vertues deutie daie by daie,
Homblie kneeling one her knee,
    As her defire was ftill to praie.

Mee thinkes I cold from morow to night
    Do no thing ells with verie good will,
But fpend the time to fpeake and writte
    The praife of my good ladies ftill;
Though reafon faith, now fhe is dead,
    Go feeke and farue as good as fhee;
It will not finke fo in my head,
    That euer the like in courte will bee.

But fure I am, ther liueth yet
    In court a dearer frinde to mee,
Whome I to farue am fo vnfit,
    I am fure the like will neuer bee;
For I with all that I can dooe,
    Vnworthie moft maie feeme to bee,
To undoo the lachet of her fhooe,
    Yet will I come to courte and fee.

Then haue amongſte ye once againe,
  Faint harts faire ladies neuer win ;
I truſt ye will conſider my payne,
  When any good veniſon cometh in ;
And, gentill ladies, I you praie,
  If my abſentinge breede to blame,
In my behalfe that ye will ſaie,
  In court is remedie for the ſame.

❡ Finis, qᵈ W. ELDERTON.

❡ Imprinted at London in Fleteſtreat
  beneath the Conduit, at the ſigne
    of S. John Euangeliſt, by
      Thomas Colwell.

The Priſoners' Petition.

To the worſhipful our good benefactor.

N all lamentable manner, moſt humbly
beſeecheth your good Worſhip, wee,
the miſerable multitude of very poore
diſtreſſed priſoners, in the hole of
Wood-ſtreet Counter, in nomber fiftie poore men
or thereabouts, lying vpon the bare boordes,
ſtill languiſhing in great neede, colde and
miſerie, who, by reaſon of this daungerous and
troubleſome time, be almoſt famiſhed and hunger-
ſtarued to death ; others very ſore ſicke, and
diſeaſed for want of reliefe and ſuſtenance, by

reafon of the great number, which dayly increaf-
eth, dooth in all humblenes moſt humbly be-
feech your good worſhip, euen for Gods fake,
to pitie our poore lamentable and diftreſſed cafes ;
and nowe helpe to relieue and comfort us with
your Chriſtian and Godly charitie againſt this
holie and bleſſed time of Eaſter. ' And wee, according to our bounden duties, do and will
dayly pray vnto Almighty God for your long
life and happy profperitie.

> We humbly pray, your Chriſtian and
> Godly charitie to be fent vnto vs by
> fome of your feruants.

A moſt pleaſant Ballad of patient Griſſell,

To the tune of the Brides Good-morrow.

NOBLE Marques as he did ride on
       hunting, '
    Hard by a forreſt fide ;
A proper mayden, as ſhe did fit a
    fpinning,
His gentle eye efpide.
Moſt faire, and louely, and of curteous grace was
    ſhe,
    Although in fimple attire ;
She fung full fweet with pleaſant voyce melod-
    iouſly,
    Which fet the lords hart on fire.

C

The more he looked the more he might,
Beautie bred his hartes delight,
   And to this dainty damſell then he went ;—
God ſpeede, quoth he, thou famous flower,
Faire miſtres of this homely bower,
   Where loue and vertue liues with ſweete content.

With comely ieſture and curteous milde behauiour,
   She bad him welcome then ;
She entertain'd him in faithful friendly maner,
   And all his gentlemen.
The noble marques in his hart felt ſuch a flame,
   Which ſet his ſences at ſtrife ;
Quoth he, faire maiden, ſhew me ſoone what is
     thy name ?
I meane to make thee my wife.
Griſſell is my name, quoth ſhe,
Farre vnfit for your degree,
   A ſilly mayden and of parents poore.
Nay, Griſſell, thou art rich, he ſayd,
A vertuous, faire and comely mayd ;
   Graunt me thy loue, and I wil aſke no more.

At length ſhe conſented, and being both contented,
   They married were with ſpeed ;
Her contrey ruſſet was changd to ſilk and veluet,
   As to her ſtate agreed.
And when ſhe was trimly tyred in the ſame,
   Her beauty ſhined moſt bright,
Far ſtaining euery other braue and comly dame,
   That did appeare in her ſight.
Many enuied her therefore,
Becauſe ſhe was of parents poore,
   And twixt her lord and ſhe great ſtrife did raiſe.

Some fayd this and fome fayd that,
Some did call her beggers brat,
 And to her lord they would her foone difpraife.

O noble Marques, quoth they, why doe you
   wrong vs,
 Thus bacely for to wed,
That might haue gotten an honorable lady,
 Into your princely bed ?
Who will not now your noble iffue ftill deride,
 Which fhall hereafter be borne ?
That are of blood fo bafe by their mothers fide,
 The which will bring them in fcorne ;
Put her therefore quite away,
Take to you a lady gay,
 Whereby your linage may renowned be ;
Thus euery day they feemde to prate,
That malift Griffelles good eftate,
 Who tooke all this moft milde and patiently.

When that the marques did fee that they were
   bent thus
 Againft his faithfull wife,
Whom he moft deerely, tenderly and entirely,
 Beloued as his life ;
Minding in fecret for to proue her patient hart,
 Therby her foes to difgrace ;
Thinking to play a hard vncurteous part,
 That men might pittie her cafe.
Great with childe this lady was,
And at length it came to paffe,
 Two goodly children at one birth fhe had ;
A fonne and daughter God had fent,
Which did their father well content,
 And which did make their mothers hart full glad.

Great royall feafting was at thefe childrens
        chriftnings,
    And princely triumph made ;
Sixe weeks together, al nobles that came thither
    Were entertaind and ftaid ;
And when that al thofe pleafant fportings quite
        were done,
    The Marques a meffenger fent
For his yong daughter, and his prety fmiling fon,
    Declaring his full intent,—
How that the babes muft murdred be,
For fo the Marques did decree,—
    Come, let me haue the children, then he fayd.
With that faire Griffell wept full fore,
She wrung her hands and fayd no more,—
    My gracious lord muft haue his will obaid.

She tooke the babies, euen from their nurfing
        ladies,
    Betweene her tender armes ;
She often wifhes, with many forrowful kiffes,
    That fhe might helpe their harmes.
Farewel, farewel, a thoufand times, my children
        deere,
    Neuer fhall I fee you againe ;
Tis long of me, your fad and woful mother
        heere,
    For whofe fake both muft be flaine.
Had I been borne of royall race,
You might haue liu'd in happy cafe,
    But you muft die for my vnworthines ;
Come, meffenger of death, faid fhee,
Take my defpifed babes to thee,
    And to their father my complaints expres.

He tooke the children, and to his noble maifter
  He brings them both with fpeed;
Who fecret fent them vnto a noble lady,
  To be nurft vp indeed;
Then to faire Griffel with a heauy hart he goes,
  Where fhe fate mildly alone;
A pleafant iefture and a louely looke fhe fhowes,
  As if this griefe fhe neuer had knowen.
Quoth he, my children now are flaine!
What thinkes faire Griffell of the fame?
  Sweet Griffell, now declare thy mind to mee.
Sith you, my lord, are pleaf'd in it,
Poore Griffell thinkes the action fit;
  Both I and mine at your command will be.

My nobles murmur, faire Griffell, at thy honor,
  And I no ioy can haue,
Til thou be banifht both from my court and pre-
    fence,
  As they vnjuftly craue;
Thou muft be ftript out of thy coftly garments
    all,
  And as thou cameft to me,
In homely gray, infteed of biffe and pureft pall,
  Now all thy cloathing muft be;
My lady thou fhalt be no more,
Nor I thy lord, which grieues me fore;
  The pooreft life muft now content thy minde;
A groat to thee I muft not giue,
To maintaine thee while I doe liue,
  Againft my Griffel fuch great foes I finde.

When gentle Griffell did heare thefe wofull
    tidings,
  The teares ftood in her eyes.

She nothing anfwered, no words of difcontent
  Did from her lips arife;
Her veluet gown moft patiently fhe flipped off,
  Her kirtles of filke with the fame;
Her ruffet gown was broght again with many a
      fcoffe,
  To beare them all herfelfe fhe did frame.
When fhe was dreft in this array,
And ready was to part away,
  God fend long life vnto my lord, quoth fhee;
Let no offence be found in this,
To giue my lord a parting kiffe.—
  With watry eyes, Farewel, my deere, quoth he.

From ftately pallace vnto her fathers cottage,
  Poore Griffell now is gone;
Full fixteene winters fhe liued there contented,
  No wrong fhe thought vpon;
And at that time through all the land the fpeaches
      went,
  The Marques fhould married be
Vnto a lady of high and great difcent;
  To the fame all parties did agree.
The Marques fent for Griffell faire,
The brides bedchamber to prepare,
  That nothing therein fhould be found awrye;
The bride was with her brother come,
Which was great ioy to all and fome;
  And Griffell tooke all this moft patiently.

And, in the morning, when they fhould to the
      wedding,
  Her patience now was tride;
Griffel was charged herfelf in princely maner
  For to attire the bride.

Moſt willingly ſhe gaue conſent to do the ſame;
  The bride in her brauery was dreſt,
And preſently the noble Marques thither came,
  With all his lords, as he requeſt:
O Griſſel, I would aſke, quoth he,
If ſhe would to this match agree;
  Me thinkes her lookes are waxen wondrous coy;
With that they all began to ſmile,
And Griſſell ſhe replide the while,
  God ſend Lord Marques many yeres of joy!

The Marques was moued to ſee his beſt beloued,
  Thus patient in diſtreſſe;
He ſtept vnto her, and by the hand he tooke her,—
  Theſe wordes he did expreſſe;—
Thou art my bride and all the brides I meane to
    haue;
  Theſe two thine owne children be!
The youthfull lady on her knees did bleſſing
    craue,
  Her brother as willing as ſhe;—
And you that enuied her eſtate,
Whom I haue made my louing mate,
  Now bluſh for ſhame, and honor vertuous life;
The chronicles of laſting fame,
Shall euer more extoll the name,
  Of patient Griſſell, my moſt conſtant wife.

FINIS.

A Newe Ballade of a Louer extollinge
his Ladye.

To the tune of Damon and Pithias.

LAS, my harte doth boyle,
    And burne within my brefte,
  To fhowe to thee, myne onely deere,
    My fute and my requeft.
My loue no toung can tell,
  Ne pen can well defcrye;
Extend thy loue for loue againe,
  Or els for loue I dye.

℩ My loue is fet fo fuer,
  And fixed on thee fo,
That by no meanes I can abftaine,
  My faythfull loue to fhowe;
My wounded harte, theirfore,
  To thee for helpe doth crye;
Extend thy loue for loue againe,
  Or els for loue I dye.

℩ Although the gods were bent,
  With greedie mynde to flaye
My corpes with cruell panges of death,
  And lyfe to take awaye.
Yet fhould my faythfull harte
  At no tyme from thee flye;
Show loue therfore for loue againe,
  Or els for loue I dye.

❡ Although the ſun were bent
   To burne me with his beames;
And that mine eyes, throw greous pangs,
   Should ſend forth bloudy ſtreames;
Yet would I not forſake,
   But ſtyll to thee woulde crye,
To ſhowe me loue for loue again,
   Or els for loue I dye.

❡ Ye though ech ſterre were tournd
   Untyll a fiery darte,
And were all ready bent with payne,
   To perce throwe-out my harte;
Yet coulde I not forſake
   To loue thee faythfullye;
Extend thy loue for loue againe,
   Or els for loue I dye.

❡ Ye though eche foule were formde,
   A ſerpent fell to be,
My corps to flay with bloudy wounds,
   And to deuower me;
Yet would I be thine owne,
   To loue full hartelye;
Extend thy loue for loue againe,
   Or els for loue I dye.

❡ Ye though the lyon were,
   With gapinge gredye jawe,
Readye with rygorus raggye teeth,
   My fleſhe to teare and gnawe;
Yet woulde I be thine owne,
   To ſerue moſt earneſtlye;
Extend thy loue for loue againe,
   Or els for loue I dye.

℃ Ye though the fifhes all,
    That fwymes in furginge feafe,
Should fwallowe me with gredy mouth,
    Yet could thee not apeafe.
My earneft harte to thee,
    To loue entyerlye ;
Extend thy loue for loue againe,
    Or els for loue I dye.

℃ Ye though the earth would gape,
    And fwallowe me there-in,
And that I fhould tormentyd be
    In hell, with euery fyn ;
Yet would I be thy owne,
    To faue or els to fpyll ;
Show me therfore lyke loue againe,
    Or els thou doft me kyll.

Finis, q M. Ofb.

Imprinted at London, in Fletftrete, at the
    figne of the Faucon, by Wylliam
        Gryffith, 1568.

The true reporte of the forme and ſhape of a monſtrous Childe borne at Muche Horkeſleye, a village three myles from Colcheſter, in the Countye of Eſſex, the xxi *daye of Apryll in this yeare* 1562.

O prayſe ye God, and bleſſe his name;
His mightye hande hath wrought the ſame.

HIS monſtrous world that monſters
  bredes as rife,
   As men tofore it bred by native
    kinde,
By birthes that ſhewe corrupted natures ſtrife,
  Declares what ſinnes beſet the ſecrete minde.
I meane not this, as though deformed ſhape
  Were always linkd with fraughted minde with
   vice,
But that in nature God ſuch draughtes doth ſhape,
  Reſemblyng ſinnes that ſo bin had in price.
So groſſeſt faultes braſt out in bodyes forme,
  And monſter cauſed of want or to much ſtore
Of matter, ſhewes the ſea of ſinne, whoſe ſtorme
  Oreflowes and whelmes vertues barren ſhore;
Faultye alike in ebbe and eke in flowd,
   Like diſtaunt both from meane, both like ex-
    treames;
Yet greatſt exceſſe the want of meane doth
   ſhrowde,

And want of meanes exceſſe from vertues
    meanes.
So contraryeſt extreames conſent in ſinne,
    Which to bewray to blindeſt eyes by ſyght,—
Beholde a calfe hath clapt about his chinne
    His chauderne, reft whence nature placed it
      right,
And ruffd, driues doubtfull ſeers to proue by ſpeache
    Themſelues not calues, and makes the faſhion
      ſtale.
In him behold by exceſſe from meane our breache,
    And midds exceſſe yet want of natures ſhape.
To ſhowe our miſſe beholde a guiltleſſe babe
    Reft of his limmes,—for ſuch is vertues want—
Himſelfe and parentes both infamous made
    With ſinful byrth ; and yet a worldlyng ſcant.
Feares midwyfes route, bewrayeing his parentes
      fault
    In want of honeſtye and exceſſe of ſinne ;
Made lawfull by all lawes of men, yet halt
    Of limmes by God, ſcapd not the ſhamefull
      marke
Of baſtard ſonne in baſtard ſhape deſcryed.
    Better, fare better, vngyuen were his lyfe,
Than geuen ſo.   For nature iuſt enuyed
    Her gyft to hym, and cropd wyth mayming
      knyfe
His limmes, to wreake her ſpyte on parentes
      ſinne ;
    Which, if ſhe ſpare vnwares ſo many ſcapes
As wycked world to breede wil neuer linne,
    Theyr liues declare theyr maims ſaued from
      their ſhapes,
Scorchd in theyr mindes.   O cruel priuye mayme,
    That feſtreth ſtyll !   O vnrecured ſore !

Where thothers quiting wyth theyr bodyes fhame
 Theyr parentes guilt, oft linger not their lyues
In lothed fhapes, but naked flye to fkyes.——

 As this may do, whofe forme tofore thine eyes
Through want thou feeft, a monftrous vglye fhape,
Whom frendly world to finne doth terme a fcape.

On Tuyfday being the xxi day of Apryll, in
this yeare of our Lorde God a thoufand fyue
hundred thre fcore and two, there was borne a
man-childe of this maymed forme at Muche
Horkefley in Effex, a village about thre myles
from Colchefter, betwene a naturall father and a
naturall mother, hauing neyther hande, foote,
legge, nor arme, but on the left fyde it hath a
ftumpe growynge out of the fhoulder, and the
ende thereof is rounde, and not fo long as it fhould
go to the elbowe ; and on the ryghte fyde no mencion of any thing where any arme fhould be, but
a litel ftumpe of one ynche in length ; alfo on the
left buttocke there is a ftumpe comming out of
the length of the thygh almoft to the knee, and
round at the ende, and groweth fomething ouerthwart towardes the place where the ryght legge
fhould be, and where the ryghte legge fhould be,
there is no mencion of anye legge or ftumpe.
Alfo it hath a codde and ftones, but no yearde,
but a lytell hole for the water to iffue out.
Finallye, it hath by eftimation no tounge, by
reafon whereof it fucketh not, but is fuccoured
wyth liquide fubftaunce put into the mouth by
droppes, and nowe begynneth to feede wyth
pappe, beyng very well fauoured, and of good
and chearful face.

❡ The aforefayde Anthony Smyth of Much
Horkefley, hufbandman, and his wyfe, were both
maryed to others before, and haue had dyuers
chyldren, but this deformed childe is the fyrft
that the fayd Anthony and his wyfe had betwene
them two ; it is a man chylde.   This chylde was
begot out of matrimony, but borne in matri-
monye ; and at the makynge hereof was liuing,
and like to continue.

❡ Imprinted at London in Fleteftrete nere
to S. Dunftons Church, by
Thomas Marfhe.

A newe Ballade.

DERE Lady Elyfabeth, which art
our right and vertous Quene,
God hath endued the wᵗ mercy and
fayth, as by thy workes it may
be fene,
Wherefore, good Quene, I counfayle thee, Lady,
Lady,
For to beware of the fpiritualtie, moft dere
Lady.

Haue you not rede of your progenitours, which
was before you many a yere,
How they endured many fharpe fhowers, as
by the cronicles it doth appere,

And many of them came to euell hap, Lady, Lady,
   And all was through the forked cap, moſt dere
     Lady ?

❡ Haue you nat rede of Wyllyam Rufus the
     ſecond kyng hereof that name,
   How he was ſlayne moſte maruelous, all through
     the curſſed ſeede of Caine ?
Tyrell kyllede hym with an arrowe, Lady, Lady,
   Yet ſome men ſayed he ſhot at a ſparow, moſte
     dere Lady.

❡ Haue you not rede of good kyng John, how
     by them he was vndone ?
   The Biſhop of Canterbury, yᵉ wicked man, ac-
     cuſed him to the court of Rome ;
They enterdyted his lande as the cronicle ſayeth,
     Lady, Lady,
   A monke poyſoned him to his death, moſte
     dere Lady.

❡ Haue you not rede of the ſecond Richard,
     who was the black princes ſonne,
   How they handled him full hard, and famiſhed
     him till lyfe was donne ?
In Powles they made him a funerall, Lady, Lady,
   To blinde the peoples eyes withall, mooſte dere
     Lady.

❡ Haue you not rede of the ſixt Henry, which
     was a good and a ſimple man ?
   The Cardinall of Wyncheſter truly made him
     loſe that hys father wanne,
The good Proteƈtor his vncle dere, Lady, Lady,
   The prieſtes kept war with him a longe yere,
     moſte dere Lady.

¶ Then came your father, King Henry yᵉ. viii.
      which was a prince of victory,
  And he depofed them all ftraight, when he had
      fpyed their idolatry ;
If this be trewe, as trewe it was, Lady, Lady,
  God graunt your grace may do no leffe, moft
      dere Lady.

¶ Then came your brother King Edward, which
      was a good and vertuous child,
  And to God's word he had regarde, but the
      wicked prieftes hath hym begilde,
And rayfed vp trentalles in euery place, Lady,
      Lady,
  And fome of them preached agaynft his Grace,
      moft dere Lady.

¶ Then came your fyfter Quene Mary, and for
      fiue yeres that fhe did rayne,
  All that was done (by) Edward and Hary her
      wicked prieftes made it but vaine ;
They brought in agayne the Romyfhe lore, Lady,
      Lady,
  Whiche was banifhed longe before, mofte dere
      Lady.

¶ Then God fent vs your noble Grace, as in dede
      it was highe tyme,
  Whiche dothe all Popery cleane deface, and
      fet vs forth God's trewe deuine,—
For whome we are all bound to praye, Lady,
      Lady,
  Longe life to raigne bothe night and day, mofte
      dere Ladye.

      Finis.   quod R. M.

The Pope in his fury doth anſwer returne
To a letter yᵉ which to Rome is late come.

I DOE eſteme your kyndnes much
　　For ſendyng worde ſo ſone,
　Your diligence it hath ben ſuch,
　　It is ariued at Rome :
But when I had pervſd your byl,
In that you ſet thereto your wyl,
And eke your mynd applyed vntyl
　　The writyng of the ſame,
I did beleue it to be true ;
But ſurely I muſt ſay to you,
It greued mee thoſe lines to vew
　　Were written in your name.

❡ And ſure it is no maruell, loe !
　　For daylye I doe heare,
The matter ſemeth to be ſo,
　　As amply doth appeare :
For euery man doth tell for true
The ſame that late was ſent of you,
But, out alas ! your tidynges new
　　Doth much appall my ſpirite,
And makes me ſweare and makes me teare,
To pull and hale, and rend my heare,
And brynges me dayly in diſpaire
　　To thinke on this deſpite.

❡ But ſith there is no remedye
　　That mine obedient chylde

D

Is hanged vp vpon a tree,
    And to-to much reuylde :
What fhoulde I doe but curfe and ban,
And hurte them toe the worft I can,
For hanging vp fo good a man
    That bare mee fuch good wyll ?
But yf I had him here at Rome,
His body fhould be fhryued foone,
And maffe at mornyng and at noone,
    With chantyng of each bell,

℃ For euer fhoulde be fayd and foung
    The deuyls to controvle,
And prayers all aboute his tombe
    With fenceyng for his foule :
That neuer a deuyll fo deepe in hell
Shoulde once prefume with him to mell,
For once approch his body tyll
    To vexe him any way,
And I wolde kepe his body fo,
That it from hence fhould neuer go,
And dyuers of my fryers mo
    For him fhould dayly pray.

℃ And gladly wolde I be reuengd
    On England, yf I might,
Becaufe they haue toe much abufd
    My Bull with great defpight :
And make thereat a laughing game,
And fet but little by my name,
And much my holynes defame,
    And dayly me difpyfe.
Their queene hath chaft the rebels all
That loued to bow their knees to Ball,
And hanged their quarters on the wall
    As meat for crowes and pyes.

℧ But I wyll walke and dayly feke
  My purgatorie thorow,
And caufe all the deuyls at my becke
  To me their knees to bow :
And whereas I may any fynde
That to their prince haue ben vnkynde,
Be fure, with mee they fhall be fhrynde
  As they deferued haue.
And cheefly now John Felton hee
Shall euer be beloued of mee,
Becaufe that he fo louinglye
  My Bull did feeme to faue.

℧ But yf that I coulde haue at once
  The paryng of his toe,
His head, his quarters, or his bones,
  That with the wynde doe bloe :
Then fhoulde they be layd vp by mee
As reliques of great dignitie,
For euery man that comes to fee
  Thofe jewels of fuch grace.
The Nortons' bones fhould be fo fhrynd
That now hanges wauering in the wynd,
Yf that I coulde deuyfe or fynd
  To bryng them to this place.

℧ And I wyll curfe and ban them all
  That fpeake againft my powre,
And feekes to make my kyngdome fall,
  My curfe fhall them deuowre :
And yf that here I might you fee,
For wrytyng lately vnto mee,
Be fure, ye fhould rewarded bee
  As beft I coulde bethynke.
And as for Wylliam Elderton
That lately fent me worde to Rome,

Be fure that he fhould haue lyke dome
   To bye him pen and ynke.

℃ Take this as written from our grace
   That vnto you we fend,
Becaufe we want both time and place
   To recompence you, frend :
As for the boyes that frump and fcoff,
And at my holynes doe laugh,
   I mynd to dreffe them wel enough,
     Yf cafe I had them here.
   And for my feruants that abyde,
   And long haue had their pacience tryde,
   From Romaine faith that wyl not flyde,
     I wyfh them all good chere.

    ℃ Finis.   S. P.

℃ Imprinted by Alexander Lacie for Henrie
Kyrkham, dwelling at the figne of the Blacke
Boy at the middle North dore of Paules
Church.

Lines underneath a Portrait of Queen Elizabeth.

LOE here the pearle,
   Whom God and man doth loue :
Loe here on earth
   The onely ftarre of light :
  Loe here the queene,
   Whom no mifhap can moue

To chaunge her mynde
    From vertues chief delight !
Loe here the heart
    That fo hath honord God,
That, for her loue,
    We feele not of his rod :
Pray for her health,
    Such as good fubiectes bee :
Oh Princely Dame,
    There is none like to thee !

❧❧❧

Ane new Ballet fet out be ane fugitiue Scottif-
man that fled out of Paris at this
lait Murther.

OW Katherine de Medicis hes maid
        fic a gyis,
        To tary in Paris the papiftes ar
        tykit,
At Baftianes brydell howbeit fcho denyis,
    Giue Mary flew Hary, it was not vnlykit;
ʒit a man is nane refpectand this number,
I dar not fay wemen hes wyte of this cummer.

ʒone mafk the Quene Mother hes maid thame in
        France,
    Was maikles and faikles, and fchamfully flane,
Bot Mary conuoyit and come with ane dance,
    Quhill princes in fences was fyrit with ane trane ;
Baith treffonabill murtheris the ane and the vther,
I go not in mafking mair with the Quene Mother.

℃ Italianes ar tyranis, and treſſonabill tratoris ;
    For gyſours, deuyſours, the Guyſianis ar gude ;
Bot Frenche men ar trew men, and not of thair
        natouris ;
    Than, Charlie, I farlie thow drank thy awin
      blude,
I wyte bot thy mother wit, wemen ar vane,
In greis neir to Ganzelon, nor grit Charlie Mane.

℃ Thy ſtyle was Treſchriſtien, maiſt Criſten
      King,
    Baith hieſt and frieſt, and neiſt the impyre ;
Bot now Proueſt Marſchell in playing this ſpring,
    And reſſoun for treſſoun prouokis God to ire ;
Beleuis thow this trumprie ſall ſtabliſche thy
      ſtyle ?
Our God is not deed, ȝit be doand ane quhyle.

℃ Suppois that the Papiſtes deuyſit this at Trent,
    To ding vs and bring vs with mony lowd
      lauchter,
With ſic cruell murther is Chriſt ſa content,
    To take the and make the ane Sanct for our
      ſlauchter ?
Albeit he correct vs, and ſcurge vs in ire,
Be war with the wand ſyne he wapis in the fyre.

℃ For better is pure men nor princes periurit,
    Baith ſchameles and fameles, we find thame ſa
      fals ;
With ſangis lyke the ſeryne our lyfis thow
      allurit ;
    Ouirſylit vs, begylit vs, with baitis in our hals ;
Or as the fals fowler, his fang for to get,
Deuoiris the pure volatill he wylis to the net.

❡ In Ilis nor in Orknay, in Ireland Oneill,
   Thay dar not, thay gar not thair lieges be
      ftickit :
Solyman, Tamerlan, nor yit the mekle Deill,
   Proud Pharao, nor Nero, was neuer fa wickit ;
Nouther Turk nor Infidell vfis fic thing,
As be their awin burreo, being ane king.

❡ Baith auld men and wemen, with babis on thair
  .   breift,
   Not luking nor huking, to hurll thame in
     Sane,
All beand murdreift downe, quhat do ʒe neift ?
   Proceffioun, confeffion, and vp Mes agane ;
Proud King Antiochus was fum tyme als haly,
And yet our God gufchit out the guttis of his
     belly.

Thy fyfter thou maryit, thy faces was four,
   Sic cuikrie for luikrie was euill interprifit ;
ʒe maid vs the Reid Freiris, and rais in an hour,
   Abhorring na gorring that micht be deuifit ;
Thou playit the fals hypocreit fenzeing the fray,
But inwart ane rageing wolf waitand thy pray.

That France was confidderat with Scotland I grant,
   Baith actit, contractit and keipit in deid ;
The kyndnes of cutthrottis we cure not to want,
   Denyis thame, defyis thame, and al thair fals feid ;
It was bot with honeft men we maid the band,
And thou hes left leifand bot few in that land.

Our faith is not warldly, we feir not thy braulis,
   Thocht hangmen ouirgang men, for gaddaring
     our geir ;

ȝe kill bot the carcaſe, ȝe get not our ſaulis,
  Not douting our ſhouting is hard in Goddis eir;
The ſame God from Pharo defendit his pepill,
And not ȝone round Robene that ſtandis in ȝour
    ſtepill.

❡ Now, wyſe Quene Elizabeth, luik to yourſelf,
  Diſpite them, and wryte thame ane bill of de-
    fyance;
The Papiſtis and Spanȝards hes partit ȝour pelf,
  As newly and trewly was tald me thir tythance;
Beleue thay to land heir, and get vs for nocht,
Will ȝe do as we do, it ſal be deir bocht.

Giue pleis God we gre ſa, and hald vs togidder,
  Baith ſurely and ſturely, and ſtoutly gainſtand
    thame;
They culd not weill conqueis vs, culd ȝe conſidder,
  For our men are dour men, and likis weill to
    land thame;
Quhen Ceſar himſelf was chaiſt, haue ȝe forȝet,
And baith the realmes be aggreit, tak that thay
    get.

❡ For better it is to fecht it, defendant our lyfis,
  With ſpeir men and weir men, and ventour our
    ſellis,
Nor for to ſe Frenchemen deflorand our wyfis,
  Diſplace vs, and chace vs, as thay haue done ellis;
I meane quhen the Ingliſmen helpit at Leith,
And gart thame gang hame agane ſpyte of thair
    teith.

❡ I cannot trow firmely that Frenchmen ar cummen,
  Perſayſand thame haifand thameſelfis into
    parrell;

The Lord faue Elizabeth, thair ane gude woman,
   That cauldly and bauldly debait will our
      quarrell
With men and with money, baith armour and graith,
As fcho hes befoir tyme defendit this Faith.

Thocht France for thair falfet be drownit in
      dangeris,
   For caufis and paufis thay plait into Pareis,
ȝit we ar in war eftait, waitand on ftrangeris,
   Not gyding, deuyding our awin men from
      Mareis ;
So weid the calf from the corn, calk me thair dures,
And flay or ȝe be flane, gif fic thing occures.

Bot how can ȝe traift thame that trumpit ȝow ellis,
   Decoir thame, do for thame, or fofter thair feid ;
And thay may anis fe thair time, tent to ȝour-
     -fellis,
  Baith haitfull, diffaitfull, ȝe deill with in deid ;
Anis wod and ay the war, wit quhat ȝe do,
And mak thame faft in the ruit gif thay cum to.

℄ God blis ȝow, my brether, and biddis ȝow gud
      nicht,
   Obey God, go fay God, with prayer and fafting,
Chrift keip this pure ile of ouris in the auld richt,
   Defend vs and fend vs the life euerlafting ;
The Lord fend vs quyetnes, and keip our ȝoung
      king,
The Quene of Inglands Maieftie, and lang mot
      thai ring.

℄ Finis, quod Simpell.

℄ Imprintit at Sanctandrois, be Robert
Lekpriuik. Anno Do. 1572.

A proper New Balad of the Bryber Gehefie.

Taken out of the fourth booke of Kinges, the v.
chapter ; to the tune of Kynge Salomon.

WAS not the bryber Gehezie
  Rewarded iuftly of the Lord,
 Which for example verelie,   .
  The Holie Scripture doth recorde ?
If this be true, as true it was,
  Of his rewarde,
Why fhould not Chriftan men, alas,
  Than haue regarde ?

When that the prophet Elizae
 Had clenfed from the leprofie
Naaman of Affiria,
 Thorow the workes of God on hye,
Then Naaman wolde him conftraine
  To take rewarde ;
But Elizae from that refrainde,
  And had regarde.

But Gehezie of falfehed minde,
 When Naaman did paffe awaie,
Did hie him fafte that was behinde,
 And unto Naaman did faie,—
Beholde, my mafter hath me fente
  For a rewarde ;
To prophetes children he is bente
  To haue regarde.

With right good will, faid Naaman,
　　Him to rewarde and did proceede ;
And Gehezie conuaide it then
　　So preuilie in verie deede,
Forgetting that the prophete tho
　　　　Of his rewarde
Could, by the fprite of God, it knowe,
　　　　And haue regarde.

Alas, how was thou, Gehezie,
　　Rauifhed in worldly gaine !
How was thou brought to mizerie,
　　Of God appointed for thy paine,
And all thy ofspringe after thee,
　　　　For thy rewarde !
The Lorde that hateth briberie
　　　　Hath his regarde.

Then Gehezie deceitfulie,
　　To-fore the prophet tooke his waie,
Who faid to hime, O Geheʒie,
　　Went not my harte with thee, I faie,
When Naaman from charret came
　　　　Thee to rewarde,
And thou haft falfelie hid the fame,
　　　　Without regarde ?

Gehezie, is it now a time
　　Thy bribes (he faid) for to receaue ?
Beholde, for this thy wicked crime
　　That leprofeie to thee fhall cleaue,
The which was vpon Naaman,
　　　　For thy rewarde,
And to thy feede thee after than,
　　　　To haue regarde.

Incontinent then Gehezie
    Departed from his prefence fo,
As the Texte doth verefie,
    A leper white as is the fnowe;
Example to fuch bribers all,
        To haue regarde;
With Gehezie at lengthe they fhall
        Haue their rewarde.

If they doe not their faultes confeffe,
    Detefting of their bryberie,
Elfe God will fpie ther wickedneffe,
    Though they it cloke with Gehezie;
And can them paie accordinglie
        The like rewarde,
As he hath done to Gehezie;
        O haue regarde!

The Lord he is that fame God ftill
    That he was than vndoubtedlie;
Such Gehezies he punifh will,
    That bribes receiue fo wickedlie,
Though they fo preuilie do hide
        Their falfe rewarde;
Yet of the Lorde it will be fpide,
        Who hath regarde.

O Lorde, vs guide in all our waies,
    That we may leade our liues aright;
To deale with trueth at all affaies,
    Giue vnto us thy Holie Sprite;
And that our Queene and her Councell
        Maie haue regarde,
In this lande bribers to expell
        That take rewarde.

❡ Finis, quod George Mell.

Imprinted at London, in Flete Streate,
beneath the Conduit, at the ſigne
of S. John Evangeliſt, by
Thomas Colwell.

❦

❡ *The ſhape of ii monſters, M D lxii.*

THIS preſent yere of oure Lord God a
thouſande fiue hundred thre ſcore and
two, one Marke Finkle, a joiner, dwelling beſide Charing Croſſe by Weſt-
minſter, had a ſow that brought forth one pigge
onely, vpon the ſeuenth of Maye, beinge Aſcen-
tion daye, the whiche pigge had a head muche
lyke vnto a dolphines head, with the left eare
ſtanding vp forked, and the right eare being like
as it were halfe a litle leafe, being deuided in the
middes, ſharpe toward thend, lying downward flat
to the head, without any holes into the headward.
The two fore feet, like vnto handes, eche hande
hauinge thre long fingers and a thumbe, bothe the
thumbes growinge on the outſides of the handes,
the hinder legges growing very much backwarde
otherwiſe then the common natural forme hath
ben ſeen, beeing of no good ſhape, but ſmaller
from the body to the middle joint then they be
from the ſame joint toward the foot. And the

taile growing an inche neare vnto the back then
it doth of any that is of right ſhape.

Theſe ſtraunge ſights the Allmighty God
ſendeth vnto vs, that we ſhould not be forgetfull
of his mighty power, nor vnthankful for his ſo
greate mercies ; the which hee ſheweth ſpecially by
geuing vnto vs his holy word, wherby our liues
ought to be guided, and alſo his wonderful
tokens wherby we are moſt gentilly warned.

But if we will not be warned, neither by his
word, nor yet by his wonderful workes, then let vs
be aſſured that theſe ſtraunge monſtruous ſightes
doe premonſtrate vnto vs that his heauy indigna-
cion wyl ſhortly come vpon vs for our monſtruous
lyuinge.   Wherfore let vs earneſtly pray vnto
God that he wyl geue vs grace earneſtly to repent our wickednes, faithfully to beleue his word,
and ſincerely to frame our liues after the doctrine
of the ſame.

❛ *An Admonition vnto the Reader.*

ET vs knowe by theſe vgly ſights,
        And eke conſider well,
    That our God is the Lord of mights,
        Who rules both heauen and hell.

By whoſe ſtrong hand theſe monſters here
    Were formed as ye ſee,
That it mighte to the world appere,
    Almightie him to bee.

Who might alſo vs men haue formde
   After a ſtraunge deuiſe,
As by the childe of late deformde,
   Appeareth in plaine wiſe.

What might theſe monſters to vs teache,
   Which now are ſent ſo rife,
But that we haue Goddes wurd well preacht,
   And will not mend our life ?

At which ſtraunge ſightes we meruel muche,
   When that we doe them ſee ;
Yet can there not be found one ſuche,
   That ſo will warned bee.

And loke what great deformitie
   In bodies ye beholde ;
Much more is in our mindes truly,
   An hundreth thouſand folde.

So that we haue great cauſe in deede,
   Our ſinnes for to confeſſe,
And eke to call to God with ſpeede,
   The ſame for to redreſſe.

Which if we wyl not fayle to doo,
   And purely to repent,
He wyl, no doubt, vs comfort ſo,
   As ſhal our ſoules contente.

Now ſith our God ſo louing is,
   And ready to forgeue,
Why doe we not abhorre all vice,
   And only to him cleaue ?

Sith he alfo his hande can fhake,
  And fone deftroy vs all,
Why doe we not then feare and quake,
  And downe before him fall?

Why doe we not amend, I faye,
  Either for loue or feare?
Why driue we of from day to daye,
  And finning not forbeare?

Good lawes of late renewde wee fee,
  Much finne for to fuppreffe;
God graunt that they fulfilde maye bee,
  To ouerthrow exceffe.

O Lord, graunt vs alfo thy grace,
  That, by repentance pure,
In heauen to haue a dwelling place,
  For euer to endure.

        Amen, quod W. F.

❡ Imprinted at London, at the Long Shop
    in the Pultry, by John Alde.

Ane Complaint vpon Fortoun.

INCONSTANT warld, fragill and
    friuolus,
    With fein3eit Fortoun, quha con-
    fides in the
Sall find his lyfe cairfull and cruellus,
    Led in this vale of wofull miſerie ;
Quhat potent princes in proſperitie,
    Hes ſho depoſd from their imperiall places !
Hir craft quotidian we may cleirly ſe,
    As men in mirrouris may behauld their faces.

The worthie Bocas, in his morall buke,
    The Fall of Princes plainly dois compyle ;
Amangs them all quha euer lykes to luke,
    Sall finde Dame Fortounis fauour for a quhyle ;
For with the one eye ſho can lauch and ſmyle,
    And with the vther lurke and play the loun ;
Sum to promotioun, and ſome to plaine exile,
    Lyke draw-well bukkets dowkand vp and doun.

℄ That variable witch makis all the warld ado !
    Quhat kingis and countreis hes ſho brocht to end !
Aſſyrians, Perſians, Grekes, and Romains to,
    The monarches foure micht not hir force defend.
Bulworkis nor battellis bydis her nocht a bend ;
    Quha may withſtand her ſtraik, quhan ſho liſt
    ſtryke ?
This nicht aneuch, the morne nathing to ſpend !
    Imago in Luna, and ſho lukis baith alyke.

E

To pen the fpeciallis it paffis mony a hunder,
　　And makis the tyme ouer tidious to declare ;
Sum fho promouis and fum fho puttis to vnder,
　　And fum rewardes with wandring heir and thair;
And fum incaftrat captiues in the fnair,
　　And fum for flatrie dois hir freindfhip find ;
To all eftates vntruethfull, quhat fould mair,
　　Turnand her volt lyke woddercok in wind?

To paint her out it paffis mine ingyne,
　　How wonderfully fhe wirkes in all thir thingis!
Sum fra thair birth brocht vp with doggis and
　　　　fwine,
　　Tane fra the pleuch and placit in fait of kingis.
The brutell beift ane barbour wolfe vpbringis
　　The firft borne Romain callit Romulus,
Quhais blude as ʒit into that regioun ringis,
　　By expectatioun of auld Amelius.

Cyrus ficlyke was be ane bitche vpbrocht,
　　Cround as a king ane cruell man of weir.
Pareis in Troy that all the toun forthocht,
　　Preferuit from flauchter be fouking of a beir.
And fwa was Thylaphus with ane hinde, I heir,
　　Medas with imates and maid ane michtie prince;
Plato with beis quha did fic prudence leir,
　　That all men meruelled of his eloquence.

Without refpect to blude royall or clan,
　　Pureanis promouit that na man wald prefume ;
Torquinius Prifcus, a baneift marchant man,
　　Chaift out of Corinth and cround a king in
　　　　Rome.
Siclyke was Seruius from ane fhipherd grome,
　　And Tullus Hoftilius fand her fauour neift ;
Is, was, and falbe quhill the day of dome,
　　Sic doubill dealing in Dame Fortounis breift !

Quha findis hir freindſhip of fauour hes aneuch,
   To warldly glore ſho gydes them all the gait;
Tuke ſho not Gordias from the ſpaid and pleuch,
   And quickly placit him in a princes ſait?
How far may Darius bragge of her debait,
   Tane fra the ſtabil ouer Perſia to ring;
Pure Agathocles from a law eſtait,
   Ane potteris boy to be ane potent King?

Of Juſtine the ſuinehird ſho maid ane empriour,
   Ouer Conſtantinople ane king and cround him
      thair;
Gyges the gait-hird ane michtie conquerour,
   To Lydia land ſhe maid him lord and aire;
And Wallancianus from his landwart fair,
   Tane fra the pleuch to place imperiall;
Cambyſes, Nero, be the contrair clair,
   Was thair awin burreois to thair buriall.

Sa Fortoun mountit neuer man ſa hie,
   Foſtered with folie, ſuppoſe ſhe make them faine;
Bot with ane tit ſho turnis the quheill, ȝe ſie,
   Doun gois their heid, vp gois their heillis againe!
Of Alexander to write I war bot vaine,
   Ouer fifty landis he lord was at the leiſt;
ȝit threttie dayis lay efter he was ſlaine,
   Unbureit in Babell lyke a brutell beiſt.

Xerxes, quhoſe armeis maid the riueris dry,
   And ſchippis ſubumbragit all the ſeyis on breid,
Did ſho not wait him with ſic foule inuy,
   Pray to Pericles, that put him to his ſpeid?
Of Julius Ceſar gif thow lykes to reid,
   In his triumphant toun victorious,
Slaine be his Senatis, ſchamefully in deid,
   By his awin kinſmen Brutus and Caſſus

Sum auld examples heir I man induce,
    To bring my purpofe to more fpeciall ;
Quha was mair worthie git I wald make rufe,
    More ftout, more trew, nor hardy Hanniball ?
Dauter of Romaines, to Carthage ane caftell
        wall,
    The onely thing quhairin he maift reioyfit ;
Do quhar he docht in deidis marciall,
·   By his awin pepill petioufly depofed.

Siclyke was Sipio, faiklefly fchot furth,
    That vinqueift Hanniball lyke a warriour wicht,
His vailiant workes was weyit bot litils worth,
    Quhen he was baneift with a bair gude nicht ;
Not lyke a captaine, nor a kindly knicht,
    Bot lyke ane beggar baneift in exile ;
Sa Fortoun montit neuer man on hicht,
    Bot fho can law him within a litill quhyle.

Alchebead of Athenis was Duke,
    Of princely parents and ane royall race,
To keip his toun fic trauell undertuke,
    He maid his fo-men fle befoir his face ;
To his rewarde he gat nane vther grace,
    Ingraitly baneift to their awin grit fkaith :
And Tymiftocles in that famin place,
    By their awin burgeffis thay wer baneift baith.

Experience teiches me not to flyte with Fortoun,
    With auld examples that dois na thing belang vs ;
Marke James of Dowglas prefent Erle of Morton,
    Ane of the beft that euer was borne amang vs ;
Danter of theuis that dayly dois ouer-gang vs,
    Key of this countre that kepit vs from fkaith ;
I fpeik na farther in feir thay fould gar hang vs,
    Preichouris and poiettis are put to filence baith.

Few things wer done bot Mortoun interprifit them,
  Dumbar and Brichane and mony vthair bloke;
Speik quhat thay pleis, he wrocht them and deuifit
    them;
  He and his freindis ay formeft in the flocke;
He faucht ʒour querrell as kein as ony cok,
  Reuengit ʒour murthers ma nor twa or thrie;
Ane nobillman and of ane ancient ftoke,
  His valiant deidis demereitis not to die.

℃ Ane of the fpeciallis did mentene ʒour croun,
  ʒour ferme protectour in ʒour tender ʒeiris;
He maid ʒow vp and all ʒour fo-men doun,
  His marciall manheid did mentein ʒour weiris;
Gif he did wrang, rewarde him as effeiris,
  Gif he did gud, God wald he fould be tret;
Bot as the prouerbe fpeikis, it plaine appeiris,
  Auld men will die and barnes will fone forʒet.

Was he not rewler ouer ʒour realme and
    rigioun,
  Quhill all was pacifeit be his prudent wit?
Stude he not ftoutly be the true religioun,
  Ane of the firft that maid the freiris to flit?
Franke on the feildis, and formeft at the bit,
  Without refpect to baggis or bodie to;
ʒour faithfull fubiect, and fua he fal be ʒit,
  To do gude feruice, as I haue feene him do.

Than at Carbarrie hill he held a day,
  With litill bludefhed Bothwell was put a-bake,
Quha flew ʒour father and fibilly fled away,
  Syne focht ʒourfelfe to bring this realme to fake.
How mony clawbackes than fuppofe thay crak,
  Conuenit with Mortoun quhan Bothwel tuk the
    chafe?

Try or ʒe tine him and trow not all thay ſpak,
    Lat workes beir witnes, vaine wordis ſould haue
      na place.

Sone efter that the Counſell cround ʒourſell,
    Quhan godly Murray as a regent rang,
ʒit thair was ſome that bauldly did rebell,
    That to ʒour lawis wald nouther ryde nor
      . gang.
Quha thair conuenit for to reuenge ʒour wrang,
    Albeit ʒour action was thocht innocent?
It was the Dowglaſſis douchtaly them dang,
    And pleit ʒour proces in that parliament.

Quha could declare our langſum lyfe in Leith,
    Fechtand all day and ſyne lay in our clais?
Gif Lindeſay lykes, that lord can tell ʒow eith,
    Quha was ʒour friendis or quha ʒour mortall fais,
Or quha gaid formeſt breiſtand vp the braies.
    I dar not pen the ſpeciallis, I do plaine ʒow;
Bot weill I wait, howeuer the warld now gais,
    Thai find maiſt freindſhip was fardeſt than again
      ʒou.

Syne at Langſyde feild ʒour grace may ken,
    Mortoun was thair ane man amang the reſt;
In Striuiling toun, out of his dowie den,
    Maiſt lyke a fox thay fyrit him in his neſt.
In Edinburgh Caſtell quhair thay war poſſeſt,
    He them deplaced that purpoſit to undo ʒow.
Quhan ʒe grow auld, I wait ʒe will confeſt,
    Mortoun hes bene ane faithfull ſaruand to ʒow.

Quhan Regentis deit and all the lytes inlaikit,
    The Counſell did conuene and ſet ane day;

Thay cheifit him Regent in that rowme that waikit,
  With fad adwife, for few or nane faid nay ;
Bot ʒit I think thay playit ʒour grace foule play,
  Gif he was knawin than of thir crymes conuict,
Gif he be faikles, furely I dar fay,
  Thay haue defamit him with ane fulich trick.

To dant the theuis had he nocht mekill ado,
  Abandoned the borders that na man durft rebell?
The Armeftrangis, Eluottis and the Johneftons to,
  With twentie vther clans I can not tell,—
During his dayis thai durft not ryde ane ell;
  The hirdis and hinde men in their labeis lay ;
Bot thair eftait, as now ʒe fie ʒourfell,
  All nicht to walke and fane to wirk all day.

Aganis grit lordis committing fmall offence,
  With iniuft challenge thay aucht na man to
    cheffoun ;
Mortoun hes ay bene vpricht with his prince,
  But fpot of cryme or ony point of treffoun.
Albeit gude faruice be not tane in feafoun,
  His workes may witnes he neuer fparit for
    perrell ;
Laitly accufit but outher ryme or reffoun,
  As findrie fchawis me for a faikles querrell.

Daft fulis defyis him becaufe thay finde him fage,
  And cowartis contrarious for his hardiment ;
Young men for glaikrie can not agrie with age,
  And waifteris inuyis him for his gouernement.
And facreit counfell can not be content
  To fuffer lorfhippis in equalitie ;
ʒit I befeik ʒour grace of gude intent,
  To play the prince but parcialitie.

Adwife ʒow weill, fen he hes not offendit;
 To keip fic fenattis it fall decore ʒour land;
Of rafche detreitis cums rew and may not
  mend it,
 As Scottifmens wifdome dois behinde the hand.
Wyfe lordis are ill ta make I vnderftand,
 And trewly in kingis is to abhorre;
This fempill counfall, fyr, is na command,
 Bot wald to God that na man louit ʒow war.

Finis, quod Sempill.

Imprintit at Edinburgh, be Robert Lekprewicke,
  dwelling at the Netherbow.

❧❦❧

The Plagues of Northomberland.

To the tune of Appelles.

HEN that the Moone, in Northom-
  berland,
 After the chaynge, in age well conne,
 Did rife with force, then to withftande
The lyght and bright beames of the Sonne,
The forowfull dolers foone began,
Through Percies pryde, to many a man.

But then anone, the Weftmere Bull
 Behelde the ryfinge of this Moone;
Thinking that fhee had byn at full,
 He haftyd then anone full foone,
With horfe and armes, and all his might,
From parfeƈt daye to vncertaine lyght.

When they in one confent were pyght,
 With them was many an ignorant man ;
The Romyfhe lawes they wold redyght,
 Through councell of fome blind Syr John,
Who neuer knewe Godes veryte,
But to rebellion then dyd agree.

For if they would of Gods word knowen,
 Longe xxx yeres they haue had tyme,
Rebellion then had not byn fowen,
 To brynge ther countre in fuch cryme ;
Their poyfon now, all men may fee,
That vnder fuger longe did lie.

What myfchyfe mouid the Perfies hart,
 This enterpryfe to take in hand,
This for to playe a Rebelles parte,
 In raifinge vp Northomberland ?
But looke, what feede by hym is fowen,
With fharp fythes downe it was foone mowen.

❡ That countre is in full fore plyght
 That doth agaynft their prynce contend,
Seeking their owne dreames to redyght,
 The Popes precepts for to defend,
Lyke brutyfhe, peruerft, ignorant men,
That feekes before a lawe to ren.

❡ This venym longe a-breedinge was,
 Which in the Perfies brefte did growe ;
The Bull in bellinge did not ceaffe,
 Till that the poyfon oute did flowe ;
So farr abroade the ftreames did ronne,
That backe agayne cold not retourne.

❡ This hatefull poyſon longe was hyde,
  Under the cloake of amytie ;
The outward treaſone was not ſpyde,
  But couerid with all courteſie ;
Their cloſe vnlawfull conſpiracion
Hath brought them to great dyſolacion.

❡ The hope vnſure was tranſytorye,
  The which was in that clowdy Moone ;
Her falſe eclypes with all the glorye,
  Her ioye vnſtable was endid ſoone ;
Her ſudden chaynge now tells vs all
That ſuger ſweet was blent with gall.

❡ What ſtate now maye hymſelfe aſſure
  Longe here to lyue in quyetnes ?
What worldely ioye maye here indure,
  In thoſe where is no ſtablenes ?
Wher lords and yerles in welth doth flowe,
From their hye ſtate muſt fall downe lowe.

❡ Now by their fall learne to be wyſe,
  Both hye and lowe in eche degree ;
Let no falſe lyght deceaue your eyes,
  As it hath done of late, you ſee.
The falſe beames of the glyſtringe Moone,
Now many a man it hath vndoone.

❡ For in the north ſhe did ſhine longe,
  But now eclypſyd is her lyght ;
The Weſtmere Bull that held ſo ſtronge,
  Hee is depreuyd of his myght ;
For many tongs of them will tell,
How theſe to yerles falſe did rebell.

And many a man more, as I heare,
　That with thefe rebelles did take part,
Which can not thinke themfelues now cleare,
　That in breft beares a doble hart ;
But as you haue begonne to brewe,
So are you found rebelles vntrue !

❡ The countre cleane you haue vndone ;
　The Lord graunt ther fome better ftaye,
Or els will many a mothers fonne
　For this curfle you another daye !
You leaue your wyues and childrene deare,
Lamentinge in moft wofull cheare.

❡ Now let vs praye, as we are bound,
　All for our Queenes hyghe maiefte,
That fhee her enemies may confound,
　And all that to rebelles agre ;
And plant true men vp in their place ;
The Lord from heauen now gyue her grace !

Finis, quod John Barker.

❡ Imprinted at London, in Fleete Streate, beneath
　the Conduyt, at the figne of Saint John
　　Euangelift, by Thomas Colwell.

*A merry new Song how a Bruer meant to
make a Cooper cuckold, and how deere the Bruer
paid for the bargaine.*

To the tune of, In Somer time.

IF that you lift, now merry be,
Lend liftning eares a while to me,
To heare a fong of a Bruer bold,
That meant a Cooper to cuckold.

The Cooper walked downe the ftreete,
And with the Bruer chanc'd to meete:
He called,—Worke for a Cooper, dame;
The Bruer was glad to heare the fame.

Cooper, quoth the Bruer, come hether to me,
Perchance I haue fome worke for thee:
If that thy doings I doe well like,
Thou fhalt haue worke for all this weeke.

The Cooper with cap and curtefie low,
Said, ready I am my tunning to fhow;
To doe your worke, fir, euery deale.
I doe not doubt to doe it well.

Then, quoth this luftie Bruer tho,
If thou my worke doeft meane to doe,
Come to me to morrow before it be day,
To hoope vp thefe olde tubs out of the way.

And fo to make vp my merry rime,
The Cooper the next day rofe betime;
To the Bruers gate he tooke his race,
And knocked there a great pace.

The Bruer leapt from his bed to the flore,
And to the Cooper he opned the dore;
He fhewed him his worke without delay;
To the Coopers wife then he tooke the way.

The Cooper he called at mind at laft,
His hatchet he had left at home for haft:
And home for his hatchet he muft goe,
Before he could worke; the caufe it was fo.

But when he came his houfe fomwhat nere,
His wife by fortune did him heare:
Alas! faid fhe, what fhift fhall we make?
My hufband is come,—you will be take!

O Lord! fayd the Bruer, what fhall I doe?
How fhall I hide me? where fhall I goe?
Said fhee,—if you will not be efpide,
Creepe vnder this fat yourfelfe to hide.

The Bruer he crept vnder the fame,
And blundering in the Cooper came:
About the fhop his tubs he caft,
To finde out his hatchet all in haft.

Then his curft wife began to prate,—
If thou let out my pig, ile breake thy pate!
A pig, faid the Cooper, I knew of none;
If thou hadft not fpoke, the pig had bin gone.

If it be a fow-pig, faid the Cooper,
Let me haue him rofted for my fupper:
It is a bore-pig, man, faid fhe,
For my owne dyet, and not for thee.

It is hard if a woman cannot haue a bit,
But ftraightway her hufband muft know of it.
A bore-pig, faid the Cooper, fo me thinks;
He is fo ramifh,—fie, how he ftinkes!

Well, fayd the Cooper, fo I might thriue,
I would he were in thy belly aliue.
I thanke you for your wifh, good man;
It may chance it fhall be there anon.

The Bruer that vnder the fat did lye,
Like a pig did affay to grunt and crie:
But, alas! his voice was nothing fmall;
He cryed fo big that he mard all.

Wife, faid the Cooper, this is no pig,
But an old hog, he grunteth fo big!
He lift vp the fat then by and by;
There lay the Bruer like a bore in a ftie.

Wife, faid the Cooper, thou wilt lie like a dog!
This is no pig, but a very old hog:
I fweare, quoth the Cooper, I doe not like him;
Ile knock him on the head ere ile keepe him.

O Lord! faid the Bruer, ferue me not fo;
Hold thy hand, Cooper, and let me goe,
And I will giue thee both ale and beere,
To find thy houfe this fixe or feauen yeare.

I will none of thy ale nor yet of thy beere,
For feare I be poifoned within feauen yeere!
Why, fayd the Bruer, if thou miftruft,
Hold here the keyes of my beft cheft;

And there is gold and filuer ftore,
Will ferue thee fo long and fomewhat more:
If there be ftore, quoth the Cooper, I fay,
I will not come emptie-handed away.

The Cooper went and filled his hat;
The Bruer fhall pay for vfing my fat!
The hooping of twentie tubs euery day,
And not gaind me fo much as I doe this way.

When he came againe his houfe within,—
Packe away, quod he, Bruer, with your broken fhin;
And vnder my fat creepe you no more,
Except you make wifer bargaines before.

*The true defcription of a monfterous Chylde,
borne in the Ile of Wight, in this prefent yeare
of oure Lord God M D lxiiij. the month of
October, after this forme, with a clufter of longe
heare about the nauell: the Fathers name is
James Johnfun, in the parys of Frefwater.*

FOR mercy, Lorde, with one accorde,
    To the we call and crye,
That fo doth fhow, in earth below,
    Thy wonderous workes daylye.

Within the rafe of fyue yeres fpace
    Moche monfterous fights hath byn,
Of fundry kynde; man, bare in mynde,
    And fone turne from thy fyn.

Repent and pray, amende, I fay,
    Leue of thy wicked wayes;
The tyme drawes on, thou muft be gone,
    Beholde this later dayes.

Of infans yonge, agone not longe,
    With calues and pigges which were,
The tookens, loo, mifhappen foo,
    Whiche cryeth to vs great feare.

Now this late fyght in Ile of Wight,
    Straungely it is to tell,
Two children borne,—neuer beforne
    Suche wonders there befell.

The one I fynde, of woman kynde,
    Hauyng her fhape all right;
The other is tranfpofed this,
    As pleafeth the Lorde of myght.

Where natures art doth not her part,
    In workyng of her fkylle,
To fhape aright, eche lyuely wight;
    Beholde, it is Gods wyll!

Loo, here you fee, before your eye,
    A man-childe to beholde;
A babe gyltles, deformyd this,
    Mofte wonderous to be tolde.

No caruer can, nor paynter then,
  The fhape more ugly make,
As itfelfe dothe declare the truthe;
  A fyghte to make vs quake!

Let vs all feare, and in mynde beare,
  This forme fo monfterous:
That no hurt wraught, nor euill hath thaught,
  What fhall become of vs.

That doth ftill fyn, and neuer lyn,
  As men heapyng vp treafure,
Agyanft the day of wrath, for aye,
  Of Gods heauy difpleafure.

Nowe praye wee all, bothe great and fmall,
  Unto the Lorde of might,
To gyue vs grace in heauen a place
  There to attayne his fight!

All ye that dothe beholde and fee this monftrous
    fight fo ftraunge,
Let it to you a preachyng be, from fynfull lyfe
    to chaunge:
For in this latter dayes trulye, the Lord ftraunge
    fyghts doth fhowe,
By tokens in the heauens hye, and on the yearth
    belowe.
This dothe demonftrate to vs, the lyfe whiche we
    lyue in;
A monfter, oughly to beholde, conceyued was in fyn:
In fhape vnparfett here to vewe, that nature hathe
    not dreft,
A chylde now borne, by porte mofte true, this
    from the mothers breft:

F

For he that doth this fhape beholde, and his owne
      ftate will knowe,
Will make the proude pecocke fo bolde, beare
      downe his tayll full lowe :
Nowe, Lorde, fende downe thy Holy Spryte, the
      confortor of joye,
For to direct owr wayes aright, to dwell with
      thee for aye ;
And graunt we maye amende our lyfe, accordyng
      to thy worde,
In euery age, bothe manne and wyfe,—nowe
      graunt vs this, good Lorde !

Finis, quod John Barkar.

❡ Imprynted at London, in Flete Strete, at the
    fygne of the Faucon, by Wylliam Gryffith, and
    are to be folde at his fhop in Saint Dunftons
    churchyarde, in the weft of London, the viij.
    daye of Nouember.

The firft part of the Marchants Daughter of Briftow.

To the tune of The Maydens Joy.

BEHOLD the touchftone of true loue,
      Maudlin the Marchants daughter
      of Briftow towne,
Whofe firme affection nothing could
      moue,—
Such fauour beares the louely browne.

℃ A gallant youth was dwelling by,
    Which many yeeres had borne this mayden
        great good will;
She loued him as faythfully,
    But all her friendes withſtood it ſtill.

℃ The young man now, perceiuing well,
    He could not get nor win the fauour of her
        friendes,
The force of ſorrowes to expell,
    To view ſtrange countries he intendes.

℃ And now to take his laſt farewell
    Of his true loue, his faire and conſtant Maudlin,
With muſicke ſweete that did excell
    He playes under her window fine.

℃ Farewell, quoth he, my owne true loue!
    Farewell, my deare and cheefeſt treaſure of my
        hart!
Through fortunes ſpight, that falſe did proue,
    I am inforc't from thee to part.

℃ Into the land of Italy
    There will I waſte and wearie out my dayes in
        woe;
Seeing my true loue is kept from me,
    I hold my life a mortall foe.

℃ Faire Briſtow towne, therefore, adue,—
    For Padua muſt be my habitation now,—
Although my loue doth lodge in thee,
    To whom alone my hart I vow.

℃ With trickling teares thus did he ſing,
    With ſighes and ſobs deſcending from his hart
        ful ſore;

He fayth, when he his hands did wring,—
　　Farewell, fweete loue, for euermore !

❡ Faire Maudlin, from a window hie,
　　Beholdes her true loue with his muficke where
　　　　he ftood,
But not a word fhe durft reply,
　　Fearing her parents angry mood.

❡ In teares fhe fpendes the dolefull night,
　　Wifhing herfelfe (though naked) with her
　　　　faithful friend ;
She blames her friendes and fortunes fpight,
　　That wrought their loues fuch luckles end.

❡ And in her hart fhe makes a vow
　　Cleane to forfake her countrey and her kinsfolke
　　　　all,
And for to follow her true loue now,
　　To bide all chaunces that might fall.

❡ The night is gone, and the day is come,
　　And in the morning very early doth fhe arife ;
She gets her downe to the lower roome,
　　Where fundry feamen fhe efpies.

❡ A gallant maifter among them all—
　　The maifter of a faire and goodly fhip was he—
Which there ftood waighting in the hall,
　　To fpeake with her father, if it might be.

❡ She kindly takes him by the hand,—
　　Good fir, fhe fayd, and would you fpeake with
　　　　any heere :
Quoth he, faire mayde, therefore I ftand.
　　Then, gentle fir, I pray you come neere.

❡ Into a pleafant parlour by,
    With hand in hand fhe bringes this feaman all
        alone,
Sighing to him moft pitteoufly,—
    She thus to him did make her mone.

❡ She falles upon her tender knee,—
    Good fir, fhe fayd, now pitty you a maydens
        woe,
And proue a faythfull friend to me,
    That I to you my griefe may fhew.

❡ Sith you repofe fuch truft, he fayd,
    To me that am unknowne, and eke a ftranger
        heere,
Be you affured, proper mayde,
    Moft faythfull ftill I will appeare.

❡ I haue a brother, fir, quoth fhe,
    Whom as my lyfe I loue and fauour tenderly;
In Padua, alas! is he,
    Full ficke, God wot, and like to die.

❡ And faine I would my brother fee,
    But that my father will not yeeld to let me go;
Wherefore, good fir, be good to me,
    And vnto me this fauour fhow.

❡ Some fhip-boyes garments bring to me,
    That I difguifd may get away from hence un-
        knowne,
And vnto fea Ile goe with thee,
    If thus much friendfhyp may be fhowne.

❡ Faire mayde, quoth he, take here my hand,
    I will fulfill each thing that now you defire:

And fet you fafe in that fame land,
    And in the place where you require.

℃ Then giues fhe him a tender kiffe,
    And fayth, your feruant, gallant maifter, I will
        be,
And proue your faythfull friend for this,—
    Sweete maifter, then forget not me.

℃ This done, as they had both decreed,
    Soone after, early, euen before the breake of
        day,
He bringes her garments then with fpeed,
    Wherein fhe doth herfelfe array.

℃ And ere her father did arife,
    She meetes her maifter as he walked in the hall ;
She did attend on him likewife,
    Euen till her father did him call.

℃ But ere the marchant made an end
    Of all thofe matters to the maifter he could fay,
His wife came weeping in with fpeed,
    Saying, our daughter is gone away.

℃ The marchant, much amazed in minde,
    Yonder vilde wretch entic't away my child,
        quoth he ;
But well I wot I fhall him find
    At Padua in Italie. ✻

℃ With that befpake the maifter braue :
    Worfhipfull marchant, thither goes this pretty
        youth,
And any thing that you would haue
    He will performe it, and write the trueth.

❡ Sweete youth, quoth he, if it be fo,
  Beare me a letter to the Englifh marchants there,
And gold on thee I will beftow,—
  My daughters welfare I do feare.

❡ Her mother takes her by the hand,—
  Faire youth, quoth fhe, if there thou doft my
      daughter fee,
Let me thereof foone vnderftand,
  And there is twenty crownes for thee.

❡ Thus through the daughters ftrange difguife,
  The mother knew not when fhe fpake vnto her
      child :
And after her maifter ftraight fhe hies,
  Taking her leaue with countenance milde.

❡ Thus to the fea faire Maudlin is gone,
  With her gentle maifter,—God fend them a
      merry wind !—
Where we a while muft leaue them alone,
  Till you the fecond part do finde.   FINIS.

*The fecond part of the Marchants Daughter
of Briftow.*

To the tune of *The Maidens Joy.*

ELCOME, fweet Maudlin, from the fea,
    Where bitter ftorms and cruel tem-
      pefts did arife :
  The pleafant banks of Italy
We may behold with ioyfull eies.

Thankes, gentle maiſter, then quoth ſhe,—
   A faithful friend in al my ſorows thou haſt
      beene;—
If fortune once doth ſmile on me,
   My thankfull heart ſhall well be ſeene.

Bleſt be the land that feedes my loue,
   Bleſt be that place whereas he doth abide.;
No trauell will I ſticke to proue,
   Whereby my good will may be tride.

Now will I walke, with ioyfull heart,
   To view the town wheras my darling doth re-
      maine,
And ſeek him out in euery part,
   Untill I do his ſight attaine.

And I, quoth he, will not forſake
   Sweete M. in al her iorneys vp and downe;
In wealth and woe thy part Ile take,
   And bring thee ſafe to Padua towne.

And, after many weary ſteps,
   In Padua they ſafe ariued at the laſt;
For verie ioy her heart it leapes,—
   She thinkes not on her perills paſt.

But now, alas, behold the lucke!
   Her own true loue in woful priſon doth ſhe find,
Which did her heart in peeces plucke,
   And greeude her gentle mind.

Condemnd he was to die, alas,
   Except he would his faith and his religion turne:
But rather then he would go to maſſe,
   In fiery flames he vowed to burne.

Now doth faire Maudlin weepe and waile,
   Her ioy is changd to weeping, forow, greefe
      and care ;
But nothing can her plaints preuaile,
   For death alone muft be his fhare.

She walkes vnder the prifon walles,
   Where her true loue doth ly and languifh in
      diftreffe ;—
Moft wofully for foode he calls,
   When hunger did his heart oppreffe.

He fighes, and fobs, and makes great mone ;
   Farwel, faid he, fweet England, now for euer ;
And al my friends that haue me known
   In Briftow towne with wealth and ftore !

But moft of al, farewel, quoth he,
   My owne true loue, fweete M., whom I left
      behind !
For neuer more I fhal thee fee ;
   Woe to thy father moft unkind !

How wel were I, if thou waft here
   With thy fair hands to clofe vp both thefe
      wretched eyes ;
My torments eafie would appeere,
   My foule with ioy fhould fcale the fkies.

When M. heard her louers mone,
   Her eies with tears, her hart with forow filled was ;
To fpeak with him no means was known,
   Such grieuous . . . on him did paffe.

Then caft fhe off her ladies attire,
   A maidens weede upon her back fhe feemly fet ;

To the iudges houfe fhe did enquire,
    And there fhe did a feruice get.

She did her dutie there fo wel,
    And eke fo prudently herfelf fhe did behaue,—
With her in loue her maifter fell,—
    His feruants fauour he doth craue.

Maudlin, quoth he, my hearts delight!
    To whom my hart in firme affections tide,
Breede not my death through thy difpight,—
    A faythful friend I will be tride.

Graunt me thy loue, faire maide, quoth he,
    And at my hands defire what thou canft deuife,
And I wil grant it vnto thee,
    Whereby thy credite may arife.

O fir, fhe faid, how bleft am I,
    With fuch a kind and gentle maifter for to meete!
I will not your requeft denie,
    So you will grant what I do feeke.

I haue a brother, fir, fhe faid,
    For his religion is now condemnde to die ;
In loathfome prifon he is laide,
    Oppreft with care and miferie.

Graunt me my brothers life, fhe faid,
    And to you my loue and liking I wil giue :
That may not be, quoth he, faire maide,—
    Except he turne, he may not liue.

An Englifh friar there is, fhe faid,
    Of learning great, and of a paffing pure life ;

Let him be to my brother fent,
   And he will finifh foone the ftrife.

Her maifter granted this requeft.
   The mariner in friars weed fhe doth aray,
And to her loue, that lay diftreft,
   She doth a letter ftraightway conuay.

When he had read her gentle lines,
   His heauy hart was rauifhed with inward ioy ;
Where now fhe was ful wel he finds,
   The friar likewife was not coy,

But did declare to him at large
   The enterprife his loue for him had taken in
       hand :
The yong man did the friar charge,
   His loue fhould ftraight depart the land.

Here is no place for her, he faid,
   But woful death and danger of her harmles life ;
Profeffing truth I was betraid,
   And feareful flames muft end our ftrife.

For ere I wil my faith denie,
   And fweare myfelf to follow damnde antichrift,
Ile yeeld my bodie for to die,
   To liue in heauen with the higheft.

O fir, the gentle friar faid,
   For your fweete loue recant and faue your
       wifhed life :
A wofull match, quoth he, is made,
   Where Chrift is loft, to winne a wife.

When fhe had wroght al means fhe might
   To faue her friend, and that fhe faw it wold not
     be,
Then of the iudge fhe claimd her right
   To die the death as well as he.

For looke what faith he doth profeffe,
   In that fame faith be fure that I will liue and dy ;—
Then eafe vs both in our diftreffe,
   Let vs not liue in miferie.

When no perfwafion would preuaile,
   Nor change her mind in anything that fhe had
     faid,
She was with him condemnd to die,
   And for them both one fire made.

And arme in arme, moft ioyfully,
   Thefe louers twain vnto the fire then did go,—
The mariners, moft faithfully,
   Were likewife partners of their woe.

But when the iudges vnderftood
   The faithful frindfhip in them al that did re-
     maine,
They faude their liues, and afterward
   To England fent them home againe.

Now was their forrowes turnde to ioy,
   And faithful louers had now their harts defire ;
Their paines fo wel they did imploy,
   God granted what they did require.

And when they were in England come,
   And to mery Briftow arriued at the laft,

Great ioy there was of al and fome,
   That heard the dangers they had paft.

Her father he was dead, God wot,
   And eke her mother was ioyful of her fight;
Their wifhes fhe denied not,
   But wedded them with hearts delight.

Her gentle maifter fhe defirde
   To be her father, and at church to giue her then;
It was fulfild as fhe requirde,
   Unto the ioy of all good men!

Finis.

Printed at London for William Blackwall.

*A briefe fonet declaring the lamentation of
  Beckles, a Market Towne in Suffolke, which
  was in the great winde vpon S. Andrewes eue
  pitifully burned with fire, to the value by eftimation of tweentie thoufande pounds, and to the
  number of fourefcore dwelling houfes, befides a
  great number of other houfes, 1586.*

To the tune of Labandalafbotte.

MY louing good neighbours, that comes
          to beholde
        Me, fillie poore Beckles, in cares many-
          folde ;
In forrow all drowned, which floated of late,
With teares all bedewed, at my wofull ftate :
With fire fo confumed, moft wofull to vewe,
Whofe fpoyle my poore people for euer may rue ;
When well you have vewed my dolefull decay,
And pittie haue pierced your heartes as it may,
Say thus, my good neighbours, that God in his ire
For finne hath confumed me, Beckles, with fire.

For one onely parifh myfelfe mought vaunt,
To match with the braueft for who but will graunt ;
The fea and the countrey me fitting fo nye,
The frefh-water river fo fweete running by,
My medowes and commons fuch profpect of health,
My fayers in fomer fo garnifht with wealth,
My market fo ferued with corne, flefh, and fifh,
And all kinde of victuals that poore men would
          wifh ;

That who but knewe Beckles, with sighing may
     faye,
Would God of his mercie had sparde my decaye!

But, O my destruction! O most dismall day!
My temple is spoyled, and brought in decay,
My marketsted burned, my beautie defaced,
My wealth ouerwhelmed, my people displaced!
My musicke is wayling, my mirth it is moone,
My ioyes are departed, my comfort is gone;
My people, poore creatures, are mourning in woe,
Still wandring, not wotting which waye for to goe,
Like sillie poore Troians, whom Sinon betrayde; A rude felt
But, God, of thy mercy releeue them with ayde! by fiering b
                                              chimney, p
                                              cured their
O daye most vnluckie! the winde lowde in skie, lamitie.
The water harde frosen, the houses so drye;
To see such a burning, such flaming of fire,
Such wayling, such crying, through scourge of
        Gods ire,
Such running, such working, such taking of payne,
Such whirling, such haling, such reauing in vaine;
Such robbing, such stealing, from more to the lesse,
Such dishonest dealing, in time of distresse;
That who so hard-hearted, and worne out of grace,
But pittie may pierce him to thinke of my case.

But, O my good neighbours, that see mine estate,
Be all one as Christians, not liue in debate;
With wrapping and trapping each other in thrall,
With watching and pryeng at each others fall,
With houing, and shouing, and striuing in lawe,
Of God nor his Gospell once standing in awe;
Lyue not in heart-burning, at God neuer wrest,
To Christ ance be turning, not vse him in iest,

Liue louely together, and not in difcorde;
Let me be your mirrour to liue in the Lorde!

But, though God haue pleafed, for finne to
      plague me,
Let none thinke there liuing is caufe they fcape
      free;
But let them remember how Chrift once did tell,
Their finnes were not greater on whom the wall
      fell:
But leaft you repent ye, thus much he doth fay,
Be fure and certaine ye alfo decaye.
Let none, then, perfwade them fo free from all
      thrall,
But that their ill-liuing deferueth a fall;
Thus, farewell!   Forget not my wofull annoye;
God fend you good new yeare and bleffe me with
      ioye!

Finis quod D. Sterrie.

Fœlix quem faciunt aliena pericula cautum.

Ech ftately towre with mightie walles vp prope,
Ech loftie roofe which golden wealth hath raifed,
All flickering wealth which flies in firmeft hope,
All glittering hew, fo haught and highly praifde,—
I fee, by fodaine ruine of Beckles towne,
Is but a blaft if mightie Ioue doe frowne.

At London:
Imprinted by Robert Robinfon, for Nicholas
Colman of Norwich, dwelling in S.
Andrewes Church Yarde.

A proper newe fonet declaring the lamentation of Beckles [a market towne in] Suffolke, which was in the great winde vpon S. Andrewes eue laſt paſt moſt pittifully burned with fire, to the loſſe by eſtimation of twentie thouſande pound and vpwarde, and to the number of foure ſcore dwelling houſes, 1586.

To Wilſon's Tune.

ITH ſobbing ſighes, and trickling teares,
  My ſtate I doe lament,
Perceiuing how God's heavie wrath
  Againſt my ſinnes is bent ;
Let all men viewe my woefull fall,
  And rue my woefull caſe,
And learne hereby in ſpeedy ſort
  Repentaunce to embrace.

For late in Suffoclke was I ſeen
  To be a ſtately towne,
Repleniſhed with riches ſtore,
  And had in great renowne ;
Yea, planted on a pleaſant ſoyle,
  So faire as heart could wiſh,
And had my markets, once a weeke,
  Well ſtorde with fleſh and fiſh.

A faire freſh riuer running by,
  To profite me withall,
Who with a criſtall cleered ſtreame
  About my bankes did fall ;

G

My fayres in fomer welthely
    For to increafe my ftore ;
My medowes greene and commons great,—
    What could I wifh for more ?

But now beholde my great decay,
    Which on a fodaine came ;
My fumptuous buildings burned be
    By force of fires flame :
A carelefſe wretch, moſt rude in life,
    His chymney fet on fire,
The inſtrument, I muſt confefſe,
    Of God's moſt heauie ire.

The flame whereof increaſing ſtil
    The bluſtering windes did blowe,
And into diuers buildings by
    Difperſt it to and fro ;
So, kindling in moſt grieuous fort,
    It waxed huge and hie ;
The riuer then was frozen, fo   ˈ
    No water they could come by.

Great was the crye that then was made
    Among both great and fmall ;
The wemen wept, and wrong their handes,
    Whofe goods confumed all ;
No helpe was found to flacke the fyre,
    Theyr paines was fpent in vaine ;
To beare theyr goods into the fieldes
    For fafegarde they were fayne.

And yet, amid this great diſtrefſe,
    A number fet theyr minde
To filtch, and fteale, and beare away
    So much as they could finde ;

Theyr neighbors wealth, which wasted lay
   About the streetes that time,
They secretly conuayde away,—
   O most accursed crime !

Thus, from the morning nyne a clocke
   Till four aclocke at night,
Fourescore houses in Beckle's towne
   Was burnd to ashes quite ;
And that which most laments my heart,
   The house of God, I say,
The church and temple by this fyre
   Is cleane consumde away.

The market-place and houses fayre,
   That stood about the same,
Hath felt the force and violence
   Of this most fearefull flame ;
So that there is no Christian man
   But in his heart would grieue,
To see the smart I did sustaine
   Vpon saint Andrewes eue.

Wherefore, good Christian people, now
   Take warning by my fall,—
Liue not in strife and enuious hate
   To breed each other thrall ;
Seeke not your neighbors lasting spoyle
   By greedy sute in lawe ;
Liue not in discord and debate,
   Which doth destruction draw.

And flatter not yourselues in sinne,
   Holde not Gods worde in scorne,
Repine not at his ministers,
   Nor be not false forsworne ;

For, where fuch vices doth remaine,
    Gods grace will neuer be;
And, in your health and happie ftate,
    Haue yet fome minde on me,—

Whofe fonges is changd to forrowes fore,
    My ioyes to wayling woe,
My mirth to mourning fighes and grones,
    The which from griefe doth growe;
My wealth to want and fcarfetie,
    My pleafure into payne,
All for the finne and wickedneffe
    Which did in me remaine.

If then you wifh profperitie,
    Be louing, meeke and kinde,—
Lay rage and rancour cleane afide,
    Set malice from your minde;
And liue in loue and charitie,
    All hatefull pride deteft,
And fo you fhall with happie dayes
    For euermore be bleft.

And thus I ende my wofull fong,
    Befeeching God I may
Remaine a mirrour to all fuch
    That doe in pleafure ftay;
And that amongeft their greateft mirth
    And chiefeft ioye of all,
They yet may haue a heart to thinke
    Of Beckles fodaine fall.

Finis, T. D.

At London:

Imprinted by Robert Robinfon, for Nicholas
Colma[n], of Norwich, dwelling in S.
Andrewes church yard.

Franklins Farewell to the World.

With his Chriftian Contrition in Prifon, before his Death.

FARWELL, vaine world, whofe com-
  forts all are cares,
  Whofe gaines are loffe, whofe liberty
   are fnares,
Whofe gold is droffe, whofe wifedome is meere
  folly,
Whofe wealth is woe, whofe feruice is vnholly,
Whofe life is death, whofe ioy is griefe and
  fadnes,
And all that's in thee is a map of madnes.
Who fo (like me) long in the world hath beene,
And hath fo many alterations feene,—
How fome from greatnes fall, fome rife from little,
How mans foundation flip'ry is and brittle,
How tranfitory things doe mount and fall
At His great pleafure, that created all?
Who fo doth note, and beare thefe things in minde,
Shall fee how Fortunes breath, like wau'ring winde,
Doth blow vp men like bladders with ambition,
And caft them headlong downe to black perdition.
That this is true the world may plainly fee,
And view a fearefull fpectacle in mee;
For I that had enough of fading pelfe,
And need not want (except I would myfelfe),—
I that had fence, difcretion, reafon, wit,
And could difcerne things fitting and vnfit,

I whom my high Creator made a creature,
Adorning me with guifts of art and nature ;—
Yet of all this I made no further vſe,
But Gods, kings, countryes, and my ſoules abuſe.
From crime to crime ſtill plundging further in,
With my continuall adding ſinne to ſinne,
Till ſinne on ſinne at laſt brought ſhame on ſhame,
And ſhame on ſhame paid the deſert of blame.
My thoughts ſurmis'd th' Almighties eyes were hid,
And that he ſaw not what I ſecret did,
But He (whoſe ſight eclipſeth moone and ſun)
Hath brought to light the deeds in darknes done ;
He, in his iuſtice, iuſtly hath reueal'd
My hainous faults, which I had long conceal'd ;
He hath laid open my notorious crimes
To bee a warning to enſuing times ;
That they ſhall neuer dare to doe the like,
Leaſt (like to me) his vengeance them doe ſtrike.
Then let a dying friend good counſell giue
To all eſtates and ſexes how they liue :
Oh, let my ending of my loathed breath
Make all men care to ſhun eternall death !
And though my life hath bin polluted foule,
Yet iudge with charity my ſinfull ſoule ;
For were the ſinnes of all the world in me,
Yet (with the eye of faith) I cleerely ſee
That Gods great mercy, like a boundles flood,
Through my bleſt Sauiour and Redeemers blood,
Hath freely pardon'd all that I haue done,
(By th' interceſſion of his onely Sonne,)
So that my ſtedfaſt faith doth me perſwade
My peace for euer with my God is made.
Hee that raiſ'd Lazarus from out his graue,
He that vpon the Croſſe the theife did ſaue,
'Tis he alone, and onely none but hee,

Hath raifd me vp from death, and faued me.
Yea, though I all my life-time haue liu'd euill,
A feruant and a flaue vnto the deuill,
Yet heer's the ioy that makes my courage bolde,—
My Sauiour Chrift hath tooke me to his folde ;
Hee true repentance vnto me hath giu'n,
And for me (through his merits) purchas'd Heau'n.
Then world, flefh, Sathan, and grim death, auaunt !
Doe all your worft, my faith you cannot daunt :
He, that for me hath conquer'd death and hell,
Hath granted me that I with him fhall dwell ;
And though my life eternall fire did merit,
Yet God in mercy hath receiu'd my fpirit.
Farwell, my countrey, by whofe iuftice I
For mine vniuft and bloody action dye !
Farewell, moft facred and renowned king,
Whofe equall iudgement through the world doth
      ring,
Whofe zeale to right, and whofe impartiall hand
Are the maine prop on which this ftate doth ftand !
Long may he raigne in his maieftick feate,
And, as on earth, bee made in Heau'n more great.
Let his pofterity and royall race
Be all infpir'd with the fupernall grace,
And of his feed let vs haue alwaies one
To fway the fcepter of Great Britaines throne !
Defend them, Lord, from foule and body harmes,
From home-bred traytors, and from foreigne
      armes,
That in thy fauour they may liue and dye,
And dye to liue with thee immortally !

FINIS.

Printed at London, for Henry Goffon.

❡ *The xxv. orders of Fooles.*

STAY a while with pacience, my freends,
   I you pray,
  Of the orders of fooles fomewhat I
   wyll fay :
Fiue and twentie iuft a quarterne is, ye know,—
Euery foole in his foolifhnes wyll I fhow.
  And, as the prouerbe doth fhow very playne,
  A hood for this foole, to kepe him from the
   rayne.

❡ Many fooles the carte of fin now-a-dayes doth
   draw,
Nowrifhyng their finne againft all right and law ;
Though that the way to hell be very playne,
Yet lyke a foole I aduife thee to returne agayne.
  If thou in foolifhnes ftyll doeft dwell,
  Thou fhalt haue a bable and a bell.

❡ He is a foole that his finnes can not hate,—
Naught young, worfe olde, fuch is his eftate :
This olde foole is glad of that name,
Defiryng all men to take parte of the fame.
  This foole muft haue in hand, without fayle,
  A bable, a bell, or els a fox-tayle.

❡ Of fooles yet I fynd another forte,
Which are caufers of lying and yll reporte ;
And he is a foole, both euen and morrow,
That nothyng wyll lend, but all thynges borrow ;

And, as the prouerbe doth fhow very playne,
A hood for this foole, to kepe him from the
    rayne.

❡ Of fooles yet another forte doth come,
Which neuer feketh for to haue wifedome;
Many fuch fooles wifedome difdayne,
Yet for their foolifhnes they fhall fuffer payne;
    And, as the prouerbe doth fhew very playne,
    A hood for this foole, to kepe him from the
        rayne.

❡ He is a foole which to others doth preach and
    tell,
And yet this foole is ready himfelf to go vnto hell:
Liue thou vprightly, be caufe of no blame,
If thou doo not, the more is thy fhame;
    And, as the prouerbe doth fay very playne,
   ·A hood for this foole, to kepe him from the
        rayne.

❡ He is a foole, and euer be fhall,
That others iudgeth, and himfelf worft of all:
This foole is blynd, frantike, and wood,
Without all reafon iudgeth bad thinges good;
    And, as the prouerbe doth fhew very playne,
    A hood for this foole, to kepe him from the
        rayne.

❡ He is a foole that wifedome doth efchue,
For no good counfell can bring him to vertue:
This foole, which fcorneth his neighbour faft,
Shall be fcorned iuftly himfelf at the laft;
    And, as the prouerbe doth fhew very playne,
    A hood for this foole, to kepe him from the
        rayne.

❡ Another foole yet I doe here fynd,
Which can not kepe cloſe the ſecrets of his mynd:
This is a naturall foole, and vndiſcrete,
Which can not hyde his owne counſell and ſecrete;
    And, as the prouerbe doth ſhew very playne,
    A hood for this foole, to kepe him from the
        rayne.

❡ He is a foole that in youth wyll not prouyde,—
In age muſt he ſterue, or in pouertie abyde:
This is a foole, and of the number one,
Which in the ſommer can make no prouiſion;
    And, as the prouerbe doth ſhew very playne,
    A hood for this foole, to kepe him from the
        rayne.

❡ He is a foole that getteth his goods wrongfullye,
For his heires after him wyll ſpend it vnthriftelye:
This fooles golde is his God, wrongfullye got,—
Why, thou foole! thy golde is muk and clay,
        knoweſt thou not?
    And, as the prouerbe doth ſhew very playne,
    A hood for this foole, to kepe him from the
        rayne.

❡ He is a foole, whether he be man or wyfe,
Whiche ſtyll deliteth in diſcorde and ſtryfe:
Such fooles their owne fleſh to the bones may gnaw,
That contendeth in matters ſcant worth a ſtraw;
    And, as the prouerbe doth ſhew very playne,
    A hood for this foole, to kepe him from the
        rayne.

❡ He is a foole that on meſſage is ſent,
And, when he is on his way, forget whether he went:

This foole is worthy of the bable and the bell,
For of all other fooles he doth excell ;
  And, as the prouerbe doth ſhew very playne,
  A hood for this foole, to kepe him from the
    rayne.

⁋ Yet of fooles a whole dozen I haue eſpyed,
And lead in a ſtryng, together they are tyed :
Theſe fooles you may know by their fauour,
For, lyke the aſpen leafe, with euery wynd they
    wauer ;
  And, as the prouerbe doth ſhew very playne,
  A hood for theſe fooles, to kepe them from
    the rayne.

⁋ He is a foole that thinketh it great wonder,
When God ſtryketh by lightnyng and thunder :
Alas! we dayly, without all dread, commit
Much curſed vice, for lacke of godly wit ;
  And, as the prouerbe doth ſhew very playne,
  A hood for this foole, to kepe him from the
    rayne.

⁋ All youth I doo lyken vnto fooles blynd,
That vnto their parents are rebels vnkynd ;
Thow vnkynd chylde, and foole diſobedient,
Remember what goods thy freends on thee ſpent ;
  And, as the prouerbe doth ſhew very playne,
  A hood for theſe fooles, to kepe them from
    the rayne.

⁋ He is a foole that greatly doth flatter and boaſt,
When he thinks leaſt, he ſhall taſt of the roſt !
This foole at laſt is caſt out of fauour,
For flatteryng pleaſeth no wiſe man of honour ;

And, as the prouerbe doth ſhew very playne,
A hood for this foole, to kepe him from the
    rayne.

⁋ He is a foole, and voyd of all prudence,
Which to vayne tales doth geue all his credence :
Therfore remember this, both low and hye,
That flatterers ſpeake fayre when they doo lye ;
    And, as the prouerbe doth ſhew very playne,
    A hood for this foole, to kepe him from the
        rayne.

⁋ He is a naturall foole, and a very daw,
That from doing good his neighbour doth with-
        draw :
Such froward fooles, all goodnes they defile,
If their neighbours doe good, then they reuile ;
    And, as the prouerbe doth ſhew very playne,
    A hood for this foole, to kepe him from the
        rayne.

⁋ He is a foole, and greatly vnprouable,
That in all his doings he is vnfortunable,
But in his misfortune he is ſo blynd,
He neuer conſidereth no remedy in mynd ;
    And, as the prouerbe doth ſhew very playne,
    A hood for this foole, to kepe him from the
        rayne.

⁋ He is a foole, that himſelf doth applye
Behynd his neighbours backe to ſclander with
        enuye :
Such beaſtly fooles commonly are well apayd,
Which thinke all is well, that falſely is wayd ;

And, as the prouerbe doth fhew very playne,
A hood for this foole, to kepe him from the
rayne.

❡ Yet more fooles there be, which be vncom-
mendable,
That vfeth yll manners alway at the table :
Of pleafant nurtour they haue no heede,
But beaftly entend as fwyne alway to feede ;
And, as the prouerbe doth fhew very playne,
A hood for thefe fooles, to kepe them from
the rayne.

❡ Many fooles there be, in thefe our dayes,
Which feeme to be wyfe, yet folow foolifh wayes ;
Therfore I haue tolde vnto you very playne,
What foolifhnes in thefe dayes in many doth re-
mayne ;
And, as the prouerbe doth fhew very playne,
A hood for thefe fooles, to kepe them from
the rayne.

❡ He is a foole, that wyll ftyll defyre
His owne death, to runne into the fyre :
And he is a foole, that hath no mynd deuoute,
But in the temple ftyll walketh aboute ;
And, as the prouerbe doth fhew very playne,
A hood for thefe fooles, to kepe them from
the rayne.

❡ God grant that all fooles wifedome may learne,
And that they may good from yll alway difcerne ;
Then no more fooles we may them call,
But wyfe men, and wifedome fhew they fhall.

God grant that on all partes we may now begin
To repent of our follye, and flye from our fin!

FINIS quod T. Gr.

¶ Imprinted at London by Alexander Lacie, for
Henrie Kyrkham, dwellyng at the figne of the
Blacke Boye, at the middle North dore of
Paules church.

The wonders of England.

·1559·

HEN date of (1553) was expirde ful,
        And Gods wrath rypt, ready to fall,
        His fworde from fheath did ferce out
                pul,
And to the heauens beganne to call,
Saying :—on England now I fhall
Plage prince, prophet, and people all,
        For contemptes fake!
Go, Death, inclofe their kyng in clay,
And, Sunne, withdraw the light of day,
        And darkenes make.

No fooner fayd, but ftraight was done,—
    The Englifh kyng Edward God tooke ;—
Light of foule from England gone,
    Darkenes made them blyndely looke ;

Truth and fayth of people forfooke,
　　Their prophetes taken from the booke,
　　　　And pryfoners made;
The bats and owles from holes out came,
Wolues and beares, and cruel Caim
　　　　Did England inuade.

When darknes thus echwhere was fen,
　　And nightly vermin rulde the roft,
No birds might fyng in that late euen,
　　By land, by fea, or by the coaft,
　　But ftraight were brought to firy poft,
　　Or els to Lolers tower toft,
　　　　And kept in cage,—
From meate and frend fomtimes fo bard,
That lomy wales they fed on hard,
　　　　Hunger to fwage.

Thys darkenes fo extremely bode,
　　That none from other fcarce were known;
On noble, fage, learned and good,
　　Thefe wormes of darknes fpared none,
　　And pourde their poifon abrod fo flowne
　　On prophet, people, and prince their own,
　　　　Whych is by name
Elizabeth,—by God nowe Quene,
To Englands ioy ryght wel is fene,—
　　　　They fought to fhame.

The fun thus quentch, and day made dark,
　　And cockes in coopes from croing kept,
Then ftraight thefe owles began to wark,
　　And to the churches fearcely lept,
　　And with new broumes them clene out fwept,
　　From God, from king and Scripture fet

Vpon the wall,
And in their ftede fet ydols long,
And made people, with prayfe and fong,
On them to call.

Thus vermin darke the maftry had
Of realme, of prince, of noble and all :
And yet not herewith fully glad,
Away they fought to faue theyr fall,
And counfayle gaue a forayne, to call
To match our quene and crowne royal,—
All for their pope
To haue their kingdome raygne alway,
And they themfelues to beare the fway,
And blindly grope.

Al this not yet their mindes fyllyng,
For no regarde to natiue land,
Fearing again Gods light fhould fpring,
Brought merfhial law forthwith in hand
Againft al fuch as would withftand
Their wicked raygne and cruell band,
And Gods part take ;
Or els in priuye places founde,
Praying to God 'proftrate on ground,
His wrath to flake.

Thus, rulyng all in darkenes blynde,
Came miferies with heape on heape ;
No lore was taught to fyl the mynde,
Godly to lyue, and good fruite reape,
But al for Church they cride and threape,—
Reftore, reftore, euen as good cheape,
As ye dyd take !
And be ye fure ye fhall attayne
To heauens blyffe wythout more payne,
And fo mendes make.

Loſſes of townes and holdes came on,
    Ruine of people beganne eche-where ;
Rich men made beggers, and captains bond,
    Armour for warre our enmyes toke clere ;
    When al thys was ſene in this realme here,
    Yet, ſayd theſe owles, we nede not feare,
        For all was well.
No loſſe haue we by heritikes gone,
Ne for Calis for whych ye mone
        Whych here do dwell.

Yet God as God, ſtyll alwaies one,
    Though angry, yet began to ſtay,
Plaging the realme and people eche one,—
    At laſt with teares beganne to ſaye :
    Oh England! England! ſore doeſt thou ſtray ;—
    My martirs bloud ſhed out thys day,
        In wofull plyght !
The infantes yong that fatherles be,
Wyth wydowes poore crying to me,
        Wythdrawes my ſpyte.

With that the ſkies their hue did change,
    And light out-ſhone in darkenes ſteede ;
Up, ſaid this God with voice not ſtrange,
    Elizabeth, thys realme nowe guyde !
    My wyll in thee doo not thou hyde,
    And vermine darke let not abyde
        In thys thy land !
Straightway the people out dyd cry,—
Prayſed be God and God ſaue thee,
        Quene of England !

Finis, quod I. A.

❡ Imprinted at London by Iohn Awdeley.

H

*A Ballad without title, having a large cut
repreſenting five figures, that of Death with his
dart purſuing them, with legends underneath
each, as follows :—*

> *The Prieſt.* " I praye for yov fower."
> *The King.* " I defende yov fower."
> *The Harlot.* " I vanqueſh yov fower."
> *The Lawyer.* " I helpe yov iiij to yovr right."
> *The Clown.* " I feede yov fower."
> *Death.* " I kill yov all."

In the background in a bower are feated the foldier, the
harlot, the lawyer, and prieſt. A feſtive board furniſhed with
viands is ſupported on the back of the clown, who reſts on his
hands and knees. Death approaching with his dart clutches
at fomething on the table. Birds of prey are hovering in the
air.

MARKE well the effect purtreyed here
          in all :
    The prelate with his dignities renowne,
    The king that rules, the lawyer in the
          hall,
The harlot and the countrey toyling clowne,
Howe and which way together they agree,
And what their talke and conference might be.
Ech to their caufe, for gard of their degree,
And yet death is the conquerour, you fee.

The biſhop vaunts to pray for thother fower,
As who wold fay, he holds the palme and prife,
And that in him and his moſt holy power
It doth depend their caufes to fuffife ;—
I pray, faith he, that Chriſts continual grace
May them conduct and guide in euery place.

The puiffant king, he claimeth to defend,
The bifhop and the other three like cafe,
In all conflictes or broyles vnto the end,
Who but his power their enemies doth deface;
He mufters men, and fends them forth afarre
In their behalf to maintaine deadly warre.

The fmiling queane, the harlot cald by name,
Stands ftiffe vpon the blafe of beauty braue;
To vanquifh all fhe makes her prized clame,
And that fhe ought the golden fpurs to haue,
For by her flights fhe can bewitch the beft,
The ftrong, the lawyer, and the reft.

The lawyer he, in title of his clame,
Prefumeth next, by law and iuftice true,
Somwhat the more to eleuate his name;
For law, faith he, all difcord doth fubdue,—
It endeth ftrife, it giues to ech his right,
And wholy doth contention vanquifh quight.

The contry clowne, full loth to lofe his right,
Puts in his foot and pleads to be the chiefe;
What can they do, faith he, by power or might,
If that by me they haue not their reliefe?
For want of food they fhould all perifh than;
What fay you now to me, the countrey man?

For want of me they fhould both liue and lacke,
For want of me they could not till the earth,
.And thats the caufe I cary, on my backe
This table here of plenty not of dearth;
I feaft them all, their hunger I appeafe,
For by my toyle they feede euen at their eafe.

Death that aloofe in ftealing wife doth ftand,
Hearing the vaunts that they begin to make,
Straight fteppeth forth, with piercing dart in hand,
And boldly feemes the quarell vp to take,—
Are they, faith he, fo proud in their degree?
Lo, here by me foone conquered fhall they bee!

And ftanding by to giue their later foode,
He entreth ftraight, the conqueft to attaine;
Thers none of them, faith he, the chiefeft bloud,
That valiant death intendeth to refraine.
Ile crop their crowne and garlands frefh and gay,
And at the laft Ile fhrine them all in clay.

I pray for you all,   I vanquifh you all,
I help you all to your right, I feede you all,
I defend you all,   I will kill you all.

(***) The authors apoftrophe to the reader.

Here may you fee what as the world might be,
The rich, the poore, Earle, Cefar, Duke and King,
Death fpareth not the chiefeft high degree,—
He triumphes ftill on euery earthly thing;
While then we liue, let vs endeuour ftill
That all our works agree with Gods good will.

❧ *A godly ballad declaring by the Scriptures*
the plagues that haue infued whordome.

REFRAIN of youth thy vain defire,
    Subdue thy lufts inordinate ;
Suppreffe the fparks, left in the fire,
    To quenche them it wilbe to late.

Thou knowfte not what a poifon ftrong,
    Thou letteft breed within thy breft,
Whiche, if thou keep within thee long,
    Wil caufe thee care and muche vnreft.

Though it feem fweet in thy conceit,
    Beware thou neuer nurifh it ;
The fifh is by a plefant bait
    Conftrained to the deadly bit.

Like as the woorm, in Affrick bred,
    Whofe fting deftroith with venem colde,
Is not fo noifome to be fled,
    As luft that reigneth vncontrolde.

If reafon cannot rule thy wil,
    But vice wil reign through appetite,
Then let the harmes, that happen ftil
    Through lufts, refrain thy fond delight.

Remember eke that in Noes dayes,
    When vice through luft was rifly growne,
The whole world by fuche wicked waies,
    By rage of rain was ouerthrowne.

The king of Egipt, Pharao,
　　Was he not plagued of God moſte iuſt?
Bothe he and all his houſe alſo,
　　Onely for he gaue place to luſt.

So read we of Abimelech,
　　The mighty king of Gerera,
That God gaue him a greuous check
　　For luſting after Saraa.

Luſt did deſtroy the Sodomites,
　　As is in Scripture manifeſt;
For luſt were ſlain the Sichamites,
　　When Sichem Dina had oppreſt.

Luſt did the wits ſo muche inchaunt
　　Of Putipher, thegipcians wife,
That Joſeph, for he would not graunt
　　Her ſute, ſhe brought nigh from his life.

Bethſaba, naked in bath,
　　Bewitched ſo king Dauids brain,
That giltles he procured hath
　　Her huſband Vry to be ſlain.

The cheef among the Iſraelites,
　　For noughty luſt and eke offence,
Wrought by the meanes of Moabites,
　　Were hanged vp by Gods ſentence.

For luſt Zimry the Iſraelite,
　　As witneſſeth Gods holy woord,
And Coſby eke the Madianite,
　　Periſhed bothe through Zimphas ſwoord.

The Ifraelites, through flefhly luft
   Towards their enmies doughters, were
Alluerd by them falfe Gods to truft,
   Whiche all their thraldomes caufed clere.

Sampfon the fonne of Monoa,
   That mighty judge in Ifrael,
For luft he had to Dalila,
   Himfelf to kil greef did compel.

Lo, him that none coulde foil in fight,
   Whofe puiffant arme the lion flew,
Whofe ftrength put thoufands vnto flight,
   By luft one woman ouerthrew.

Luft in the tribe of Beniamin
   Caft twenty thoufand down and fiue ;
So that in all, for that one fin,
   Were but fix hundred left on liue.

If Ammons luft had not defilde
   His fifter Thamar with inceft,
He had not of his life been fpoild,
   At Abfolon his brothers feaft.

If luft had not impaird the name
   Of Salomon, that witty king,
He had not loft his roiall fame,
   Nor fallen to idolls worfhiping.

If Herod, in his finful life,
   Had not by luft been fore mifled,
He had not kept his brothers wife,
   Nor ftricken of John Baptifts head.

℃ Now what be thefe but tokens fure,
    That God wil plage all thofe that vfe
To lead their liues in luft vnpure,
    And without fear themfelues abufe?

But fome doo think God dooth not fee,
    To eche mannes dooing in all things,
Becaufe fome feem ful fafe to be,
    And profper ftil in il liuings.

But if fuche wil geue ear vnto
    Gods woord, which dooth the truth vs tel,
Shal foon perceiue thofe that liue fo
    Shall fudenly go down to hel.

Therfore to God now let vs pray
    That he wil gide our harts aright,
To flee from filthy lufts alway,
    And him to pleafe with all our might.

And alfo for our gracious Queene,
    That God long profper her, and then
Good dayes among vs may be feene,
    Whiche unto vs he graunt.   Amen!

Finis, A. I.

℃ Imprinted at London, at the long fhop adioin-
    ing vnto Sainct Mildreds churche in the Poul-
    trie, by John Allde, Anno Domini 1566,
    Nouembris 25.

*A merie newe Ballad intituled, the Pinnyng
of the Baſket : and is to bee ſonge to the tune of
the doune right Squire.*

TWAS my hap of late to heare
    A pretie ieſte,
The which by me, as may appeare,
    Is here expreſte,—
With tantara, tantara, tantara,—
    For this belonges thereto;
With bitter broyles, and bickeryng bloſe,
    And ſtrife, with muche adoe.

Marke then, for now this maruell ſtrange
    I will declare :
A joigner ſent his man to change
    Money for ware,—
Tantara, tara, tantara ;—
    Unto the toune he goſe,
And haſted to the chandlers ſhop,
    His money to diſpoſe.

But ſee the chaunce, the chandler drie
    Was gone to drinke,
Or els, poore ſoule, to plaie thereby
    At ſice and ſincke,—
Tantara, tara, tantara,—
    Whereat his wife did chafe,
And out ſhe went then, in a rage,
    To ſeeke her good man, Rafe.

She ranged forthe, and could not refte
  Vpon the molde,
When fhe hym founde, the bedlam beafte
  Beganne to fcolde,—
Tantara, tara, tantara ;—
  Quoth fhe,—Vnthriftie knaue,
If thou be at the good ale tappe,
  Thou haft that thou wouldeft haue !

This quiet man acquainted was
  With her rough talke,
And paciently doeth with her paffe,
  And homeward walke,—
Tantara, tara, tantara ;—
  At home fhe founde hym plaie,
Till he had ferued his cuftomer,—
  And then beganne the fraie. ·

For hauyng doen,—Hold here, quoth he,
  The bafket, dame ;
Goe, goffip, giue it hym, and fee,
  You pinne the fame,—
Tantara, tara, tantara ;—
  Now doeth the fporte beginne ;
Knowe thou, quoth fhe, fir knaue, that I
  The bafket will not pinne !

Her houfebande, fore infenfte, did fweare
  By ftockes and ftones,
She fhould, or els he would prepare
  To bafte her bones,—
Tantara, tara, tantara ;—
  Quoth he, Ile tame your tongue,
And make you pinne the bafket to,
  Doubt not, ere it be long.

Then with a baftian that ftoode by,
   Whiche he did fmell, .
At her he freely did let flie,
   And bumbde her well,—
Tantara, tara, tantara,—
   Vnguentum Bakaline
Did make this houfwife quickly pinne
   The bafket paffyng fine.

This paftyme pleafed well the page,
   That all this while
Sat on his horfe, and fawe this rage
   And bitter broyle,—
Tantara, tara, tantara ;—
   The good wife doeth retire,
And fwears fhe will no more deny
   Her houfebandes iuft defire.

The bafket pinde, the page departes,
   When all is paied ;
He fpurres his cutte, the jade ftartes,
   He was fo fraied,—
Tantara, tara, tantara ;—
   In hafte he homewarde rides,
Yet when he comes, for tariyng long,
   His maifter chafes and chides.

His miftres too, as one halfe madde,
   Beganne to raue ;
Becaufe too long he taried had,
   She calde hym knaue,—
Tantara, tara, tantara ;—
   He fpake his miftres faire,
And tolde her fhe fhould knowe the caufe
   Of his long tariyng there.

Then boldly he began his tale,
    And tolde them all,
Betwixt thefe two, how Beaudly Ale
    Had bred a braull,—
Tantara, tara, tantara ;—
    Quoth he, the chandlers wife
Would not intreated be to pinne
    The bafket for her life,

Till he to beate her did beginne,
    With bounfyng bloofe,—
Then quickly fhe in pofte to pinne
    The bafket goofe,—
Tantara, tara, tantara ;—
    The joigner ioyes at this,
But fure his wife, to heare this tale,
    Was quite bereft of bliffe.

The joigners wife .   .   .   .   .   .   ame,
    Whofe gallant grace
Was chaunged, now beganne to frame
    A frounyng face,—
Tantara, tara, tantara ;—
    Quoth fhe,—For all his bloofe,
The knaue the bafket fhould haue pinde
    Hymfelf, fpight of his nofe !

Here then her houfebande did beginne,—
    Quoth he,—If I
Should bid you, wife, the bafket pinne,
    Would you deny ?—
Tantara, tara, tantara ;—
    To hym fhe plainly tolde
That fhe the bafket would not pinne,
    Thereof he might be bolde !

Then thei hereof for to conferre
   Doe hafte to bedde,
And here you fee a feconde iarre,
   The bafket bredde,—
Tantara, tara, tantara ;—
   The thirde doeth now beginne,—
The fillie page, to get fome meate,
   In hafte doeth hye hym in.

No whit amazde, vnto the maide
   He ftraight doeth goe,
The queane of hym no more afraide,
   Beganne to crowe,—
Tantara, tara, tantara,—
   Caulyng hym knaue and fot,
And vfed hym, that, in the ende,
   A broken head he got.

Henceforthe take heede of makyng ftrife,
   Thou knaue, quoth fhe,
Betwixt thy maifter and his wife,
   Where loue fhould be,—
Tantara, tara, tantara ;—
   With greef her wordes he heares ;
But yet it grieued hym more to feele
   The blood about his eares.

Yet vp he ftept full ftoutly then,
   And bomde me Jone ;
That fhe lent he fo paide againe,
   He made her grone,—
Tantara, tara, tantara,—
   And getts his fupper too,
And made her fitte and eate with hym,
   Although with muche adoe.

His maifter on the morowe nexte
  Of this was glad ;
His miftres was herewith fo vexte,
  It made her mad,—
Tantara, tara, tantara ;—
  This happe brynges ioye and care,
For now the joigners wife to pinne
  The bafket muft prepare.

Her houfebande by his mans good happe
  Doeth hope to winne,
And makes her now, fpite of her cappe,
  The bafket pinne,—
Tantara, tara, tantara,—
  Againe he doeth replie ;
Will you the bafket pinne or no ?
  She ftoutly doeth denie.

Then with a bedftaffe he to bafte
  Her doeth beginne :
Yet would fhe not, for all his hafte,
  The bafket pinne ;—
Tantara, tara, tantara,—
  This combate beyng doen,
Unto a Juftice houfe hard by,
  In hafte this dame doeth runne.

And to this ioylly Juftice wife
  Difcoueryng all,
Betwixt her fpoufe and her what ftrife
  Did late befall,—
Tantara, tara, tantara,—
  Whom fhe would faine haue bounde
Unto the peace, if by the happe
  There might fuche meanes be founde.

Of this her frende the francke confent
   She fone had wone,
To doe for her incontinent
   What might be doen,—
Tantara, tara, tantara,—
   This Juftice wife now gofe, ·
Her goffipps fute in hafte vnto
   Her houfebande to difclofe.

Her houfebande, hearyng by this tale
   How all thynges ftood,
In mynde he at this iefte fo ftale
   Did laugh a-good;
Tantara, tara, tantara,—
   A little more adoe,
This Juftice would have taught his wife
   To pinne the bafket too.

Now all good wiues, beware by this
   Your names to blot;
The bafket pinne with quietneffe,
   Denie it not,—
Tantara, tara, tantara,—
   Be counfailed by your frende;
And of this bafkettes pinnyng now
   Enough, and fo an ende.

Finis, quod T. Rider.

❦ Imprinted at London, for Henrie Kirkham,
and are to be fold at his fhop, at the little North
doore of Paules, at the figne of the Blacke Boye.

HIS present yeare of our Lord God, a thousand, fyue hundred, three score and two, one Robert Martin of Hamsted, in the countie of Mid. besyde London, had a sow, the which brought forth viii piggs, the xvi day of October, whereof vii were of right shape and fassion, but the eight was a wonderous monster, and more monstrous then any that hath bene seene before this time, as you may se by this picture. It hath a head contrary to all other of that kynd ; it hath a face without a nose or eyes, sauing a hole standing directly betwen the two eares, which eares be broad and long, lyke the eares of a bloude-hound, and a monstrous body, like vnto a thing that were flean, without heare. It hath feet very monstrous with the endes of them turning vpwards, lyke vnto forked endes. This monster lyued two houres, and the rest of them lyued about halfe a day.

❡ These straunge and monstrous thinges Almighty God sendeth amongest vs, that we shuld not be forgetfull of his almighty power, nor vnthankeful for his great mercies so plentifully powred vpon vs, and especially for geuyng vnto vs his most holy word, whereby our lyues ought to be guyded: and also his wonderful tokens, wherby we ought to be warned. But if

we will not be inftructed by his worde nor warned
by his wonderfull workes, then let vs be affured
that thefe ftraunge monftrous fightes do forefhew
vnto vs that his heauy indignation wyl fhortly
come vpon vs for our monftrous liuyng. Wherefore let vs earneftly pray vnto God that he wyll
geue vs grace fpedely to repent our wickedneffes,
faithfully to beleue his holy Gofpel, and cencerely
to frame our lyues after the doctrine of the fame,
to whome be all prayfe, honour, and glory.
Amen.

℃ Imprinted at London, by Alexander Lacy, for
Garat Dewes, dwellyng in Poules church yarde,
at the eaft end of the church.

℃ *A very proper Dittie :*

To the tune of Lightie Loue.

℃ Leaue lightie loue, Ladies, for feare of yll name,
And true loue embrace ye, to purchace your Fame.

BY force I am fixed my fancie to write,
  Ingratitude willeth mee not to re-
  fraine :
Then blame me not, Ladies, although
  I indite
What lighty loue now amongft you doth raigne.
Your traces in places, with outward allurements,
Doth mooue my endeuour to be the more
  playne :

I

Your nicyngs and ticings, with fundrie procure-
     mentes,
  To publifh your lightie loue doth mee con-
     ftrayne.

❡ Deceite is not daintie, it coms at eche difh,
  Fraude goes a fifshyng with frendly lookes ;
Throughe frendfhip is fpoyled the feely poore fifh,
  That hoouer and fhouer vpon your falfe hookes ;
With baight you lay waight, to catch here and
     there,
  Whiche caufeth poore fifshes their freedome to
     lofe :
Then loute ye and floute ye, wherby doth appere
  Your lighty loue, Ladies, ftyll cloaked with
     glofe.

❡ With DIAN fo chafte you feeme to compare,
  When HELLENS you bee, and hang on her
     trayne :
Mee thinkes faithfull Thifbies be now very rare,
  Not one CLEOPATRA, I doubt, doth remayne ;
You wincke and you twincke, tyll Cupid haue
     caught, .
  And forceth through flames your louers to fue :
Your lyghtie loue, Ladies, too deere they haue
     bought,
  When nothyng wyll mooue you their caufes
     to rue.

❡ I fpeake not for fpite, ne do I difdayne
  Your beautie, fayre ladies, in any refpeét :
But ones ingratitude doth mee conftrayne,
  As childe hurt with fire, the fame to negleét ;
For proouing in louyng, I finde by good triall,
  When beautie had brought mee vnto her becke,

She ftaying, not waying, but made a deniall,
  And, fhewyng her lightie loue, gaue mee the
    checke.

❦ Thus fraude for frendfhip did lodge in her breft;
  Suche are moft women, that, when they efpie
Their louers inflamed with forowes oppreft,
  They ftande then with Cupid againft their replie:
They taunte, and they vaunte; they fmile when
    they vew
  How Cupid had caught them vnder his trayne;
But warned, difcerned the proofe is moft true
  That lightie loue, Ladies, amongft you doth
    reigne.

❦ It feemes, by your doynges, that Creffed doth
    fcoole ye,—
  Penelopeys vertues are cleane out of thought:
Mee thinkes, by your conftantneffe, Heleyne doth
    rule ye,
  Whiche both Greece and Troy to ruyne hath
    brought.
No doubt, to tell out your manyfolde driftes,
  Would fhew you as conftant as is the fea fande:
To trufte fo vniuft, that all is but fhieftes,
  With lightie loue bearyng your louers in hande.

❦ If ARGVS were lyuyng, whofe eyes were in
    nomber
  The peacockes plume painted, as writers replie,
Yet women by wiles full fore would him cumber,
  For all his quicke eyes, their driftes to efpie;
Suche feates, with difceates, they dayly frequent,
  To conquere mennes mindes, their humours to
    feede,
That bouldly I may geue arbittrement
  Of this your lightie loue, ladies, indeede.

℃ Ye men that are fubiect to Cupid his ftrooke,
    And therin feemeth to haue your delight,
Thinke, when you fee baight, theres hidden a
        hooke,
    Whiche fure wyll bane you, if that you do bight :
Suche wiles and fuche guiles by women are wrought,
    That halfe their mifchefes men cannot preuent ;
When they are moft pleafant vnto your thought,
    Then nothyng but lightie loue is their intent.

℃ Confider that poyfon doth lurke oftentyme
    In fhape of fugre, to put fome to payne,
And fayre wordes paynted, as dames can define,
    The olde prouerbe faith, doth make fome fooles
        faine !
Be wife and precife, take warning by mee ;
    Truft not the crocodile, leaft you do rue ;
To womens faire wordes do neuer agree,
    For all is but lightie loue, this is moft true.

℃ Anexes fo daintie example may bee,
    Whofe lightie loue caufed yong Iphis his woe ;
His true loue was tryed by death, as you fee,
    Her lightie loue forced the knight therunto ;
For fhame then refrayne, you ladies, therfore,
    The cloudes they doo vanifh, and light doth
        appeare ;
You cannot diffemble, nor hide it no more,
    Your loue is but lightie loue, this is moft cleare.

℃ For Troylus tried the fame ouer well,
    In louyng his ladie, as Fame doth reporte ;
And likewife Menander, as ftories doth tell,
    Who fwam the falt feas to his loue to reforte,
So true, that I rue fuch louers fhould lofe
    Their labour in feekyng their ladies vnkinde,

Whofe loue thei did prooue, as the prouerbe
    now goes,—
Euen very lightie loue lodgde in their minde.

❡ I touche no fuche ladies as true loue imbrace,
    But fuche as to lightie loue dayly applie ;
And none wyll be grieued, in this kinde of cafe,
    Saue fuche as are minded true loue to denie ;
Yet frendly and kindly I fhew you my minde ;
    Fayre ladies, I wifh you to vfe it no more ;
But fay what you lift, thus I haue definde,
    That lightie loue, ladies, you ought to abhore.

❡ To truft womens wordes in any refpect
    The danger by mee right well it is feene,
And loue and his lawes who would not neglect,
    The tryall wherof mofte peryllous beene ?
Pretendyng the endyng if I haue offended,
    I craue of you, ladies, an anfwere againe ;
Amende, and whats faid fhall foone be amended,
    If cafe that your lightie loue no longer do rayne.

❡ Finis.   By Leonarde Gybfon.

❡ Imprinted at London, in the vpper end of
Fleetlane, by Richard Jhones ; and are to be
folde at his fhop, ioyning to the South-wefte
Dore of Saint Paules church.

Sapartons Alarum to all fuch as do beare
the name of true fouldiers, in England or elf-
wheare.

L Mars his men, drawe neere,
    That warlike feates embrace,
Sit downe a while, and harken heere,
    A feruinge fouldiers cafe.

Laye downe the fhiuered fpeare,
    And eke the battered fhielde;
From trumpets found withdraw thine eare,
    And harke, in open field,

The true complaint of one,
    Whofe gaine by feruice got
Will fcarfely yelde a hungry boone
    To caft into the pot.

If euer warlike wighte .
    Hath ferued his time in vaine,
In hope to haue bin well requighte,
    And hath receiued difdaine,—

In faith, then, I am he,
    Such one that for my parte
Haue ready bin full willinglye,
    With hand and eeke with harte,

To ferue my prince in fielde,
    Whiles life had bearing breath,—
As one that minded not to yelde,
    Nor forced life or death.

The fiery cannons thump
   The cragged ſcull that riues,
Whoſe force by inwarde charge is wonte
   To ſpoyle poore ſouldiers liues,

Could neuer force me yet
   The enemies face to ſhonne,
If captaines courage ſemed fit
   The conqueſt to haue wonne.

And for the time, perchaunce,
   I was accepted then,
And promiſed to haue aduaunce
   As ſoone as other men.

I ſpeake as founde I haue ;—
   What thoe ? I am contente,—
For Saparton now waxeth graue,
   Some youthfull yeares are ſpente.

Tis not the curled head,
   Nor yet the friſled heare,
That courage giues in time of neede
   To weld thunweldy ſpeare.

Some youthfull imps I knowe,
   That beares a paſſing grace,
If they to pitched fielde ſhould goe,
   Durſt ſcarſly ſhew their face.

But when that all is don,
   Tis manhood makes the man ;—
Match not the candell with the ſunne,
   No praiſe deſerue you than.

If courage craues a fame,
   Remaining in the breaſt,

Then manhood needes muſt make his claime
  For to excell the reſte.

Though Venus ſtriue with Mars
  To get the vpper grounde,
At length yet ſhall the barded horſe
  Exceede both hauke and hounde.

And, luſtie laddes, to you,
  Let not your courage quell;
Good hap hereafter may enſue,
  Though I good hap do fell.

℃ Coaſte on apace, althoe
  Light horſeman trace the ſoyle;
Encounter ſharpely with thy foe,
  Make hauocke of the ſpoyle.

Eſteeme not my yll hap,
  Nor weye it ought at all;
The wight that ſcapes the cannons clap
  Runnes yet to further thrall.

O Mars, bewaile thy man,
  Becauſe he hath ſuche wronge!
In dolefull tunes, O ruſtick Pan!
  Now helpe to waile this ſonge.

So thus my leaue I take;—
  O ſouldier, now farewell:
No more to do now will I make,
  But God preſerue Queene EL.

          Finis.   Iohn Saparton.

Imprinted at London, in Fleeteſtreete, by William
  How, for Richard Johnes, and are to be ſolde
  at his ſhoppe vnder the Lotterie houſe.

A godly ditty or prayer to be fong vnto God
for the preferuation of his Church, our Queene
and Realme, againft all Traytours, Rebels, and
papifticall enemies.

Preferue thy feruaunt, Lord,
   Elizabeth, our Queene;
Be thou her fhield and fword,—
   Now let thy power be feene.
That this, our queene annoynted,
   May vanquifh al her foes;
And, as by thee appoynted,
   Let her lay fword on thofe.

Geue, Lord, true faythful hartes
   To vs, her fubieftes al,
That we play not the partes
   Of thefe traitours that fal
Both from their God and prince,
   And from their lawful othes;—
All fuch, O Lord, conuince,
   And geue them ouerthrowes.

Syng this after the tune of the cxxxvij Pfalme, which begins,
When as we fat in Babilon;—or fuch lyke.

UR liuyng God, to thee we cry,
   Now tend vnto our playnt;
Behold thy church and family,
   Which enmies feeke to faynt;
And though our fyns haue moued thee
   Juft plagues on vs to poure,
Yet let thy Chriftes death fhortly
   Thy wrath vp cleane deuour.

Correct vs, Lord, by thine own hand,
   And leaue vs not to thofe
That do thee and thy truth withftand,
   Like diulyfh deadly foes;
For better is it for vs, Lord,
   Into thy handes to fall,
Then vnto them for to accord
   Which in hell perifh fhall.

Behold, O Lord, thine enmies rage
   Againft thee and thy Chrift;
Not our fyns they feeke to afwage,
   But thy truth to refift.
And fhall our fyns then be a let
   For thee them to withftand,
Seing againft thee they be fet?
   No, Lord, fet to thy hand.

For thine the glory is, not ours,
   Which they feeke to fuppres;
Bend, therfore, Lord, thine hoft of powrs,
   And this thy caufe redres;
Refift thefe rebels and traytours,
   With papiftes euery one,
Which thy poore people fo deuours
   In euery nacion.

Let not the wicked thus preuayle,
   To vexe thy church and fayntes;
But ftroy them from the head to tayle,
   Let none bewayle their playntes!
Lord, heare the cry of fatherles
   And wyddowes, which do mone,
The which thefe enmies do oppres
   With mifchiefes many one!

Defend, O God, our gracious queene
   From pope, rebel, and all ;
And as by her thy woorkes be feene,
   So let thy wrath now fall
Upon all thofe that vexe thy truth,
   Our queene, our realme and ftate,
And let their vicious prankes of ruth
   Light vpon their own pate !

So fhall thy name be magnified ;
   So fhall thy power be knowne ;
So fhall our Chrift be fanctified
   By them that be his owne :
Wherefore, O Lord, graunt our requeftes,
   Which here to thee we make,
And make vs loue and lyue thy heftes
   For thy Chrift Jefus fake !

Finis, quoth Ioh. Awdely.

℃ Imprynted at London, by Iohn Awdely.

***

*The Groome-porters lawes at Mawe, to be
obferued in fulfilling the due orders
of the game.*

1.

IF you chaunge hands, it is the loffe of
the fet.
   2. If you renounce, it is the loffe of
the fet.
   3. If you leade when your mate fhoulde, it is
the loffe of that game and vied cardes.

4. If you lofe dealing, it is the loffe of fower cardes; but if the lofer of the dealing deale not againe, you acquite the fower, and no gaine to either of both parties.

5. If you looke either on the afked carde or the bottome carde, it is the loffe of that game and vied cardes, in whom the fault is found.

6. If you roub (not hauing the ace) you lofe fower and al the vied cards, although you lay downe the fame carde which you tooke vp.

7. If you make out the carde when your mate rubbeth, it is the loffe of fower, for the roubber muft make out the carde himfelfe.

8. If you turne vp the ace of hartes, you gaine fower thereby.

9. If you turne vp the ace of hartes, and thereby make either partie aboue xxvj, the contrary part muft haue liuings; but if the contrary parte bee xxv, by meanes whereof liuings fets them out, then is he who turned vp the ace of hartes to make for the fet, fo that he make not one game nor the firft tricke, without the confent of both parties.

10. The partie that afketh a carde may not vie any carde before the firft tricke be played.

11. You may not vie it after your card is led, but the contrary part may.

12. Three cardes croffed, no carde by any meanes giuen backe.

13. Neither partie may giue backe his owne vied card, though none be croffed.

14. You may not afke a carde to fet the contrary parte or your felfe at liuings or out.

15. Prouided alwaies that, if the contrary parte bee xxiij or aboue, by reafon that fower fets the

other partie behinde the liuinges, it fhalbe lawfull for the partie which is behinde to afke a carde,
although the carde fo afked put the other to liuings.

16. Prouided alfo that, if you meane to lead
a helpe, you may vie it vpon your owne afked
carde, fo as it be done before the helpe be out of
your hand; the contrary part may pledge you a
card after he feeth your helpe vpon the boord, fo
as it be done before his owne card be played.

ℂ *Of the horrible and wofull deſtruction of Sodome and Gomorra.*

To the tune of the Nine Mufes.

THE Scripture playne doth fhow and
    tell
  How Lot in Sodome towne did dwell,
    Amongft the Sodomites vile;
He did rebuke their noughty liues,
Both yong and olde, both men and wiues,—
  Why do you yourfelues defile?
He often times, with watry eyes,
  Their caufe he did lament.
He wept in hart, in greeuous wife,
  And bad them to repent,—
Defiring, and praying,
  From finne they fhould refrayne,
Leaft body and foule bee
  In euerlaftyng payne.

❡ God doth abhorre that whorifh bed,
Whiche thoufands now therin are led,
    And therin ftyll doth dwell;
They yeld their foules for facrifice
To filthy finne in diuers wife,
    Vnto the paynes of hell.
You rauenyng needy men, quoth he,
    That riches haue in ftoare,
Geue to the poore, I fay to thee,
    The whiche coms to thy doore;
To fatherleffe and wydowes, too,
    To pyttie them take payne;
You furffetters and dronkardes, now
    From this your finne refrayne.

❡ Then all in vayne Lot preached ftyll,
They all did folow their felfe wyll,
    For that was their defire;
For his counfell good they paffed fmall,
In filthy finne they wallowed all,
    As filthy fwyne in myre;
Then did the Lorde commaund that Lot,
    That he fhould foone depart
From amongft the Sodomites fo whot,
    For they fhould feele great fmart;
The angell then to hym he faide,—
    Come, Lot, and hafte awaye,
For tyll the tyme that thou be gone,
    Nothynge be done there maye.

❡ The angell faid, Looke you not backe,
To fee that wofull fight and wracke,
    Which on them now fhall light;   .
For you out of the towne are brought,
And are efcaped from their wicked thoughts,
    Wherin they do delyght:

Yet Lots wyfe ſhe turnde backe agayne,
  As ſoone as ſhe was gone;
For her offence ſhe turned was
  Into a huge ſalt ſtone,
Where ſhe doth ſtande continually,
  By Goddes decreed judgement,
Becauſe ſhe brake, and did forſake
  Goddes good commaundement.

℃ The gates of Heauen God opened than,
So fyer and brymſtone from thence came,
  And on Sodome downe did rayne:
Gomorra towne they did excell,
As thicke as hayle the fyre it fell,
  And deſtroyed was euery man;
Both man and beaſt were burnd to mucke,
  And babes in mothers lap,
And eke the chyldren that did ſucke
  On mothers tender pap;
With fier were they burned,—
  O wofull, grieuous ſight!—
They cryed and ſhryked,
  To healpe no boote it might.

℃ The damſelles teare their coſtly guyſe,
Their yelow lockes downe to their eyes,
  And their heare like ſiluer wyer;
Their ſownde did reach vnto the clowdes,
With bitter teares they cryed alowde,
  All burnynge in the fier!
Theſe townes like gold that ſhyned ſo bright,
  With flamyng fier is conſumed;
The mighty God hath deſtroyed quite,
  And brought it to the grounde,
That nought is left, the trueth to ſay,
  But ſtinkynge pooles and welles,

Whiche was a place of braue delyghtes,
　　And eke of pleaſant ſmelles.

❡ Thus were theſe towns brought to decay,
Both all and ſom, the trouth to ſay,
　　Sauyng Lots houſeholde then :
And Lot hymſelfe was counted iuſt,
Tyll his doughters tempted hym to luſt,
　　As the ſtory ſheweth playne ;
Loe, wanton girles whiche ſo doth burne
　　In Venus pleaſant games,
If that they may content their turnes,
　　And eake their youthfull flames,
They do deſire their fathers bed,
　　The cankred fleſh to pleaſe :
Alas, that ye ſo wanton bee,
　　That you wyll neuer ceaſe !

❡ Thou mightie God that ſitteſt on hie,
O turne our hartes for thy mercie,
　　That now amend we may !
O Lorde, thou ſaydſt, and it may ſo be,
The Sodomits ſhould witnes be
　　Againſt vs at the latter day :
O heauy ſayng ! yf that theſe men
　　Shall ſooner mercy craue,
Then we which know Gods ſainges, then
　　What iudgement ſhall we haue ?
O let vs bewayle vs,
　　Our ſinnes doth ſo abound,
For in ſhort ſpace, I feare, the Lorde
　　In wrath wyll vs confound !

❡ O England, thou like Sodome art,
In filthy ſinne doth play thy part,—

What finnes are found in thee!
Thou dooeft exceede Sodome in finne,
Thou careft not for Lots preaching;
  O, thefe heauy newes wyll be!
Ye, be thou fure, and fure agayne,
  The ftones that lieth in wall,
Becaufe we doo fo fore offend,
  To God for plagues wyll call;
Therfore let fee, amends to be,
  And euery one amende:
Good Lorde, I fay, graunt this allway,
  And thus I make an end.

❡ Finis.

❡ Imprinted at London, by Richard Johnes, for
Henrie Kyrkham, dwellyng at the figne of the
Blacke Boy, at the middle North dore of Paules
church.

❡ * ❱

❡ *A mery balade, how a wife entreated her*
hufband to haue her owne wyll.

IN May, when floures fwetely fmel,
  The people romyng abrode ful ryfe,
A mery tale I fhal you tel,
  That then was herd, but no great
    ftrife;

K

In clofe a yong man and his wife
  Sate reafonyng fore, but for none yl;
She faid, I am wery of this lyfe,—
  Good hufband, let me haue mine owne will.

℘ Wyfe, quoth he, then muft I nedes know
  What is your wyll, then, for to haue:
At me you muft neither mocke nor mow,
  Nor yet loute me, nor call me knaue;
Nor VENVS game vpon me craue,
  Nor yet your honeftye for to fpill,
And make me neyther boy nor flaue,
  But do good, and therin take your owne wyl.

℘ Tufh, quoth fhe, fir, as for that
  I wyll be honeft, to dye therefore;
But, hufband, hufband, wot ye what?
  I haue bene your wyfe this month and more,
And haue not gone but to the dore,—
  Such keping in my heart doth fpyll;
By houfe-kepers neighbours fet no ftore,—
  Good hufband, let me haue mine owne wyll!

℘ Wyfe, quoth he, be you content;
  You fhall to church and to market go,
And to neighbours to, at time conuenient,
  But not to goffip, the truth is fo;—
Tauernes to haunt? no wyfe, no, no!
  Nor yet alehoufes, with Jacke nor Gyll;
You know my mynd for friend or fo,—
  Doe good, and therein take your owne wyll.

℘ Hufband, quoth fhe, you be to blame
  To kepe me in, and fo playne withall;
Me thinke I fhuld be a fyne dame,
  Whereby great prayfe to you might fall:

I being fayre, nice, and fmall,
  Yf I had gay clothes my body to hyll,
Then gentlewomen for me wold call,—
  Good hufband, let me haue myne owne wyll.

ℂ No, wyfe, quoth he, it wyll not be borne
  For you to go fyne and gayly clad;
To go as I will haue you, thinke ye no fcorne,
  That is, comely and cleane, fober and fad;
Wherefore, be you neyther ficke nor yet mad,
  Becaufe ye may not your mynd fulfyll,
For your defyre is wicked and bad,—
  Doe good, and therein take your owne wyll.

ℂ Not mad, quoth fhe; alas, good man,
  What woman culd your wordes abyde?
I entreatyng you as fayre as I can,
  And yet my wordes you fet afyde;
Though I be fayre, I loue no pryde,
  For I ferue your fwyne with draffe and fwyl;
Unto my friendes I wold fayne ryde,—
  Good hufband, let me haue myne owne wyll.

ℂ Wyfe, quoth he, what nedeth all this?
  You craue a great deale more then neede;
Your friendes haue no need of vs, I wis,
  Wherefore be ftayed, good gentle Beede:
Now let vs plow and fow our feede,
  Our wynter land is yet to tyll;
How to thryue let vs firft take heede,
  And do good, and therin take your owne wyl.

ℂ Oh hufband, quoth fhe, I am but yong,
  Wherefore, I pray you, graunt me one thyng,
At libertie let me haue my toung,
  Eyther to chyde, or els to fyng;

To daunce, to kyffe, not ouer-workyng,
　　But once a weke to go to myll;
My time is fhort, my death is cumming,—
　　Good hufband, let me haue mine owne wyll.

❡ No, wyfe, quoth he, I am your head,
　　Wherefore, I pray you, my counfell take,
And let fuch tricks in you be dead,
　　Leaft that for it your bones doe ake;
Therefore learne betime to brue and bake,
　　And liue no longer in ydleneffe ftyll;
Wherefore, for your owne eafe fake,
　　Doe good, and therein take your owne wyll.

❡ Alas, quoth fhe, what chaunce haue I,
　　To couple myfelfe with fuch a one,
That had rather to fee me dye,
　　Then to decke me gay, as I wold haue gone,
To chyde, nor fyng, nor to daunce alone?
　　I wold I had maried John Goofequyll,
Then nede I not to haue made this mone,
For by him I might haue had all my wyll.

❡ No more of thefe twayne culd be hard,
　　But home they went together playne;
But let no wyues this wyfe regard,
　　For her requeft was all in vayne.
And yet with fhrewes fome men take payne,
　　And abydeth the iob of the deuylles byll,
From the which, all good wyues, refrayne!
　　God geue vs all grace to doe his wyll.   Amen.

❡ Finis, quod T. W. T.

❡ Imprinted at London by Alexander Lacy.

The Othe of euerie Freeman of the City of London.

YE fhall fweare that yee fhall bee good and true to our Souereigne ladie Queene Elizabeth, &c, and to the heires of our faid fouereigne ladie the Queene. Obeyfant and obedient ye fhall be to the Mayor and Minifters of this citie. The franchifes and cuftomes thereof yee fhall mainteine, and this citie keepe harmeles in that that in you is. Ye fhall be contributorie to all manner of charges within this citie, as fummons, watches, contributions, tafkes, tallages, lot and fcot, and all other charges, bearing your part as a freeman ought to doo. Yee fhall colour no forreines goods, vnder or in your name, whereby the Queene or this citie might or may loofe their cuftomes or aduantages. Ye fhall know no forreine to buy or fell anie marchandife with any other forreine within the citie or the franchife thereof, but yee fhall warne the Chamberlaine thereof, or fome minifter of the chamber. Yee fhall implead or fue no freeman out of this citie, whiles yee may haue right and law within the fame citie. Yee fhall take none apprentice, but if hee bee free borne (that is to fay) no bond man's fonne, nor the childe of any alien, and for no leffe terme then for feuen yeeres; within the firft yeere yee fhall caufe him to be enrolled, and at his termes end ye fhall make him free of this citie, (if he haue well and truely ferued you.) Ye fhall alfo keepe the Queenes peace in your

owne perſons; ye ſhall know no gatherings, con-
uenticles, nor conſpiracies made againſt the Queenes
peace, but ye ſhall warn the Mayor thereof, or let
it to your power.   All theſe points and articles
yee ſhall well and truely keepe, according to the
lawes and cuſtomes of this citie to your power.
So God you help, and by the holie contentes of
this Booke.   God ſaue the Queene.

Printed at London, by Hugh Singleton.

A Balade declaryng how neybourhed, loue,

and trew dealyng is gone.

NOW ſtraunge it is to men of age,
  The which they ſe before their
     face,
  This world to be in ſuch outrage,
It was neuer ſene in ſo bad caſe.
  Neibourhed nor loue is none,
  Trew dealyng now is fled and gone.

Where ſhall one fynde a man to truſt,
  Alwaye to ſtande in tyme of neede?
The moſt parte now they are vniuſt,
  Fayre in wordes, but falſe in deede.
    Neybourhed nor loue is none,
    True dealyng now is fled and gone.

Who can flatter now beſt ſhall ſpeede ;
   Who can deceyue is gaynes well won :
Of deceytfull tongues who can take hede ?
   Many a man they haue undone.
      Neibourhed nor loue is none, &c.

The wickedneſſe that doth abounde,
   More then I can with tongue expreſſe,
To ſee vnfaithfull men are founde ;
   Of frendſhip there was neuer leſſe.
      Neiborhed nor loue is none, &c.

On couetouſneſſe moſt men deſyre ;
   Their neibours houſe ſome doth procure,
And ouer his hed they wyll it hyre,
   Or bye a leace to make it ſure.
      Neiborhed nor loue is none, &c.

To pourchace and bye, for lucre and gaine,
   Both leace and houſe, both wood and grounde,
Thei double the rent, to poore mens payne ;
   Of landlordes nowe fewe good are founde.
      Neiborhed nor loue is none, &c.

This is vſed now euery where,
   And wyll be tyll we haue redreſſe ;
With them I thought the Lorde dyd fere,
   Becauſe his worde they doo profeſſe.
      Neiborhed nor loue is none, &c.

What neiborhed is this you call,
   That one another doth backbite,
And daily wyll both ſkolde and brall
   With ſlaunderous wordes in moſt deſpite ?
      Neyborhed nor loue is none, &c.

For matters fmall fome fuffre wronge,
  Upon difpleafure in prifon caft,
And there fhall lye, without pitie, long,
  Tyll that his goodes are fpent and waft.
    Neyborhed nor loue is none, &c.

Thungodly riche the poore oppreffe,
  On them few haue compaffion ;
Their caufe is here remedileffe,
  Without all confolacion.
    Neyborhed nor loue is none, &c.

If any membre be hurte in man,
  The whole body lamentes therfore ;
The poore oppreft, who cureth than
  Or helpes him for to falue his fore ?
    Neiborhed nor loue is none, &c.

The percialneffe that now doth raigne
  With fome that haue fuche caufe in hande,
The riche men doth the poore difdayne,
  And fekes the meanes to make them band.
    Neyborhed nor loue is none, &c.

Truly to deale one with another
  In thefe dayes now ar very fewe ;
The fifter wyll begyle the brother,
  The brother agayne deceyte wyll fhewe.
    Neyborhed nor loue is none, &c.

The father wyll deceyue the chylde,
  The chylde the father likewife agayne ;
Thus one another dothe begylde,
  By falfe deceyt that now doth raigne.
    Neyborhed nor loue is none, &c.

To fpeake fomwhat of vfurye,
   The whiche the Lorde doth daily curfe ;
Yet fome doo vfe it priuely
   To fyll their vncontented purfe.
      Neyborhed nor loue is none, &c.

To ftriue or fpeake it is no boote,
   In couetoufneffe there is no order ;
Of mifchiefe it is the very roote,
   All thinges it fpoyles in euery border.
      Neyborhed nor loue is none, &c.

Our preachers with Gods word doth cry
   On couetoufmen that wyll not ceffe ;
Their wordes are herde with yeres fo flye,
   Their filthy gaynes they ftyll encreffe.
      Neybourhed nor loue is none, &c.

How many doth their rentes abate,
   Or now a dayes their tenentes eafe ?
They fet their rentes at a new rate,
   Both fines and leaffes they daily reafe.
      Neybourhed nor loue is none, &c.

Couetoufneffe hathe now the way,
   Wronge and briberye dothe not refrayne ;
In euery coft pride bereth the fway,
   Amonges the whole now it doth raygne.
      Neybourhed nor loue is none, &c.

What is the caufe neibourhed is gone,
   Which here hath reigned many a daye ?
I heare the poore men make great mone,
   And fayth hit is falne in decaye.
      Neibourhed nor loue is none, &c.

True dealyng dare not once appeare,
  Deceit hath put him out of place ;
Euery where, both farre and nere,
  He raigneth now in moſt mens face.
    Neibourhed nor loue is none, &c.

Graunt, oh God, for thy mercyes ſake,
  That neigbourhed and dealyng trewe
May once agayne our ſprites awake,
  That we our lyues may chaunge a-new ;
    That neybourhed and loue alone
    May come agayne to euery one.

        quod Jhon Barker.

Imprinted at London, by Richard Lant.

A proper newe Ballad ſheweing that philoſo-
phers learnynges are full of good warnynges.
And ſonge to the tune of my Lorde Marques
Galyarde, or the firſte traces of Que paſſa.

PHILOSOPHERS learnings are ful of
        good warnings,
      In memorye yet left to ſcoole vs,
So be ther contayned, in poietries
        fained,
  Great documentes to rate and rule vs ;
As well for continuance of life, helth, and ſubſtance,
  Whoſe vanities the world requireth,
As for the derection of life by correction
  From lyberties that luſt deſireth.

Menander being aſked what life was, he anſwered,
  A miſerie that neuer ceaſeth,
Tormenting minds worldly for goods goton hardly,
  With contraries as time increaſeth,—
Wherin is no ſurance of hope nor induraunce,
  But jeoberdies as fortune ſendyth ;
Now ſicklie, now helthie, now poorelie, now welthy,
  With caſualties as life contendith.

Of Chilo thus reed we, whoſe councel moſt need
    we,
  No memorye ought more to moue vs,
Then for to know throwly ourſelues and our dewty,
  To notifie what doth behoue vs ;
And as we ſeeme faultie, reiecte folyes noughtie,
  With practeſinge all waies to ſhone them ;
So may we, triumphing, geue praiſe to ech good
    thing, .
  Recomfortinge that we haue done them.

Exceſſe that delighteth, as Plutarche well writeth,
  In greedines that life requireth,
In ſurfeitinge diſſhes, ill workinge, ill wiſhes,
  Suche filthines as fleſhe deſyrethe ;
Withdraw wyth their pleaſurs dame natures dew
    meaſures,
  Whoſe gouernaunce is ſo defaced ;
What man can diſpoſe them when luſt ouerthrows
    them,
  To temperaunce that ſhould be placed ?

Periander of liuinge good counſell once geuinge,
  Said merilie, Looke well within thee ;
If conſience accuſe thee, ill reſt will abbuſe thee,
  No libertie hath leaue to win thee.

Kepe concience then clearly, that life may liue
        chearly,
    As Socrates doth wifelie will thee ;
No corzye fhall greeue thee, found fleepes fhall
        reliue thee,
    Unquietnes can no waye fpill thee.

If fortune difpleafe vs, whofe wrackes may difeafe
        vs,
    Let Sophacles his doctrine fkoole vs,—
Who writes that no furetie on earth getteth victrye,
    But pacience in paines to rule vs ;
In fuche pointes prefifely, good counfel moft wifely
    Exuperate blinde fortunes fcourges,
As the marriner fteareth the fhip when he feareth
    The violence of falt fea fourges.

Ten thoufand and ten to of theafe and like men to,
    Lyke documentes haue left behinde them ;
Methinks that thefe pagons may counfel good
        Chriftians
    With diligence to heare and mind them.
Sith life hath no fuertie, nor longe time of puertie,
    For accedence that can preuaile vs,
Let wifdome now win vs to plant vertue in vs,
    With penitence, eare life doth faile vs.

            ℂ Finis, qd W. Elderton.

ℂ Imprinted at London, in Fleeteftreet, beneath
    the Conduit, at the Signe of Sainte John
        Evangelift, by Thomas Colwell.

A Balade of a Preiſt that loſte his noſe,
For ſayinge of maſſe, as I ſuppoſe.

HO ſo liſt, heare of a wonderous
    chaunce !
    Of late I mette with one did me tell,
The craftieſt prieſt in England or
    Fraunce,
Hath loſt his noſe, and how ſhould he ſmell ?
He went to his freinde his mynde to diſcloſe,
And, as he came home, one cut of his noſe.

It is a gentleman, a prieſt he tolde me,
    To tell you his name I do not much paſſe ;
It is olde ſyr John, the vycar of Lee,
    Which rayles at Gods boke and reeles at his
        maſſe.
His cankarde mynde he cannot kepe cloſe,
Yet he ſerued him ſhrewdly that cut of his noſe.

His ſmeller is ſmitten cleane from his face,
    Yet was there but one, as he did ſaye,
Which caught him and pluckt of his noſe in that
        place ;
    A hie man, a lowe man, a foxe or a graye ?
Tenne ſhillinges, he ſaith, in his purſe he did loſe ;
I thinke he lied therof, but not of his noſe.

Great ſerching was ſence that ſmeller to ſeke ;
    Some for haſt left their ſcabbert at home,
Some had gunnes, ſome halberts, ſome forked
        pikes,
    Some in ſhyrts of maile like a luſty mome :

There was neuer fene before, I fuppofe,
Such toffing and tombling for a prieftes nofe.

Som men that thought him no harme in ther life,
    But becaufe they feare God and do go about
To liue with pure confcience and be without ftrife,
    Thei ar bound to the peas now for a priefts
        fnout ;
But becaufe he can kepe mens horedom fo clofe,
Therfore they make fuch a worke for his nofe.

Becaufe his fcollers did mock at his maffe,
    He faid he wolde make bloud run by their heles,
But God hath turned the plage from their arfe,
    And he with his nofe did bloudy the ftiles.
With bloud, I hard faye, as red as a rofe ;
He dronke well, belike, before he loft his nofe.

What maner of nofe was it, fir, ye fought for ?
    A black nofe, a red nofe, or one like my fift ?
To be without nofe was the marke of an whore,
    And now it is the marke of an whorifhe prieft.
And now you are ryd right well of the pofe,
Why do you make fuche a worke for your nofe ?

Or was your nofe fomewhat wan or pale ?
    A blewe nofe, a bottle nofe, or was it yellowe ?
Nos autem haue fene it fometime at the ale ;
    Libera nos, falua nos, from the fwap of the
        fwalowe.
But why did ye vfe, fyr, to lye fo and glofe ?
Was it any meruayle though ye loft your nofe ?

Some men are liuing to whom he did fay,
    Seing he knew the truth, if euer he fayd maffe,

He wifht that fome membre might be cut away ;
  Now at his requeft it is come to paffe.
Much work he doth make for the lomp he did
     lofe—
Well, what will ye geue, fyr, for a newe nofe ?

But what fhal we fay, yf men do not lye ?
  Who cut of the prieftes nofe it is harde to iudge,
But he himfelf, I think, did it of enuy,
  And then to bewite it to them he did grudge,
That therby they might ther kingdom vp clofe,
As fometime Sopirus did fnap of his nofe.

For fometime he fayth it was but a mome,
  And eftfone a talle man this he doth name ;
But ftyll he affyrmeth it was but one,
  Which caught him and brought his nofe oute
     of frame.
Could one man fo do it, as you fuppofe,
Except he were willing to haue of his nofe ?

Remedie is none, but this thinge is true,
  His fnout is fnapt of, howfoeuer it was ;
I thinke it were beft to make him a new,
  As fone he may do it as God at his maffe ;
Yf he cannot make him a fnout, I fuppofe,
He can not make God no more then his nofe.

Seïng the true God is gone from your towne,
  And god Pean and Baccus doth rule in his ftede,
With hoyfty and foyfty ouer fhoulder and crowne,
  Yet hath he no more life then a lompe of leade ;
Yf he haue, then charge him that man to difclofe,
Which met you and caught you, and cut of your
     nofe.

But yf you do vſe the true God to mocke,
  And geue his honor to your god in the purſe,
Loke whom ye bleſſe, and in blyndneſſe rocke,—
    The liuing God will you and your bleſſinges
        curſe ;
And at length your falſehed to all men diſcloſe,
And then, no dout, your head wyl folow your
        noſe.

Take hede, I ſaye, you chaplyns of Balle,—
  Though ye haue fed longe at Jeſabels borde,
Not longe but Helias ſhall geue you a fall ;
  Repent and returne to the liuinge Lorde.
Though ye pricke till bloud runne by your toes,
Ther wil a worſe chance com then leſing your
        noſe.

I wyll not pray for you,—let them do that liſte,—
  For feare God with me ſhould be miſcontent,
Seyng of purpoſe the Holy Ghoſt you reſiſte ;
  And if ye haue cleane forgotten to repent,
When God ſhall the ſecretes of all men diſcloſe,
Ye ſhal haue as much help as the preiſt of his noſe.

But you haue a vauntage, ſyr, if you mark all ;
  If a mous catch your god, when ye haue made it,
Then ye may catche the mouſe faſt by the walle,
  For how can you hurt your noſe except ye
        had it ?
The prouerbe is true in you, I ſuppoſe,—
He cannot tell where to turne his noſe.

FINIS.

God ſaue the Quene.

The true difcripcion of this marueilous ftraunge
Fifhe, whiche was taken on Thurfday was fen-
night, the xvj. day of June, this prefent month,
in the yeare of our Lord God, M.D.lxix.

¶ A declaration of the taking of this ftraunge Fifhe, with
the length and bredth, &c.

OOING you to vnderftande that on
Thurfdaye, the xvj. daye of this prefent
month of June, in the yeare of our
Lord God M. D. lxix. this ftraunge
fifhe was taken betweene Callis and Douer, by
fertayne Englifh fisfher-men whych were a fyfh-
ynge for mackrell. And this ftraunge and mer-
ueylous fyfhe, folowynge after the fcooles of
mackrell, came rufhinge in to the fifher-mens
netts, and brake and tore their nettes marueilouflie,
in fuch forte, that at the fyrft they weare muche
amáfed therat, and marueiled what it fhould bee
that kept fuche a fturr with their netts, for they
were verie much harmed by it with breking and
fpoyling their netts.

And then they, feing and perceiuyng that the
netts wold not ferue, by reafon of the greatnes of
this ftraung fifhe, then they with fuch inftrue-
ments, ingins, and thinges that they had, made
fuch fhift that they tooke this ftraung fifhe. And
vppon Fridaye, the morowe after, brought it vpp
to Billyngefgate in London, whyche was the xvij.
daye of June, and ther it was feene and vewid of
manie, which marueiled much at the ftraungnes of

L

it ; for here hath neuer the lyke of it ben feene :
and on Saterdaye, being the xviij. daye, fertayne
fifhe-mongers in New Fifhftreat agreeid with them
that caught it, for and in confideracion of the
harme whych they receiued by fpoylinge of ther
netts, and for their paines, to haue this ftraunge
fifhe.   And hauinge it, did open it and flaied of
the fkinn, and faued it hole.   And, adiudging the
meat of it to be good, broyled a peece and tafted
of hit, and it looked whit like veale when it was
broiled, and was good and fauerie (though fum-
what ftraung) in the eating, and then they fold of
it that fame Saterdaye to fuche as would buy of
the fame, and they themfelues did bake of it, and
eate it for daintie ; and for the more fertaintie
and opening of the truth, the good men of the
Caftle and the Kinges Head in new Fifhftreat did
bui a great deale and bakte of it, and this is mofte
true.
    The ftraunge fifhe is in length xvij. foote
and iij. foote broad, and in compas about the
bodie vj. foote ; and is round fnowted, fhort
headdid, hauing iij. ranckes of teeth on eyther
iawe, maruaylous fharpe and very fhort, ij. eyes
growing neare his fnout, and as big as a horfes
eyes, and his hart as big as an oxes hart, and likewyfe his liuer and lightes bige as an oxes ; but all
the garbidge that was in hys bellie befides would
haue gone into a felt hat.   Alfo ix. finns, and ij. of
the formoft bee iij. quarters of a yeard longe from
the body, and a verie big one on the fore parte
of his backe, blackifh on the backe, and a litle
whitifhe on the belly, a flender tayle, and had but
one bone, and that was a great rydge-bone, run-
ninge a-longe his backe from the head vnto the

tayle, and had great force in his tayle when he was in the water. Alſo it hath v. gills of eache ſide of the head, ſhoing white. Ther is no proper name for it that I knowe, but that ſertayne men of Captayne Haukinſes doth call it a ſharke. And it is to bee ſeene in London, at the Red Lyon in Fleteſtreete.

Finis, quod C. R.

Imprynted at London, in Fleetſtreate, beneathe the Conduit, at the ſigne of Saint John Euangeliſt, by Thomas Colwell.

❦ *The fantaſies of a troubled mannes head.*

Y fortune, as I lay in bed, my fortune was to fynd
  Such fancies as my careful thought hath brought into my mynd;
And when each one was gone to reſt, all ſofte in bed to lye,
I would haue ſlept, but that the watch did folow ſtyl mine eye.
And ſodeinlie I ſaw a ſea of wofull ſorrowes preſt,
Whoſe wicked wayes of ſharpe repulſe bred mine vnquiet reſt :
I ſaw this world, and how it went, ech ſtate in his degree,
And that from Wealth ygraunted is both lyfe and libertie :

I faw eke how Envie did raigne, and bare the
      greatift price,
Yet greatter poifon is not found within the cock-
      atrice:
I faw alfo how fowle Difdaine oft times, to forge
      my woe,
Gaue me the cup of bitter fweete, to pledge my
      mortal foe:
I faw alfo how that Defier to reft no place could
      fynd,
But ftyl conftraind, in endles paine, to follow
      natures kynd:
I faw alfo (moft ftraunge of all) how Nature did
      forfake
The bloud that in her womb was wrought, as doth
      the lothed fnake:
I faw how fancie would retaine no longer then
      fhee luft,
And as the wynd how fhee doth chaunge, and is
      not for to truft:
I faw how fteadfaftnes did flye with wynges of
      often chaunge,—
A flyeng bird but feldome feen, her nature is fo
      ftraunge:
I faw how pleafaunt times did paffe, as flowers do
      in the mede,
To-day that rifeth red as rofe, to-morow falleth
      deade:
I faw my time how it did run, as fand out of a
      glaffe,
Euen as each owre appointed is from time and
      tide to paffe:
I faw the yeares that I had fpent, and loffe of all
      my payne,
And how the fporte of youthly plaies my follie
      did retayne:

I faw how that the little ants in fomer ftyl doth
  rome,
To feke their foode, wherby to liue in winter for
  to come.
I faw eke Vertue how fhee fate, the threede of
  life to fpin,
Which fheweth the end of euery worke before it
  doth begin;
And when all thefe I thus behelde, with manie
  mo pardie,
In me, me thought, each one had wrought a
  perfect propertie ;
And then I faid vnto myfelfe, a leffon this fhall bee
For other that fhall after come, for to beware by
  mee.
Thus all the night I did diuife which way I might
  conftrayne
To forme a plot that wit might worke thes
  braunches in my brayne.

❡ Finis. I. C.

༺✿༻

Of euyll tounges.

EUYLL tounges, which clap at euerie
  wynd,
  Ye flea the quicke, and eke the dead
  defame ;
Thofe that liue well fome fault in them ye fynd,

Ye take no thought in fclaundring their good
    name.
Ye put iuft men oft times to open fhame ;
Ye ryng fo lowde, ye found vnto the fkyes,
And yet in proofe ye fowe nothyng but lyes.

❡ Ye make great hatred where peace hath ben of
    long,
  You bring good order to ruine and eke decaye ;
Ye plucke downeright, ye doe enhaunce the wrong,
  Ye tourne fwete myrth to wo and wallawaye.
Of mifcheifs all you are the ground, I faye,—
Happie is he that liueth on fuch a forte,
That nedes not feare fuch tounges of falfe reporte.

❡ Finis, quod I. Canand.

❡ *Of Truft and Triall.*

WHO trufts before he tries may foone
    his truft repent,
  Who tries before he trufts doth fo his
    care preuent ;
Thus truft may not be caufe of triall, then, we fee,
But triall muft be caufe of truft in ech degree.

❡ Finis. B. G.

A Strife betwene Appelles and Pigmalion.

WHEN that Appelles liued in Grece,
　　Pigmalion alſo raigned than :
　Theſe two did ſtriue to frame a pece,
　　Which ſhould amaze the ſight of
　　　man,
Whereby they might win ſuch a name,
As ſhould deſerue immortall fame.

❧ Appelles then ſtrayed euerie where,
　　To marke and viewe ech courtlie dame,
And when he heard where any were
　　Did well deſerue the prayſe and fame,
He thither rode, with willyng harte,
Of her to take the cumlieſt parte.

❧ And when he had, with trauaile great,
　　A thouſand wights knit vp in one,
He found therewith to wurke his feat,
　　A paterne ſuch as earſt was none ;
And then with ioye retourned backe,
For to thoſe limmes but lyfe did lacke.

❧ Pigmalion eke, to ſhew his arte,
　　Did then conclude in iuorie white
To forme and frame in euerie parte
　　A woman fayre to his delighte,
Wherein was euerie limme ſo coucht,
As not a vayne he lefte vntoucht.

❡ When their two cunnings ioyned were,
    A worlde it was to fee their wurke;
But yet it may greue euerie eare,
    To heare the chaunce did therein lurke;
For through the pece they framed had,
For loue Pigmalion did run mad.

❡ Which feene, Appelles fhut his booke,
    And durft no longer viewe that fight;
For why? her comelie limmes and looke
    In one did paffe ech other wight;
And while Appelles wiped his eye,
The pece did mount vnto the fkye.

❡ Whereas Dame Nature toke it ftraight,
    And wrapt it vp in linnen folde,
Efteeming it more then the waight
    Had ten times ben of gliftryng golde;
Shee lockt it vp faft in a cheft,
To pleafure him that fhee loued beft.

❡ Appelles then, difmayed much,
    Did throw his booke into the fire;
He feared left the gods did grutch
    That wurkemen fhould fo high afpire;
Yet once agayne he trauailed Grece
With leffe effect, and made a pece,

❡ Which long time did hold great renowne,
    For Venus all men did it call,—
Tyll in our dayes gan Nature frowne,
    And gaue the workemannes worke a fall;
For from her cheft, t'auoyde all ftryfe,
Shee tooke the pece, and gaue it lyfe;

❡ And for a token gaue the fame
   Vnto the higheſt man of ſtate,
And ſaid, Since thou art crownd by Fame,
   Take to thee here this worthie mate,—
The ſame which kyld the caruers ſtrife,
Before that Nature gaue it life.

❡ Lorde! yf Appelles now did know,
   Or yf Pigmalion once ſhould heare,
Of this their worke the worthie ſhow,
   Since Nature gaue it life to beare;
No doubt at all her worthie prayſe
Thoſe ſelie Grekes from death wold rayſe.

❡ Then thoſe that daylie ſee her grace,
   Whoſe vertue paſſeth euerie wight,—
Her comelie corps, her chriſtall face,—
   They ought to pray, both day and night,
That God may graunt moſt happie ſtate
Vnto that Princeſſe and her mate.

❡ Finis. Ber. Gar.

❡ Imprinted at London without Alderſgate, in
   Little Britaine, by A. Lacy.

❦

A new Ballad againſt Unthrifts.

WHEN raging louts, with feble braines,
   Moſte wilfully wyl ſpend awaye,
   And eke conſume more then their
      gaines,
   In riotyng al the longe day,
And ſpend with him that wil ſpend moſte,
 Yet of their gaine they need not boſte.

When drunken drunkerds will not fpare
   The alehous daily for to plye,
But fit and tipple there full fquare,
   And to their gaines will haue no eye,
Nor will not ceafe, I warrant ye,
So long as they haue one penny.

When rufling roifters wil beftowe
   Vpon their backs fuche fine aray,
And be not wurth that whiche they owe,
   Falling therby into decay;
Yet wil they fet theron a face,
And bragge and crake it out a-pace.

When liuely lads wil plye the dice,
   Confuming there away their good,
No man wil count them to be wice,
   But rather to be mad or wood ;
For when that all their money is gone,
Then are they drefled like a mome.

When lafie loiterers will not wurk,
   And honeftly their liuings get,
But had rather in corners lurk
   Then that they wold with labor fwet,
Therfore no welth they can attain,
But liue in trouble and in pain.

When doting doltes wil enterprife
   To wurk fuche feates as I haue tolde,
Not ceaffing for to exercife
   Worfe deeds then thofe with courage bold,
Then fome do lay their cotes to gage,
Til that they haue receiued their wage.

Then fome the Counter oft doo kiffe,
   If that the money be not paid,
Or if that they their day doe miffe,
   For whiche to gage their cote was laid ;
Yet wil they not by this take heed,
But ftil continew to proceed.

Then fome therby their credit lofe,
   So that no wife man wil them truft,
Wherfore they can no lenger glofe,
   But rub and reuel not they muft,
For wherfoeuer they be come,
They are not fo wel truft as knowne.

Then fome at length do beg their bread,
   Who, if in time they had been wife,
Might wel haue had inough to fed
   Themfelues, their children, and their wiues ;
But when that all is gone and fpent,
It is to late then to repent.

Then fome to pilfer doo begin,
   But affone as they be efpied,
With whips they are laid on the fkin,
   At a carts ars being wel tied ;
But al this can not thofe amend,
That wil doo mifchefe to the end.

Then fome proceed to rob and kyl,
   Counting al fifh that comes to net ;
And yf that they might haue their wil,
   For right or wrong they wuld not let,
Til at the laft they fall in bands,
And can not efcape out of hands.

Then fome at Newgate doo take fhip,
  Sailing ful faft vp Holborne Hil;
And at Tiborn their anckers piche,
  Ful fore indeed againft their wil;
But then it is to late, I fay,
To cal againe the yefterday.

Wherfore al ye that vfe this trade,
  Leaue of betimes, yf ye be wife,
Left that perchaunce this way ye wade
  Ful fore againft your owne deuife;
For heer ye fee the end of fuche,
As litle haue and wil fpend muche.

℄ Finis, quoth W. F.

℄ Imprinted at London, at the long fhop adioining vnto Saint Mildreds Churche, in the
Poultry, by John Alde.

A newe Secte of Friars, called Capichini.

THESE newe frefhe come Friars, being
            fprong vp of late,
      Doe nowe within Andwarpe keepe
            their abidinge,
Seducinge muche people to their damned eftate,
  By their newe falfe founde doctrine the Gofpel
            deridinge;
Sayinge and affirminge, which is no newe falfe
      tidinge,

That all fuche as doe the Popes doctrine
    difpife,
As damned foules to hell mufte be ridinge;
    For they doe condemne them with their newe
    found lies.
Thefe be the children of the worlde counted wife,
    Whofe wifedome is folly to God and his elect;
But let Sathan worke all that he can deuife,
    God it is alone which the Gofpel doeth protect.

*The firft part of the faire Widow of Watling
ftreet and her 3 daughters, and how her wicked
fonne accufed her to be a harlot, and his fifters
baftards, only to deceiue them of their portions.*

To the tune of Bragandary.

OF the kind Widdow of Watling ftreet
    I will the ftory tell,
    Who by her hufband deere was left,
      In fubftance rich and well;
A prodigall fonne likewife had fhe,
And faire yong daughters louely three;—
      Great mifery, forrow and mifery,
      Commeth for want of grace.

¶ For by his dayly practifes,
    Which were both lewd and ill,
His fathers hart from him was drawne,
    His loue and his good will;
But yet, what chance fo ere befell,
His mother loued him deerely well.

❡ When he in prifon lay full poore,
  For debt which he did owe,
His father would not ftur out of doore,
  For to releafe his woe ;
But when his mother his griefe did fee,
She found the meanes to fet him free.

❡ And when her hufband fell full fick,
  And went to make his will,—
O hufband, remember your fonne, fhe faid,
  Although he hath beene ill ;
But yet no doubt he may returne,
Repenting the euill that he hath done.

❡ Remember, wife, what forrow and care
  Through him I dayly found ;
Who, through his lewd vngratious deeds,
  Hath fpent me many a pound ;
And therefore, let him finke or fwim,
I meane not for to deale with him.

❡ And therefore fole executor here
  I do thee onely make,
To pay the debts and legacies,—
  The reft vnto thee take.
Not fo, my hufband deare, quoth fhe,
But let your fonne be ioynd with me ;

❡ For-why he is our child, fhe faid,—
  We can it not deny,—
The firft that euer graced you
  With fathers dignity ;—
O, if that euer you did me loue,
Graunt this requeft for his behoue.

❡ Thy loue, deere wife, was euermore
   Moſt precious vnto me,
And therefore, for thy ſweet loues ſake,
   I graunt thy ſuite to thee;
But, ere the yeare is fully ſpent,
I know thou wilt the ſame repent.

❡ Now was his ſonne receiued home,
   And with his mother deere
Was ioyn'd executor of the will,
   Which did his courage cheare.
The old man dying, buryed was,—
But now behold what came to paſſe.

The funeral being ended quite,
   It fel vpon a day
Some friends did fetch the widdow foorth,
   To driue conceits away.
While ſhe was forth, and thought no ill,
Her wicked ſonne doth worke his will.

Poſſeſſion of the houſe he took
   In moſt deſpitful wiſe,
Throwing his ſiſters out of dores,
   With ſad lamenting cryes.
When this they did his mother ſhow,
She would not beleeue he would do ſo.

But when ſhe came vnto her houſe,
   And found it true indeed,
She cald vnto her ſon, and ſaid,—
   Althogh her hart did bleed,—
Come down, my ſonne, come downe, quod ſhe,
Let in thy mother and ſiſters three.

❡ I will not let in my mother, he ſaid,
    Nor ſiſters any one;
The houſe is mine, I will it keepe,
    Therefore, away! be gone!
O ſonne, canſt thou indure to ſee't,
Thy mother and ſiſters to lie in the ſtreete?

❡ Did not thy father, by his will,
    For terme of this my life,
Giue me this houſe for to enioy
    Without al further ſtrife;
And more, of all his goods, quoth ſhe,
I am executor ioynd with thee.

❡ My father left you the houſe, he ſaid,
    But this was his intent,—
That you therefore, during your life,
    Should pay me yearely rent;
A hundred pound a yeare, therefore,
You ſhall me giue, or giue it ore.

❡ And ſith the citties cuſtome is,
    That you the thirds muſt haue
Of all my fathers moueables,
    I graunt what law doth craue;
But not a peny more will I
Diſcharge of any legaſie.

❡ O wicked ſonne, quoth ſhe, that ſeekes
    Thy mother thus to fleece,—
Thy father to his daughters gaue
    Three hundred pound a peece:
Tell me who ſhall their porcions pay,
Appointed at their marriage day.

❧ Then, with a fcornefull fmile, he faid,
 What talke you of fo much?
Ten pound a peece I will them giue,—
 My charitie is fuch.
Now fie vpon thee, beaft, quoth fhe,
That thus doth deale with them and me!

❧ But ere that they and I will take
 This iniury at thy hand,
The chiefeft peeres of England fhall
 The matter vnderftand.
Nay, if you go to that, quoth he,
Mark well what I fhall tell to thee :—

Thou haft a fecret harlot bin,
 And this ile proue full plaine,
That in my fathers lifetime did
 Lewd ruffians entertaine,
The which did then beget of thee,
In wicked fort, thefe baftards three.

❧ No daughters to my father then
 Were they in any wife,
As he fuppofd them for to be,
 Thou blinding fo his eyes ;
Therefore no right at all haue they
To any peny giuen this day.

❧ When fhe did heare her fhameles fonne
 For to defame her fo,
She with her louely daughters three,
 With griefe away did goe ;
But how this matter forth did fall,
The fecond part fhall fhew you all.
 Great mifery, forow, &c.   Finis.

Imprinted at London for T. P.

M

The fecond part of the Widdow of Watling-

ftreete and her three Daughters.

To the tune of the Wanton Wife.

HE beautifull widdow of Watling
  ftreete,
  Being thus falfly accufde by her
  fonne,
With her three daughters of fauor fo fweet,
 Whofe beauty the loue of fo many had wonne,
With her daughters three, for fuccour went fhe,
Vnto the kings counfaile of noble degree.
  Now fie vpon falfhood and forgerie fraile,
  For great is the truth, and it fhall preuaile !

❦ Her fonne by a writ now fommoned is
 At the Star-chamber with fpeed to appeare,
To anfwere there the abufes of his ;—
 The Lords of the Counfel the matter will heare.
The news was brought; his wits he fought,
Which way his villanie beft might be wrought.

❦ Then vp and downe the citty fo faire
 He feeketh companions to ferue his turne,—
A fort of vacabonds, naked and bare,
 The which to worke murders for money is won:
Thefe wretches behold, for money and golde,
He hired for witneffes his lyes to vphold, &c.

❦ My maifters, quoth he, my mother by name
 To be a lewd ftrumpet accufed I haue ;

And, hauing no witneffe to proue that fame,
 Your ayde and affiftance herein I do craue :
Therefore, without feare, before the Lords there,
Yet this thing is certaine, you fixe fhall it fweare.

℄ The firft two, quoth he, fhal fweare on a booke,
 That fixteene yeares paft they plainely did fee,
As they through the garden hedge fadly did looke,
 That fhe in one houre was abufed by three ;
And how it fell, as they markt it wel,
That iuft nine moneths after fhe had hir firft
  girle.

℄ The fecond couple fhall fweare in this fort,
 That at Briftow Faire, about xvij. yeares paft,
She with her owne apprentife did fal in fuch fport,
 That her fecond daughter was got at the laft.
Now truft vs, quod they, weele fweare what you
  fay,
Or anything elfe for money, this day, &c.

And thus the third couple their oath now fhal
  take,
 That as at the bath fhe ftaid on a day,
For ach in her bones, as the fcufe fhe did make,
 How fhe with a courtier the wanton did play ;
And how well you wot, in the pleafant plot,
Her deareft yong daughter for certaine was got.

But now, you mafters, your names let me know,
 That I may prouide you apparell with fpeed ;
Like fixe graue cittizens fo muft you go,
 The better your fpeeches the Lords will heed ;
So fhal I with fcorne, ere Saturday morne,
Proue her a harlot, my fifters bafe borne, &c.

❡ My name is Make-fhift, the firft man did fay ;
    And Francis Light-finger, the fecond likewife ;
Cutbert Creepe-window, the third to difplay ;
    And Rowland Rob-man, with foule ftaring
        eyes ;
Jack Shameles comes then, with Hary Steale-hen.
You are, quod the widdow, fome right honeft
        men!

❡ Before the lords moft prudent and graue,
    This wretch doth with his witneffe come :
The mother complains, and juftice doth craue
    Of all the offences that he hath her done.
My Lords, then quod he, I pray you heare me,—
The law for my deeds my warrant fhall be.

I fay, fhe is a harlot moft vilde,
    And thofe be her baftards that ftandeth in
        place,
And that fhe hath often her body defilde
    By very good witnes ile proue to her face.
This thing of thy mother thou oughtft for to
        fmother,—
'Tis fhame for a child to fpeake [fo] of his mother!

❡ But if this matter be proued vntrue,
    And thou a falfe lyar be found to thy face,
Worfe then an infidell, Pagon, or Jew,
    Thou oughtft to be punifht and plagd in this
        cafe ;
And therefore draw neere, and now let vs heare
What faies the witnes that here doth appeare.

❡ When the firft couple did come for to fweare,
    They quiuerd and quakt in moft wondrous fort ;

The lords very countenance did put them in feare,
   And now they knew not what to report ;
The fecond likewife ftard fo with his eyes,
They ftamberd and knew not what to deuife.

℄ The lords, perceiuing the cafe how it went,
   Did afke the laft couple what they had to fay,
Who fell on their knees incontinent,
   Saying, they were hird for mony that day :
Quoth they, it is fo, the truth for to fhow,
Againft the good widow no harme we do know.

℄ Thus was the widow deliuered from blame,
   With her three daughters of beauty moft bright,
Her fonne reproached with forrow and fhame,
   Hauing his iudgment appointed him right,—
To loofe, at the leaft, the goods he poffeft,
To loofe both his eares, and banifht to reft.

When he heard this iudgment pronounced to be,
   The teares full bitterly fell down from his face,—
To mother and fifters he kneeled on his knee,
   Confeffing that lucre had wrought his difgrace ;
That for my own gaine I fought to detaine
My fifters three portions, this lye I did faine !

Therefore, deare mother, forgiuenes I craue
   Of you and my fifters, offended fo fore ;
My body from perill if you will but faue,
   I fweare I will grieue and offend you no more.
The lords then replide,—the law iuftly tride,
The punifhment now thou art like to abide :

℄ Therefore to prifon now thou fhalt go,
   Where thou fhalt the king's pleafure abide ;

From thence to be brought, with fhame and with
     wo,
   To fuffer the punifhment due to thy pride :
Then out of hand, thou fhalt vnderftand
That prefently thou fhalt be banifht the land.

℃ Now, while in prifon this prifoner did reft,
   Himfelfe he hanged in defperate wife—
Such horror of confcience poffeffed his breft ;
   And being caft forth, the rauens pickt out his
     eies.
All children, behold what here hath bin tolde,
Accufe no man falfly for lucre of golde !

     Now fie vpon falfhood and forgerie fraile,
     For great is the truth, and it will prevaile.

FINIS.

Imprinted at London for T. P.

℃ *Almightie God I pray his Holy Spirite to fend,*
The iuft mannes hart ftedfaft to ftay, and wicked
     liues to mend.

RUE   tryall   touchyng   truth   time
          trimly here doth trye,
     E xcept the fcribes therfore we paffe
          in righteoufnes, we dye.
M yndes many mooued bee all truth to eftablyfh ;
P apes popifh, puft in Plutoes pride, all popery
          here doe wyfh ;—

V oyde from them all, good men, which godly
      be in mynde,
S ith Sathan affaileth fome fo fore, and ftyl their
      harts doth blynde.

E mbrace and loue the truth; on Chrifts fyde
      ftifly ftand;
D eny the Pope, Sathan, the Turke, reiect them
      quite from hand.
A nd neuer wifh in wyll with wicked men t'agree,
X pe faith we can not their wayes hould, and
      eke his feruaunts be.

R eiect and expell quite that which difpleafe
      God may;
E ncline to Chrift, the truth embrace, be fure
      thereon to ftay;
R eioyce, though rigour raunge, and run for to
      obtayne;
V pon thee perfecution beare, great ioyes to haue
      agayne;
M ufe nothyng on thefe dayes, but wey the time
      now frayle.

T he tryed truth time vndertreades,—in time truth
      wyl preuayle,
I n time the wicked laugh, in time the iuft lament:
M ufe not, therfore, the iuft to trie, the Lordes
      wyl now is bent;
E mploy thy wyll and mynd to the Scriptures
      deuine.

B e not feduced in no wyfe, from truth doe not
      decline;
R efufe (yf faith thou haft) a Chriftian dumme to
      bee;

Y elde out thy talent with encreafe, and looke thy
    faith be free.
N o doubt, yf dumme thou lurke, clokyng thy
    faith for feare,
G od wyl thee plague, and to good men thy faint
    faith wyl appeare ;
E nclyne thine eare hereto, and this well vnder-
    ftand ;—
T rie out the fence hereof by truth,—all wicked-
    neffe withftand ;
H eauen with the Lorde of Lordes we fhall not
    inherite
E xcept our righteoufnes far paffe the fcribe and
    hipocrite.

A ll wicked men we fee now glorie much in
    mynd,
L ookyng for maffe, an idoll which to them hath
    ben full kynd.

T ruely thofe naughtie men thinke now, within
    fhort time,
H ere, for Jefus Chriftes true worde, to plant
    Sathans doctrine ;
Y ea, ftyll they hope indeede, and ftyll looke for
    a day,
N o doubt, Chrifts gofpel to exclude, and popes
    lawes to beare fway.
G od faue our noble queene, Lorde, graunt this,
    we requyre ;
E mong vs here long fhee may raigne, and cut
    fhort papes defyre ;
S end out thy wrath, O Lorde, confound with
    open fhame

T hofe which in hart vnto her grace long lyfe
    doe not proclaime !
O ut pull thofe hatefull harts, which in fpight
    rage and boyle

A gainft thy truth, her grace, good men; O Lorde,
    thou canft them foyle.
N othyng but wickedneffe, fuch in their hartes
    embrace,

E mong vs here although they fay, and beare out
    a fmooth face.
N ow, Lorde, thy flocke defend ; Lorde, bleffe
    thine heritage ;
D irect thy fpirit ouer vs all, in this our time and
    age ;
E ncourage vs againft rageyng Sathan alway.

Q uicken our myndes, ftrength vs herein, O
    Lorde, to thee we pray ;
V ouchfafe eke on thofe men thy heauenlie fpirite
    to fend ;
O Lorde, enfpire them with thy grace, their err-
    yng liues t'amend ;
D eftroy all errours here, illuminate their hart.

C all home all thofe which haue run wyde, to the
    truth them conuart ;
H eale thofe which broken be, O Lorde, I fay,
    in mynd !
R educe and bryng to thee in truth all wicked
    Jewes vnkynd,
I nfidels and eke Turkes, Paganes which know
    thee not :
S o fhall we all be to thee one inheritaunce and
    lot.

T read vnder and fuppreffe all vice, and eke
  expell
O ur hollow-harted hipocrites, which loue not
  thy Gofpell;
P ut in their harts fuch grace, O Lorde, that they
  may now
H ope in thee, their eternall God, and to thee
  their hartes bow!
E uer to watch and pray, as thou haft taught the
  fame,
R eady to be with oyle in lampe, heauen with thee
  to attaine.

W ee, hopyng on thee thus, all vayne hope now
  confound,
I n heauen with thee at length wyl we thy worthy
  praife forth found.
L orde, graunt that we may raigne in ioyes ce-
  leftiall;
S uch as wyl ftyl thy foes remaine, fhall to paynes
  infernall.
O Lorde, graunt this requeft,—Lorde, let thy
  kyngdome cum :
N ow watch and pray we wyll ;—for whye? Tem-
  pus edax rerum.

℄ Finis, quod Chriftopher Wilfon.

A Song againſt the Maſs.

SOME hope you ſee,—
　　The more pitie,—
　　　　Not in the Lorde of might ;
　　Whoſe harts and mynd
His wayes ſhould fynd,
　　To prayſe him day and night.

❡ With hart and voyce
They ſhould reioyce
　　Onely in Chriſt, I ſay ;
And not to hope
To ſee the pope,
　　With his lawes to beare ſway.

❡ Lament I doe,
Here to ſee nowe,
　　The ioyes that ſome be in,—
Wyſhyng for Maſſe,
I ſay, alas !
　　The cloke of filthy ſin !

❡ I may here write,
And truth endite,
　　Affyrme plainely, and ſay :
The worde of truth,—
The more is ruth,—
　　Is ſowne in ſtonie way.

❡ For all teachyng
And true preachyng,

Some harts be hard as fteele;
There is no way
Their harts to ftay,
 Or caufe them truth to feele.

❧ But ftoute they be
In all poperie,
 As by this man doth feeme;
Whofe fhamelefle face
Put forth this cafe,
 And bad his neighbours deme:

❧ Where beft fhould be,
To make, quod he,
 An aulter for our Mafle?
Let vs firft be
Herein, quod he,
 It wyll thus come to pafle.

❧ This freend of popes
Offred ten grotes
 This aulter there to make,
Where mafle fhould be;
Haue here, quod he,
 This money mine here take.

❧ Lorde, our Queene faue,
We cry and craue,
 In godlie ftate alway;
Defend her grace
Long time and fpace
 Emong vs here, we pray!

❧ Imprinted at London without Alderfgate, in
 little Britaine, by Alex. Lacy. The 16 of
 Auguft, 1566.

The Daunce and Song of Death.

At the four corners four engravings, with verſes.

1. Under a picture of the Miſer (or rich man) counting his gold, with Death at his elbow, the following quatrain.

> From your gold and ſiluer
>> To graue ye muſt daunce ;
> Though you loue it ſo deare,
>> And haue therein affiaunce.

2. Over a picture of a Priſoner fettered to an iron ring, with Death at his ſide.

> Thy pryſon and chaynes
>> From graue cannot keepe ;
> But daunce, though in paynes,
>> Thou ſhalt thereto creepe.

3. Engraving of a Judge upon the bench of juſtice, with Death beſide him, theſe lines under :—

> From trone of iuſt iudgement,
>> Syr Judge, daunce with vs ;
> To graue come incontinent
>> From ſtate ſo glorious.

4. A Man careſſing a Lady in a bower, a table ſpread with wine and fruit, Death ſeated behind them ; the following inſcribed.

> Ye dallying fyne louers,
>> In mydſt of your chere,
> To daunce here be partners,
>> And to graue draw ye nere.

In the centre a figure playing the pipe and tabor upon a feat
made of crofs-bones, mattock, and fhovel, acrofs a yawning
grave, with this placard, " Sycknes, Deathes minftrel."
Around him in a circle, joined hand in hand, are the
following figures, Death leading the dance, the king,
the begger, the old man, the childe, the wyfe man, the
foole, with thefe lines.

Come, daunce this trace, ye people all,
    Both prince and begger, I fay ;
Yea, old, yong, wyfe, and fooles I call,
    To graue, come, take your way.
        For ficknes pipes thereto,
        By griefes and panges of wo.

A Ballad intituled, Prepare ye to the plowe.

To the tune of Pepper is blacke.

❡ The queene holdes the plow, to continew good feede;
    Truftie fubieftes, be readie to helpe, if fhe neede.

LOOKE vp, my Lordes, and marke my
            wordes,
        And heare what I fhall fing ye:
        And fubiefts all, both great and fmall,
    Now marke what word I bring ye.
Parnafo Hill, not all the fkill
    Of Nimphs or Mufes fayned,
Can bring about that I finde out,
    By Chrift himfelfe ordayned.

Let wifdom be, as it is, I fee,
    A gift moſt worth the telling,
Which neuer was fo brought to paſſe
    Where Pagans haue ben dwelling,
Is now, in fine, by power deuine,
    Among vs Engliſh planted;
Which many a day was kept away,
    And many a one it wanted.

And by that wifdom haue we had
    Such proofe as yet was neuer,
To judge and deeme both good and bad,
    To our great comfort euer.
Which fithes we haue, now let vs hold,
    This tutchſtone is the triall,
To beate the baggage from the gold,
    And truth from falfe deniall.

And by this knowledge we do know
    That euery thing is vaine
Beneath the fonn, which heare below
    We couet to attaine.
Let not the fpright geue vs delight
    To labour and attend vs,
To feke to haue before our graue
    The ioy that Chriſte may fend vs.

In feking that, then, muſt we nat
    Build on the fandy furges,
Nor fow our feede where euery weede
    His grace and bounty vrges;
Nor put our hope in Preeſte or Pope,
    In maſſe or other matters,
Or, by our dole, to fave our foule
    With filling empty platters.

Or by a pardon to appeafe
　　The furfits of our finning,
Although our fathers had all theafe
　　By wicked mens beginning.
Nor let vs make our ftock and ftore
　　A burden to accufe vs ;
For, doing fo, fo much the more
　　We tempt GOD to refufe vs.

Neither let vs once prefume fo far,
　　Of mercy or of meekenes,
To counterfait, to make or mar
　　This image or this likeneffe,
That our forefathers did beleue
　　Were Gods to giue and guide them :
Such follies did the Chriftians greeue,
　　And Pagans now deride them.

Remember once the latter law—
　　Left yet in Moyfes table,—
That neighbourly to liue in awe
　　It is moft commendable :
Then fhouldft thou not defire to craue
　　Thy neighbours loffe or lacke ;
Neither exceffe defire to haue,
　　That puts thy foule to wracke.

Neither vfery, nor vfe at all
　　Of women, wealth, or wine ;
Neither of aboundance, great or fmall,
　　Ill gotten, fhould be thine :
Neither fhould contencion, craft, increafe,
　　Nor fwearing beare the fway,
Nor God vnferued—men as beafts
　　Would break the Sabboth day.

Then would the honour duly hit,
    To parents, lord, or king;
Then would ther be no doubt a whit
    To haue ſtore of euerything:
All this the new law, with the old,
    Doth nip vs to remember,
Euen as the froſt, that waxeth cold,
    Doth nip vs in December.

And as, vpon a ſodain heat,
    We ſoone forget that freeſing,
When God doth of his mercy great
    Spare vs for lack of leeſing,—
So let vs think, as Sommer ſhows
    Grene graſſe to our deliting,
We ſe that all the graſſe that growes
    Goth down with litle ſmiting;

And when the mowyer coms to mowe,
    'Tis ſone both ripe and rotten:
This tale, I truſt, of hye and low
    Will neuer be forgotten.
On Gods good booke then let vs loke
    For that which neuer faileth;
Without which boke, by hooke or crooke,
    No worldly wit preuaileth.

God ſaue her Grace that holds the plow,
    To ſowe this truſty treaſure;
Though many a one be ſtubborn now,
    And harrow it but at leaſure:
God graunt that he that harrowed Hell
    In guardon ſtill may haue her,

N

And fend you grace that thinke not well
    Of God, that fo doth faue hir.

W. Elderton.

❡ Imprinted at London, in Fleeteſtreete, by
    William How for Richard Johnes : and are
    to be folde at his Shop, ioyning to the
    fouthweſt doore of Paules Church.

An Epitaph on the death of the vertuous Mat-
rone the Ladie Maioreſſe, late wyfe to the right
Honorable Lorde (Alexander Auenet,) Lord Maior
of the Citie of London, who deceaſed the vij. daie
of July, 1570.

HELPE nowe, ye Mufes nyne, powre
            out your noates of woe!
        Aide me, with pitious piercing plaints,
            the loſſe of her to ſhoe,
Whofe virtues, maugre Death! ſhall lyue and
    laſt for aye,
As fliyng Fame in golden trump doth cherefully
    difplay.
Ye ladyes, leave your fportes, your paſtymes fet
    afyde ;
To weepe this ladyes fatall fine, conduictes of
    ſtreames prouide :
Caſt off your coſtly ſilkes, your juelles nowe for-
    fake,

To decke yourfelues in mournynge weedes, now
    poaftynge hafte do make.
Helpe now, ye faythfull wyues, to wayle this
    faythfull wyfe,
Whofe flowynge vertues were not hyd whyle fhe
    enioyed lyfe ;—
As well to frende as foe her curtefie was knowne ;—
But now the goddes haue thought it good to
    clayme agayne their owne.
Lvcina hath forgot her chardge, the fatall Fates
    haue don ;
Clotho hath left the rocke of lyfe, and Lachas
    longe hath fpon.
Thefe werie of their wonted toyle, at mightie
    Ioves decree—
To whom the heauens, the earth, and fea, and
    all thynges fubiect bee,—
The fifter dire, fearce Atropos, with fchortchyng
    cuttynge knyfe,
Hath fhred the threede that longe dyd holde this
    godly ladies lyfe ;
Whofe loffe, deare dames, bewayle, and weepe
    with many a teare,
For you fhall miffe a matrone graue in daunger
    you to cheare,
Whofe counfell in their neede her neighbours
    could not want.
Her helpe vnto the comfortleffe could neuer yet
    bee fcant ;
Vnto the poore, oppreft with fickeneffe, griefe and
    payne,
To minifter and giue reliefe her hart was euer
    fayne.
The poore haue loft a nurfe to helpe their nedie
    ftate,

The ritche fhall want a perfecte frende, as they
    can well relate.

Thus ritche and poore fhall want her aide at
    euerie neede ;

For both eftates in daunger deepe fhe laboured to
    feede,—

The ritche with counfelles fwete to chearifh ftyll
    fhe thought,

The poore by almes and lyberall giftes to tender
    longe fhe fought.

But who fhall haue the greateft loffe I knowe is
    not vnknowen,—

Her beft beloued, the wight whom fhee accompted
    for her owne,

The Lorde MAIOR, whiche nowe doth rule in
    LONDON, noble citie,

Shall want her fight,—the greater griefe to miffe
    a mate fo wittie ;

A phenyx rare, a turtell true, fo conftant in her
    loue,

That Nature nedes muft fhowe her force, her
    hufbandes teares to moue.

Who for the loffe of fuche a wyfe can fobbyng
    fighes refrayne,

In whom fo many vertues dyd continue and
    remayne ?

You damfelles deare domefticall, whiche in her
    houfe abyde,

Haue caufe to wayle, for you haue loft a good and
    godly guide,

Whofe lenytie and gentell hart you all haue
    knowen and felt,

For vnto you in courteous forte her giftes fhe
    euer dealt.

You officers, that dayly ferue her lorde at euery
    neede,

Can teftifie that you haue loft a ladie kynde in
        deede,—

So gentell, graue, demure, and wife, as ye your-
        felues expreffe,

That needes ye muft gufh foorth your teares, and
        weepe with bytterneffe.

In fyne, both ritche and poore haue iuft caufe
        giuen to wayle ;

The ritch in counfell lacke a frende, the poore
        their comfort fayle.

The troupe of maryed dames, whiche fhall her
        vertues knowe,

Haue offered caufe in bytter teares fome tyme
        for to beftowe.

But fith it is the goddes decree, to whom all flefh
        muft bende,

To take this ladie from the earth, and bringe her
        dayes to ende,

Who can withholde that they wyll haue? who
        dare their wyll withftande?

To vayne it were for mortall men the caufe to take
        in hande.

Her vertues were fo great, that they haue thought
        it meete

To take from hence vnto the heauens her chriftall
        foule fo fweete,

Which now inclofed is with aungelles rownde
        aboute.

Suche hoape we haue, no other caufe is giuen vs
        for to doubt.

Her corps fhall fhrowde in claye, the earth her
        right doth craue,

This ladie yeldes her parent too, her tombe, her
        cell and graue ;

From whence no kynge nor keyfar can, nor rulcr
        bearynge fwaye,

For all their force and puiſſaunce, once ſtarte or
      go awaye.
All fleſshe ſhall haue an ende, as goddes do graunt
      and wyll,
And reape rewarde as they deſerue, hap good, or
      hap it yll.
But thoughe that death haue done his worſte, this
      dame to take awaye,
In ſpite of death her vertues ſhall endure and laſt
      for aye.
℃ Farewell, O ladye deare ! the heauens haue
      choſen thee,—
Receyue this VALE ; I haue done ; thou getteſt no
      more of mee.

   Poſt funera viuit virtus, quoth John Phillip.

   Imprinted at London by Richarde Johnes.

℃ *A famous dittie of the joyful receauing of
the Queens moſte excellent maieſtie by the worthy
citizens of London, the xij. day of Nouember,
1584, at her graces comming to Saint James.*

     To the tune of Wigmores Galliard.

HE twelfe day of Nouember laſt,
     Elizabeth, our noble queen,
  To Londen-warde ſhe hied faſt,
     Which in the cuntry long had been.
  The citizens went then apace,
  On ſtately ſteeds, to meet her grace,
  In veluet coats and chaines of golde,
  Moſte gorgiouſly for to beholde.

❡ Each company in his degree
　　Stood orderly in good aray,
To entertaine Her Maiefty,
　　As fhe did paffe along the way.
And by each man did duly ftand
A wayter with a torch in hand,—
Becaufe it drue on toward night,—
Along the way her grace to light.

❡ The people flocked there amain,
　　The multitude was great to fee ;
Their joyful harts were glad, and fain
　　To view her princely maiefty,
Who at the length came riding by,
Within her chariot openly ;
Euen with a noble princely train
Of lords and ladies of great fame.

❡ Her maiefty was glad to fee
　　Her fubiects in fo good a cafe,
Which then fell humbly on their knee,
　　Defiring God to faue her grace.
And like a noble prince that day
For them in like forte did fhe pray ;
And curteoufly fhe anfwered ftill,
I thank you all for your good will.

❡ And bowing down on euery fide,
　　Mofte louingly vnto them all,
A poor man at the length fhe fpied,
　　Which down before her grace did fall.
And curteoufly fhe then did ftay,
To heer what he had then to fay ;
To whome he did prefent anon,
An humble fupplication.

Then plefantly fhe paffed on,
   Til fhe vnto Saint James came,
And alwaies, as fhe went along,
   The people cri'd with might and main,—
O Lord, preferue your noble grace,
And all your fecret foes deface!
God bleffe and keep our noble queen,
Whofe like on earth was neuer feen!

What traitors hart can be fo hard
   To hurt or harme that princely flower?
What wretch from grace is fo debard,
   That can againft her feem to lower,
Which is the onely ftar of light,
That doth amaze all princes fight,—
A mofte renowned virgin queen,
Whofe like on earth was neuer feen?

The daughter of a noble king,
   Defending of a royall race,
Whofe fame through all the world doth ring,
   Whofe vertues fhines in euery place;—
The diamond of delight and ioy,
Which guides her cuntry from anoy;
A mofte renowned virgin queen,
Whofe like on earth was neuer feen.

❡ The peerles pearle of princes all,
   So ful of pitty, peace, and loue,
Whofe mercy is not proued fmall,
   When foule offendors doo her mooue.
A phenix of mofte noble minde,
Vnto her fubiects good and kinde;
A mofte renowned virgin queen,
Whofe like on earth was neuer feen.

❡ The feruant of the mighty God,
  Which dooth preferue her day and night,
For whome we feel not of his rod,
  Although the pope hath doon his fpite.
The cheef maintainer of his Woord,
Wherein confifts our heauenly food ;—
O Lord, preferue our noble queen,
Whofe like on earth was neuer feen!

❡ And fuch as hollow-harted be,
  Partakers of the Romifh rout,
Which thinketh mifcheef fecretly,
  The Lord wil fuerly finde them out,
And giue them their deferuings due,
Which to her grace is found vntrue ;
But, Lord, preferue our noble queen,
Whofe like on earth was neuer feen !

❡ In many dangers hath fhe been,
  But God was euermore her guide ;
He wil not fee our gratious queen
  To fuffer harme through traitors pride ;
But euery one which fought her fall,
The Lord did ftil confound them all,
And fuch as thought her life to fpill
Themfelues mofte defperately did kil.

❡ And euery traitor in this land,
  Whofe wicked thoughts are yet vnknown,
The Lord confume them out of hand,
  Before they be more riper grown ;
Whofe harts are fet with one accord
Againft th' annointed of the Lord ;
But, God, preferue our noble queen,
Whofe like on earth was neuer feen !

℃ Lord, ſend her long and happy daies,
   In England for to rule and raigne,
Gods glory euermore to raiſe,
   True Juſtice alwaies to maintain,—
Which now, theſe ſix and twenty yeers,
So royally with vs appeers;—
O Lord, preſerue our noble queen,
Whoſe like on earth was neuer ſeen!

      Finis.   Richard Harrington.

℃ At London: printed by Edward Allde for
   Yarath James, and are to be ſolde in Newgate
   Market againſt Chriſt church gate.   1584.

A meruaylous ſtraunge deformed Swyne.

HERE, good reader, ſhalt thou beholde
a ſtraunge and deformed ſwyne,
farowed and brought foorth in Den-
marke, and there bought and brought
ouer by an Engliſhman, which hath it at this
preſent; and is to be ſeen aliue, the proportion
wherof is wonderous ſtraunge to beholde and
vew; the forepart therof from the ſnoute beneath
the foreſhoulders are in al pointes like vnto a
ſwine, except the eares only, which reſemble the
eares of a lion; the hinder parte (contrarie to
kinde) is proportioned in all pointes like vnto a
ram, hauing ſofte wooll, both white and blacke,
mixed monge the hard heare, and ſo groweth

from the fhoulders downewarde, all the body ouer ; and it is a boare pyg, howbeit there doth nothing appeare outwarde, but onely the pyfell vnder his belly ; but if a man lift to feele and gripe it in the grindes, there ye may feele his coddes within his belly ; and the moft ftraungeft thinge of all is the mifshapen and deformed feete, wheron grow certayne tallents and very harde clawes, doubling vnder his feete, euery claw fo byg as a mans fynger, and blacke of colour, and the length of euery of them are full x inches, very ftraunge and wonderfull to beholde. It feedeth and eateth diuers and fundrie thinges, as well haye and graffe as breade and apples, with fuch other thinges as fheepe and fwyne do feede on.

⁋ *An exhortacion or warnynge to all men, for amendment of lyfe.*

Come neere, good Chriftians all,
   Beholde a monfter rare,
Whofe monftrous fhape, no doubt, fortels,
   Gods wrath we fhould beware.
His wondrous works we ought not iudge,
   As toyes and trifles vaine ;
Whither it be childe or brutifh beaft,
   Forwarnings they are playne.
As now this mingled brutifh beaft
   Gods creature is, we fee,
Although as ftraunge of fhape and forme
   As poffyblie may be;
For if you do way well ech poynt,
   His nature and his fhape,

I feare, refembles fome of thofe
   As on the fame do gape ;
For-why moft fwinifh are our liues,
   And monftrous, that is fure.
Though we refemble fimple fheepe,
   Or lambes that be moft pure,
But euery tree itfelfe will try,
   At laft by his owne fruite ;
Though on our backs we cary woll,
   Our confcience is pollute ;
Though fmilingly, with flattering face,
   We feeme Gods word to loue,
Contrary wife fom hate the fame,
   As well their deedes did prooue,
Who ment the ruine of our realme;
   As traytours to our queene,
Som white-fafte lambs, haue fought to do,
   Nay, monftrous fwine, I weene.
I meane not here at large to fhowe
   Offences as they bee,
In whom they raigne, in hie or low,
   I name here no degree ;
But generally I fay to all,
   Repent, amend your life ;
The greedy rich, the needy poore,
   Yea, yong man, maide, and wife !
The proteftant, the papift eke,
   What fecte fo that ye be,
Gripe your own confcience, learne to do
   As God commaundeth ye ;
For all are finners, Dauid faith,—
   Yea, do the beft we may,
Vnprofitable feruaunts ftill we be,—
   We can it not denay.
Judge ye therfore how far amiffe
   All thofe their liues do frame,

That outwardly profeffe Gods truth,
   And inward hate the fame.
Judge ye againe that hate your prince,
   And feeke the realme to fpoyle,
What monftrous fwine you proue at length,
   For all your couert coyle.
Experience late by Felton falfe,
   And Nortons two, I weene ;
Their treafon known were wondred at,
   As they had monfters been ;
And furely I can iudge no leffe
   But that they monfters were,
Quite changed from true fubjects fhape,
   Their deedes did fo appere.
Then let their deedes example be
   To vs that fubiects are,
For treafon ends by fhamfull death,—
   Therfore by them beware.
I fpeake not here of monftrous pride
   In man, in mayde, and wife ;
Nor whoordom, which is daily vfde
   In England ranke and rife.
Of couetoufneffe what fhould I fay,
   Or vfery daily don ?
It booteth not to fpeake therof,
   So much therby is wonne.
But if they well do count their cardes,
   How God they do offend,
I wis their fweete ill-gotten gaines
   Hath fowre and bitter end.
From the which end deliuer vs, Lord,
   And graunt both hie and low
To become thy feruaunts iuft and true,
   And then our end we know.
God grant our gracious fouerain queen
   Long ouer vs may raigne ;

And this life paſt, with Chriſt our Lord
   Heauens ioyes ſhe may attaine!

Finis, I. P.

Imprinted at London by William How, for
   Richard Iohnes, and are to be ſolde at his
   ſhop ioyning to the ſouth weſt doore of Paules
   Churche.

Love deſerveth Love.

YOONGE man that on VENVS ſporte
        doth raunge,
  Taking delight his miſtreſeſſe to
        chaunge,
In lewe of LOVE doth hope to be regarded,
And with a gentle looke to be rewarded.
He proffers ſeruice, vowing all he maye,
That, were ſhe deade, there neuer would be daie!
Saying then,—Phœbe, thow art more deuine,—
Shee borroweth Phœbus light, and Phœbus thine;
And one the top his eſtridge plumed helme
He beares her gloue, his foes to ouerwhelme;
And for reward he nothinge doth requier
But loues ſweet-water to aſſwage luſte' fier;
He ſeekes not for abundance out of meaſure,
But loue's reward is all his hop'te for treaſure.

T. W.

A ſpell for Ione.

TELL me, ſweete girle, how ſpellſt thou
     Ione;
    Tell me but that, is all I craue,—
I ſhall not neede to lye alone,
  When ſuch a louely mate I haue.
That thou arte one who can denye,
  O one whoſe praiſe no tonge can tell?
And all will graunt that I am I,—
  O happy I, if right thou ſpell;—
If I am I, and thou art one,
Tell me, ſweete wench, how ſpellſt thou Ione?

IONE.

Ile tell you, ſir, and tell you true,
  For I am I and I am one,
So can I ſpell Ione without you,
  And ſpelling ſo, can lye alone:
My I to one is conſonant,
  But as for yours, it is not ſo;
If then your I agrement want,
  I to your I muſt aunſwer no;
Wherfor leaue of your ſpelling plea,
And let your I be I per ſe.

RES.

Your aunſwer makes me almoſt blind,
  To put out one and leaue one I;
Unleſs herein ſome hope I find,
  Therfor I muſt diſpayre and dye;

But I am you, when you doe fpeake ;—
    O fpeak againe, and tell me fo !
My hart with forrow canot break
    To heare fo kinde a graunting, no ;
For this is all for which I fue,
That I may be turnd into you.

IONE.

Nay, if you turne and wind and prefs,
    And in the crofs-row haue fuch fkill,
I am put down, I muft confefs ;
    It bootes me not to crofs your will.
If you fpeak tru, fay I ftand to it,
    For you and I are now but one ;
And I will ly that you may doe it,—
    Now put together we fpell Ione ;
But how will Ione be fpeld, I wonder,
    When you and I fhall part afunder ?

A Paradox.

WHAT lyfe is beft to lead in citty or in
        towne ?
    In thone both witt and wealth, court
        getts vs great renown ;
The country keepes in health, bringes quietnes of
        mind,
Where wholfome ayre with exerfice and pretty
        fportes we find.
Wed, and thou haft a bed of follace and of ioye ;
Wed not, and haue a reft without anoy ;

The fetled loue is fafe, fwete is the loue at large;
Thy children are thy comforters, no childrun are
      no charge;
Youth lufty is and getts, age honnord is and wife;
Then not to dye or be vnborne is beft, by my
      aduife.

     *   *   *   *   *

Thefe verfes found I thus placed on a wall,
For want of ink, twas written with a coale,
By one who fince hath chaungd his ftat of lyf,
For liuing fingle now hath gott a wife.
So that, howere we men think ftraung to mary,
It is our cheif defyr, though long we tary;
Witnefs this party, who thefe lines hath penned,
Which doutles then was of an other mind.
But graunt this tru, that here is fayd of menn,
Much more in maydes and widowes I thinke then;
Yett left I fhould proue tedious with my rime,
Here will I end, wifhing you a good hufband in
      time.   I. G.

The Ficklenefs of Women.

Dust is lighter then a fether,
And the wind more light then ether;
But a womans fickle minde
More light then feather, duft or wind.

o

An Epitaph on Edmund Sandford, written in gould.

M Y fand ftill refts, though lyfe doth paffe
      Fleete as the ford, parting my name ;
So parte remaines, though run my glafs,
      For what was fand is ftill the fame.
Thus death dicaies not all my truft,
For fand I was, and now am duft.

*The forme and fhape of a monftrous Child,
borne at Maydftone in Kent, the xxiiij. of
October,* 1568.

As ye this fhape abhorre
In body for to haue,
So flee fuch vices farre
As might the foule depraue.

In Gods power all flefh ftands,
As the clay in the potters hands,
To fafhion euen as he wyll,
In good fhape or in yll.

A T Maydftone in Kent there was one
Marget Mere, daughter to Richard
Mere, of the fayd towne of Maydftone,
who, being vnmaryed, played the
naughty packe, and was gotten with childe, being
deliuered of the fame childe the xxiiij. daye of
October laft paft, in the yeare of our Lord 1568,
at vij. of the clocke in the afternoone of the fame

day, being Sonday; which child, being a man-child, had firſt the mouth ſlitted on the right ſide, like a libardes mouth, terrible to beholde, the left arme lying vpon the breſt, faſt therto ioyned, hauing as it were ſtumps on the handes, the left leg growing vpward toward the head, and the ryght leg bending toward the left leg, the foote therof growing into the buttocke of the ſayd left leg. In the middeſt of the backe there was a broade lump of fleſh, in faſhion lyke a roſe, in the myddeſt whereof was a hole, which voyded like an iſſue. Thys ſayd childe was borne alyue, and lyued xxiiij. houres, and then departed this lyfe,—which may be a terrour as well to all ſuch workers of filthynes and iniquity, as to thoſe vngodly liuers who (if in them any feare of God be) may mooue them to repentance and amendement of lyfe, which God for Chriſtes ſake graunt both to them and vs. Amen! Witneſſes hereof were theſe : William Plomer, John Squier, glaſier, John Sadler, goldſmith, beſides diuers other credible perſons, both men and women.

A warnyng to England.

THIS monſtrous ſhape to thee, England,
　　Playn ſhewes thy monſtrous vice,
If thou ech part wylt vnderſtand,
　　And take thereby aduice.

For waying firſt the gaſpyng mouth,
　　It doth full well declare
What rauine and oppreſſion both
　　Is vſed wyth greedy care.

For, for the backe and gorging paunch,   ` `
   To lyue in wealth and eafe
Such toyl men take, that none may ftaunch
   Their greedy minde, nor pleafe.

For in fuch fort their mouthes they infect
   With lying othes and flaightes,
Blafpheming God, and prince reiect,
   As they were brutifh beaftes.

Their filthy talke and poyfoned fpeech
   Disfigures fo the mouth,
That fom wold think ther ftood the breech,
   Such filth it breatheth forth.

The hands which haue no fingers right,
   But ftumps fit for no vfe,
Doth well fet forth the idle plight
   Which we in thefe daies chufe.

For rich and poore, for age and youth,
   Eche one would labour flye ;
Few feekes to do the deedes of truth,
   To helpe others thereby.

The leg fo clyming to the head,
   What meaneth it but this,
That fome do feeke not to be lead,
   But for to leade amis ?

And as this makes it moft monftrous
   For foote to clyme to head,
So thofe fubiects be moft vicious
   That refufe to be lead.

The hinder part doth ſhew vs playne
  Our cloſe and hidden vice,
Which doth behind vs run amayne
  In vyle and ſhameful wyſe.

Wherefore to ech in England now,
  Let this monſter them teach
To mend the monſtrous life they ſhow,
  Leaſt endles death them reach.

℘ Imprinted at London by John Awdeley, dwellyng in Little Britain ſtreete without Alderſgate,
the xxiij. of December.

*A mournfull Dittie on the death of certaine
Judges and Juſtices of the Peace, and diuers
other Gentlemen, who died immediatly after
the Aſſiſes holden at Lincolne laſt paſt.*

To the tune of Fortune.

ECOUNTING griefes and dolors long
      tyme done,
      Or blazyng forth the danger none
        can ſhon,
Might ſeeme a ſtudy altogether vayne;
Yet outwarde words oft eaſeth inward payne.

Then patiently my woefull tale attend,
Where ſorrowe doth each ſeuerall peryod end,
And euery word a bitter ſigh doth ſound,
For thoſe great plagues which we haue often found.

At Oxford firſt the iuſteſt judge of all
Our earthly judges firſt to count dyd call,
And ſecondly at Exceſter againe;
And laſt of all did Lincolne witnes plaine

How ſore for ſinne the Lord offended was,
How ſore for ſinne his wrath from him did pas,
And how for ſinne the prudent of our land
Hath felt the force of his moſt heauie hand.

Come, Shute, I ſaie, make vp the number then,
Thou worthie judge among vnworthie men;
Thy godly zeale and wiſedome plaine did ſhow,
Thou waſt too good for wretched men below.

Thy ſodaine death at Lincolne Siſes wrought,
Remaines a terror to each ſeuerall thought;   ·
Although with life thou didſt from thence depart,
Yet there did ſicknes ſlaie thy tender hart.

And like lament for Hollice may we make,
Whoſe life likewiſe moſt cruell death did take;
A vertuous man and juſtice of the peace,
Whom Creſſus wealth cannot from graue releaſe.

Copartner with theſe breathles perſons here,
Lies maiſter Tyrwhite, bound vpon the beere;
O fickle life, how brittle is thy ſtate,
And how vncertaine is thy finall date!

And Littlebury, by birth a good eſquier,   ·
Whoſe ſeruice then the lawe did well requier,
The foreman of a jurie there was he,
Whom death areſted with a deadly fee.

The ſkilfull clarke which to the peace pertaind,
That long in credit in the place remaind,
Welby, I ſaie, his name was called ſo,
Which at that place receiude a deadly blo.

Nor could graue Cauthron ſcape from cruel death,
Though likely long to harber vitall breath;
His wit, his wiſedome, and his ſage aduice
With life was loſt and turned to a trice.

Where ſhould I finde meete wordes for to expreſſe
Our inward woe, our griefe and heauines,
For Butlers death, a man of good degree,
And for the loſſe of many more then hee.

Let this ſuffice, that our eternall God
In ſecret wiſedome had prepard this rod
For our examples that remaine behind,
To cleere our eyes that Sathan ſo did blind.

Thrice in this ſort our judges haue bin ſlaine,
At three Aſſiſes, as is proued plaine,
And warning thrice herein our eies haue ſeene,
But more then thrice haue our offences beene.

Some iudge of this, and ſome doe iudge of that,
Some ſpeak and prate, and ſaie they know not what;
Then learne of Chriſt this leſſon tolde to thee,
Judge not at all, leaſt that thou iudged be.

The cauſe hereof to God is onely knowen,
No cauſe at all by any man was ſhowen;
Yet without cauſe God neuer wrought the ſame,
As chiefeſt cauſe ourſelues our ſinnes may blame.

And like as men, by naturall defcent
From Adams loines, to wicked finne is bent,
So may I faie, the lawyer is not cleere
From vile corruption, while he liueth heere.

Then they, as we muft both with one accord,
Repent their finnes before the mightie Lord,
Leaft in his wrath a greater plague be fent
On flintie hearts that would not once relent.

Vprightly deale with euerie poore mans caufe,
Againft the truth wring not nor wreaft the lawes,
And haue a confcience in your common fees,
For God, thou knowft, all inward motions fees.

Let not your hearts with bribes polute your hands,
And by oppreffion do not inlarge your lands;
For curfed gold fell not your foules away,
A practife found too common at this day.

Haue thou an eare vnto the wronged wight,
Defpife not him that fimple is in fight;
Do right and iuftice vnto each degree,
Then in the end thou fhalt moft bleffed bee.

And for our queene of moft exceeding fame,
Let vs defire, in Jefus Chriftes name,
That God will ftill preferue her royall grace,
That fhe may runne a long and ioyfull race.

FINIS.

Imprinted at London by John Wolfe, for
William Wright.   1590.

❡ *A diſcription of a monſtrous Chylde, borne*
at Chycheſter in Suſſex, the xxiiii. daye of May.
This being the very length, and bygnes of the
ſame. MCCCCCLXII.

[Here is an engraving of the child, 6⅝ inches in height.]

HEN God for ſynne to plage hath
   ment,
 Although he longe defarde,
 He tokens truly ſtraunge hath ſent
To make hys foes afearde ;

That they thereby might take remorce
 Of their yll lyfe miſpent,
And, more of loue then feare or force,
 Their formall faultes repent.

Before the earth was ouerflowen
 With waters huge throughout,
He ſent them Noe, that holy one,
 Who dayly went about

To call them then to godly lyfe,
 At whome they laughte and fumde ;
He was contemde of man and wyfe,
 Tyll they were all conſumde.

Loth did preache moſt earneſtly,
 But it did not preuayle ;
When fyre and brymſtone verèly
 Upon them doune did hayle.

Pharaoes heart had no remorce,
    Though wounders ftraunge he fawe,
But rather was therfore the worce,
    Without all feare or awe;

Untyll bothe he and his therfore,
    By iuftice fent of God,
In raginge feas were all forlore,
    And then he felt the rod.

Ten tymes truely were the Jewes
    In captiue brought and led;
Before eche tyme, our God did vfe
    Hys tokens ftrange, we red.

The yeare before Vafpatian came,
    The Jewes a heyfer dreft,—
Whiche beynge flayne, did calue a lame,—
    This fygne they fone did wreft,

As others doe, and ftyll haue done,
    In making it as vayne;
Or els good lucke, they faye, fhal come,
    As pleafe their foolifh brayne.

The heathen could forefe and faye
    That when fuche wounders were,
It did forefhew to them alwaye
    That fome yll hap drew nere.

The Scripture fayth, before the ende
    Of all thinges fhall appeare,
God will wounders ftraunge thinges fende,
    As fome is fene this yeare.

The felye infantes, voyde of fhape,
   The calues and pygges fo ftraunge,
With other mo of fuche mifhape,
   Declareth this worldes chaunge.

But here, lo ! fee, aboue the reft,
   A monfter to beholde,
Procedinge from a Chriftian breft,
   To monftrous to be tolde!

No caruer can, nor paynter maye,
   The fame fo ougly make,
As doeth itfelf fhewe at this daye,
   A fight to make the quake !

But here thou hafte, by printing arte,
   A figne therof to fe;
Let eche man faye within his harte,—
   It preacheth now to me,

That I fhoulde feke to lyue hencefoorth
   In godly lyfe alwaye,
For thefe be tokens now fent foorth
   To preache the later daye.

Alfo it doeth demonftrate playne
   The great abufe and vyce,
That here in Englande now doeth raygne,
   That monftrous is the guyfe.

By readinge ftories we fhall fynde,
   In Scripture and elles-where,
That when fuche thinges came out of kynde,
   Gods wrath it did declare.

But if we lightely weye the fame,
   And make but nyne dayes wonder,
The Lord our ftoutnes fone will tame,
   And fharpely bringe vs vnder.

Then ponder wel, be tymes long paft,
   The fequel of fuche fignes,
And call to God by prayer in haft
   From finne to chaunge oure myndes.

Repent, amende, both hygh and lowe,
   The woorde of God embrace,—
To lyue therto as we fhould doe
   God gyue vs all the grace!

      Quod Jhon D.

❡ The father hereof is one Vyncent, a boutcher;
bothe he and hys wyfe being of honeft and quiet
conuerfation, they hauing had chyldren before
in natural proportion, and went with this her
full tyme.

❡ Imprynted at London by Leonard Afkel, for
Fraunces Godlyf, in the yeare of oure Lorde
1562.

❡ *A new balade entituled as foloweth :*

❡ To fuch as write in metres I write
 Of fmall matters an exhortation,
By readyng of which men may delite
 In fuch as be worthy commendation.
 My verfe alfo it hath relation
 To fuch as print, that they doe it well,—
 The better they fhall their metres fell.

❡ And when we haue doen al that euer we can,
Let vs neuer feke prayfe at the mouth of man.

ORACE, that noble poet, did write
 In his learned booke, the Arte of
 Poetrie,
 Notable thinges of which to refite ;
One is now to be noted fpeciallie
 In thefe our dayes, and wot ye whie ?
For fome there be, take matters in hand
 Chiefly in metre, to fhew their fancie,
As did in his dayes a certaine band.

❡ Read in his bookes, and then vnderftand,
 They vexed his eares, they troubled his eyes,
With metres in number compared to the fand,
 And lacked not fuch as wolde to the fkyes
 So prayfe their workes—fuch was their guyfe,—
And alfo extoll their metres fo
 With wordes freuolous and manifeft lyes,
That lyke vnto them there was no mo.

❡ But what faith HORACE, afore we go
 Any further herein ? Becaufe they did vfe
To procure freendes, left that their fo
 Shoulde paint them out, and fo accufe

Their doinges in verſe and their abuſe,
Which men to praiſe them were not ſo preſt,
    As Horace agayne wolde ſtyll refuſe
To admit that number into his breſt.

❡ Suche coulde not dwell in his ſtudie or cheſt.
    Lvcilivs, with other in Horace dayes,
Was one which he coulde not diſgeſt ;
    His verſe in wordes or ſence alwayes
    For the moſt parte deſerued ſmall prayſe,
And why ? becauſe he had more reſpeɕt
    To couet the garland of lawrel or bayes,
For number rather then verſe ſeleɕt.

❡ For when by writing men doe deteɕt
    Their wyſedome or els their follie in deede,
Yf it be fooliſh, they doe correɕt,
    Or ought that can, and that with ſpeede,
    As Horace did, the vnſkylfull breede
Of poets that wrote in his time, I ſay ;
    The workes of ſuch, as ye may read,
Continue not long, but fall away.

❡ Such ſpices and wares as come from the ſea,
    They be good to vſe from towne to towne,—
To the pedler they be a right good ſtay
    To put in his ſtuff, blacke, white or browne ;—
    Good for the maſter, and good for the clowne ;
So make—as ye know—the matter cleane,
    Good to take vp, and good to caſt downe ;
When ye haue doen, ye know what I meane.

❡ Your balades of loue, not worth a beane,
    A number there be, although not all ;
Some be pithie, ſome weake, ſome leane,
    Some doe runne as round as a ball ;—

Some verſes haue ſuch a pleaſant fall,
That pleaſure it is for any man,
    Whether his knowledge be great or ſmall,
So that of a verſe ſome ſkyll he can.

℄ But ſome yf ye take in hand to ſkan,
    They lacke their grace, they lacke good ſence ;
The printer ſhoulde, therfore, with his fan
    Pourge chaff from corne, to avoyde offence ;
    And not for lucre, vnder pretence
Of newes, to print what commeth to hand,
    But that which is meete to bring in pence
Let him print, the matter well ſcand.˙

℄ Our Englyſhmen, ſome out of the land,
    A ſorte of rebelles ſturdye and ſtoute,
With our pope, holy men, that ouerthwart band,
    At Louaine, with open ſclander breath oute
    What enuie can doe, to bryng in doubte
The godly workes, well written of late
    Of learned men, and now go aboute
To ſtirre vp againſt vs warre and debate.

℄ Wherfore let vs not open a gate,
    Eyther the printer, or they which write,
To ſuch as they be, knowyng their ſtate,—
    Their ſclanderous pen doth cruelly byte.
    Let them not ſay that thoſe which endyte
Lacke knowledge in that the pen doth expreſſe ;
    Let them not ſay that a rauenyng kyte
Is as good as a larke at a printers meſſe.

℄ But now, leſt ye thinke me to vſe exceſſe,
    I wyll to an end myſelf prepare,
Wyſhyng àll them that wyll adreſſe
    Their pen to metres, let them not ſpare

To folow Chawcer, a man very rare,
Lidgate, Wager, Barclay and Bale,
  With many other that excellent are,
In thefe our dayes, extant to fale.

❡ Let writers not couet the bottom or dale,
  Yf they may come to the hyll or brinke ;
And, when they haue written their learned tale,
  The printer muft vfe good paper and inke,
  Or els the reader may fometime fhrinke,
When faulte by inke or paper is feene ;—
  And thus euery day, before we drinke,
Let vs pray God to faue our queene.   Amen.

❡ Finis.   By R. B.

❡ Imprinted at S. Katherins, befyde the Towre
  of London, by Alexander Lacie.

❡ *O maruelous tydynges, both wonders old and new,*
The Deuyll is endited, yf many mens wordes be tru.

I N all chriftendom Chriftes godfpell now
          is rad
      Of man, woman and chyld ; it maketh
          their harts glad,
Whiche with fhamefull fyns before were full fad ;—
  O wounders good tydynges, yf al fayinges be tru !

❡ It is rad fo oft, and with foch diligence,
That no text is wrefted thorow raifche negligence ;

Playn declaracions help moche to the true fenfe.
    We all haue caufe to reioyfe, yf thefe tydyngs
        be tru.

Now after Chriftes rule all folk do lead theyr lyfe,
They abhor all chydyng, braulyng, fyghtyng,
        and ftryfe;
Grete feruent charytie is betwyne man and wyfe,
    No worfe wordes then honycomb, fweet hart
        of gold moft tru.

❡ One neybur reforteth fryndly to another,
As though all were kynsfolk, lyke brother and
        brother;
Greter loue was neuer betwyne chyld and mother.—
    This world is no world, yf all tydynges be tru;

It is rather lyke heuyn, or pleafaunt paradyfe,
The folk be lyke angels, difcrete, fober, and wyfe;
If one fall through fraylty, he, repentyng more
        then twyfe,
    Ryfeth ftyll a new man, a good Chriftian and
        tru.

❡ Folk faft, pray, and ferue God not hipocritically,
Only to be feen of men for folyfh vayn glory,
But from the very hart, the Lord God to gloryfy,
    Defpyfyng fond fantafyes, as falfe thynges and
        not tru.

❡ Euery body now, in fom trade of lyuyng,
Doth labour for his foode with trauell or fwetyng;
Som dyggyng, fom fpynnyng, fom wrytyng, fom
        redyng,
    Som geuyng good counfell, lyke honeft folk
        and tru.

P

¶ They knowe that they muſt make a rekenyng
    to God
Of theyr diſpenſacion, they feere gretely Gods rod;
The ryche do helpe the poore with roſt meat or
    with ſod,
   None lye ſtaruyng in ſtreets, yf all mens
    tonges be tru.

¶ Great ryche men be afrayd leaſt they dye
    ſodaynly,
Leaſt theyre goods (after them) be ſpent in foolery;
Leaſt God wyll call them fooles, therfore liberally
   They ſpend moche in theyr lyfe vpon poore
    folk and tru.

¶ They be redy, alſo, ſomwhat to pryſons to ſend,
If any through frayltie chaunſe folyſhly to offend;
But now priſons be empty; the world doth ſo
    amende,
   There be but iiij. ſcore and ten in Kynges Benche,
    it was tru.

¶ Of them that be in pryſon ſom be tyed with
    clogges,
Som gnaw broun cruſtes of bred, ſom burniſh
    boones like doggs;
Som wyſh to fyll theyr gutts with catts, ratts,
    myſe, or froggs;
   Specyally this deere yere, now, they ſay, they
    wyll be tru.

How many be in Ludgate and Neugate I can
    not tel,
But they that be abrode be afrayd, I truſt well,
And fall to wourk luſtely thorow theyr exampell,—
They abhorre Clinkerum, they ſay they wyll be
    tru.

❡ A man may goo now ouer Fynſbery fylde
Without ſweard and buckler, without ſpeare or
    ſhylde,
With an houndred poundes, as ſafe as with a nylde,
   In a myſty mornyng and by nyght, yf tales be
   tru.

❡ All England and Spayn, all Scotland and
    Germany,
All Fraunce and Ireland, all Denmark and
    Hungary,
Be purged ſo, I truſt, from vice and idolatry,
   That the Turk doth beghyn to thynk the
   Godſpele tru.

❡ The Saracens and Jewes, I truſt, do now conuert,
Moued with godlynes that is in Chriſtians harte;
They fere leaſt Chryſts ſcourge wyll make theyr
    bones to ſmart,—
   I truſt they receyue baptyme, and belyue the
   Godſpell is tru.

They hire it ſo diſcuſſed by calculacyon
That Doomeſday is at hand; yf mens ſpeculacion
In aſtronomye be tru, the worldes transformacyon
   Wyl be within x. yeres, ſtraunge newes yf it be tru.

❡ I—one of xl. yeres—thought to prouyde for
    age,
Houſe for one and twenty yere, or ſom fat
    perſonage,
Som prebend, deanery, or ſom vicarage,
   But now I pas not moche, yf aſtronomers be tru.

❡ Yea, whither aſtronomers be true eyther no,
Or that generall iugement be commyng to or fro,
This one thyng I kno ſure, that I ſhall hence go,
   I kno nor day nor ooure, nothyng is more tru.

❡ And douteles yf all men wolde be of my mynde,
We wold fom better way for to lyue here out fynde;
Men fhulde be fet awurk, onleffe they were ftark
      blynd,
   Yea, blynde fhuld do fomwhat to kepe them-
    felfe tru.

❡ Helthy folke lackyng wourk fhuld reforte to
      a place
With theyr tooles and inftrumentes, as fom vfe
      to fhew their face;
Then fet awourk, or fed, of mens fauour and grace,
   With fom comon purfe, to kepe themfelfs tru.

❡ So that it fhuld be a ftraunge thyng for to fee
Any theft or murder euer committed to be,
As—thankes be to God'!—folk burne fo in
      charytie,
   That no knauery raigneth, yf all mens wordes
    be tru.

❡ The Deuyll hath ben a knaue, and hath kylde
      many men,
Yea, both foule and body, moe perchaunfe then ten;
Now he is endyted, as witneffeth my pen,
   His queft is empayneld, he is founde falfe, not
    tru.

Here folowe the names of the xij. men that goo vpon
the Deuyll.

❡ Gen. iii. 1 Paralip. xxj. Job i. ii. Sapien. ii.
   Chrift in Math. xiij. and in Luke viij. Math. iiij.
   Mar. i. Luke xxij. Joan xiij. and 1 Joan iij.
   Paull to the Ephefians vj. 1 Pet. v. Jacob iiij.

C It wyl be hard to kyll fuche an immortall knaue,
He recoueryth fo oft, though a ftronge hoofte we
    haue ;
Call in Turkes and Saracens, that they alfo may
    be faue,—
    Through Gods help, we may breke Satans hed,
        it is tru.

C To breke Satans hed, of all wayes this is one,
With the buckler of fayth to refyft fuggeftion,
And ftrongly to belyue that Chriftes paffion,
    Chriftes wordes and myrakels all, be moft furely
        tru.

All Chriftian kyngs do now theyr wittes bende
Theyr letters in print to the Turkes for to fende,
With many New Teftamentes, theyr blynd lyfe to
    amend,
    For fere of hell fyre, I truft it wyl be tru.

C When Satan the Deuyll feeth fuch a great
        hooft,
Suche a fort of Chriftians, to diminifh his booft,
He muft nedes be compelld to graunt his great
        ftrenght loft,
    When his pate is broken, God graunte this may
        be tru.

C Then the golden world, I truft, wyll com agayn,
That folk may lyue eafyly without any great
        payn ;
Many egges for a peny at London I wolde fe fayn,
    Flefche and fifche better chepe, I truft it wyl be
        tru.

❡ All other thynges good chepe I truſt to ſe er I
      dye,
Coynes, meaſures, and weyghtes in good vnifor-
      mitie
Thorow all the world, I truſt to ſe ſchortely,
   Onles that diuerſitie doth more good, it bé tru.

Jentyll reder, farewell! Thou knoeſt part of my
      mynde,
There lye in my harte many ſuch thynges be-
      hynde;
Whiche towards the brekyng of Satans hed I fynde,
   That all may be mery and wyſe in Chriſt: It
      is tru.

    ❡ Printed by Cornelis Woltrop, dwellyng
        at Saynt Antonies.

As pleaſant a dittie as your hart can wiſh,
Shewing what vnkindnes befell by a kiſſe.

MY miſtris ſings none other ſong,
    But ſtil complains I do her wrong;
Beleeue her not, it is not ſo,
     For I did but kiſſe her,
     For I did but kiſſe her,
      And ſo let her goe.

  And now ſhe ſwears I did—but what?
  Nay, nay, I muſt not tell you that;

And yet I will, it is fo fweet,
  As teehe taha,
  As teehe taha,
    When louers do meete.

But womens words they are heedles,
To tell you more it were needles;
I ran and caught her by the arme,
  And then I kift her,
  And then I kift her,
    Was this any harme?

Yet out, alas! fhees angry ftill,
Which fheweth but a womans will;
She bites the lippe, and cries, fie, fie!
  And kiffing fweetly,
  And kiffing fweetly,
    Away fhe doth fly.

Acteon for one fight did die,
So for one fillie kiffe muft I;
Vnwares fond loue did me betray,
  When I gaue her vantage,
  When I gaue her vantage,
    And fhe fled away.

She ftriued and wrangled ful fore with me,
And cryedft,—For fhame, let it be!
You doe me wrong to vfe me fo,—
  Therefore be quiet,
  Therefore be quiet,
    And now let me goe.

Yet ftill I held her by the hand,
Her words could not my will withftand;

She fround, fhe pouted, fhe lookt fower,
  And ftill I held her,
  And ftil I held her
    Within my power.

At laft fhe gan for anger cry,
And then my hart with griefe did die;
I could no longer her containe,
  But thus we parted,
  But thus we parted,
    Vnto my great paine.

And fince, when I with her do meete,
With words vnkind fhe doth me greet;
At me her wanton head fhe fhakes,
  And as a ftranger,
  And as a ftranger,
    My fauours fhe takes.

But yet her looks bewrayes content,
And cunningly her brawles are ment,—
As louers vfe to play and fport,
  When time and leafure,
  When time and leafure
    Is too-too fhort.   Finis.

At London: printed for T. P.

*The true discription of two monsterous children,
laufully begotten betwene George Steuens and
Margerie his wyfe, and borne in the parish
of Swanburne in Buckynghamshyre the iiij. of
Aprill, Anno Domini 1566; the two children
hauing both their belies fast ioyned together, and
imbracyng one another with their armes : which
children wer both alyue by the space of half an
hower, and wer baptized and named the one
John, and the other Joan.*

READ how Affrique land was fraught,
   For their most filthy life,
With monstrous shapes confuzedly,
   That therin wer full rife.

❧ But England now pursues their vyle
   And detestable path,
Embracyng eke all mischeefs great,
   That moues Gods mightie wrath.

❧ As these vnnaturall shapes and formes,
   Thus brought forth in our dayes,
Are tokens true and manifest
   How God by dyuers wayes

Doth styrre vs to amendment of
   Our vyle and cankred lyfe,
Which to-to much abused is
   In man, in chylde, and wyfe.

❡ We wallow fo in filthie fin,
    And naught at all regarde,
Nor wyll not feare the threats of God,
    Tyll we, for iuft rewarde,

Be ouerwhelmd with mifcheefs great,
    Which, ready bent for vs,
Full long ago decreed wer,
    As Scriptures doth difcus.

❡ Both tender babes and eke brute beaftes
    In fhape disfourmed bee;
Full manie wayes he plagues the earth,
    As dayly we may fee.

❡ Thus mightie Ioue, to pearce our harts,
    Thefe tokens ftraunge doth fend,
To call vs from our filthie lyfe,
    Our wicked wayes t'amend.

And thus, by thefe two children here,
    Forewarnes both man and wyfe,
How both eftates ought to bewayle
    Their vile and wretched lyfe.

❡ For fure we all may be agaft
    To fee thefe fhapes vnkynd,
And tremblyng feare may pearce our harts,
    Our God to haue in mynd.

For yf we printed in our breft,
    Thefe fignes and tokens ftraunge
Wold make vs from our finnes to fhrinke,
    Our liues anew to chaunge.

⁊ But fome proude boaftyng Pharifie
   The parents wyll detect,
And iudge with heapes of vglie vice
   Their liues to be infect.

⁊ No, no; but leffons for vs all,
   Which dayly doe offend;
Yea, more, perhaps, then hath the freends
   Whom God this birth did lend.

⁊ For yf you wyll, with fingle eye,
   Note well and view the text,
And marke our Sauiours aunfwer eke
   That thereto is annext,

Where his difciples afked him,
   To know therein his mynd,
Yf greatter wer the parents finnes,
   Or his that was borne blynd.

⁊ To whom Chrift aunfwered in a breef,
   That neither hee nor they
Deferued had that crooked fate,
   Although they fin each day;

But to the end Gods glorie great,
   And miracles diuine,
Might on the earth apparaunt be,
   His workes for to define.

⁊ Such lyke examples moued me,
   In thefe forgetfull dayes,
To rue our ftate, that vs among
   Vice beares fuch fwings and fwayes;

❡ Wherein the goodneſſe great of God
   We way and ſet ſo light;
By ſuch examples callyng vs
   From ſin both day and night.

Where we doe runne at randon wyde,
   Ourſelues flatteryng ſtyll,
And blazyng others faults and crimes,
   Yet we ourſelues moſt yll.

❡ But if we doe conſider right,
   And in euen balaunce way
The ruine great of hartie loue
   Among vs at this day;

And well behyld, with inward eyes,
   Th' embracyng of theſe twinnes,—
That God by them vpbraides vs for
   Our falſe diſcemblyng ſinnes;

We would with Niniuie repent
   Our former paſſed yeares,
Bewaylyng eke our ſecret ſinnes
   In ſackecloth and in teares.

❡ Therfore in time amend your ſtate,
   And call to God for grace,—
Bewayle your former lyfe and ſinnes,
   While you haue time and ſpace.

     ❡ Finis, quod John Mellys Nor.

❡ Imprinted at London by Alexander Lacy, for
  William Lewes, dwellyng in Cow Lane, aboue
  Holborne Cundit, ouer againſt the ſigne of the
  Plough.

A newe Ballade intytuled, Good Fellowes muſt go learne to daunce.

GOOD fellowes muſt go learne to daunce,
  The brydeall is full nere a ;
There is a brall come out of Fraunce,
  The tryxt ye harde this yeare a ;
For I muſt leape, and thou muſt hoppe,
  And we muſt turne all three a ;
The fourth muſt bounce it lyke a toppe,
  And ſo we ſhall agree a.
I praye thee, mynſtrell, make no ſtoppe,
  For we wyll merye be a.

The brydegrome would giue twentie pounde
  The mariage daye were paſte a ;
Ye knowe, whyles louers are vnbounde,
  The knotte is ſlyper faſte a ;—
A better man maye come in place,
  And take the bryde awaye a.
God ſend our Wilkin better grace,
  Our pretie Tom, doth ſaye a,—
God vycar, axe the banes apace,
  And haſte the mariage daye a.

A bande of belles, in bauderycke wyſe,
  Woulde decke vs in our kynde a ;
A ſhurte after the Moryce guyſe,
  To flounce it in the wynde a.
A wyffler for to make the waye,
  And Maye brought in withall a,
Is brauer then the ſunne, I ſaye,
  And paſſeth round or brall a ;

For we will trype fo tricke and gaye,
   That we wyll paffe them all a.

Drawe to dauncinge, neyghboures all,
   Good fellowfhyppe is beft a,
It fkylles not yf we take a fall,
   In honoringe this fefte a.
The bryde wyll thanke vs for oure glee,
   The worlde wyll vs beholde a;
O where fhall all this dauncinge bee,
   In Kent or at Cotfolde a?
Oure Lorde doth knowe, then axe not mee,—
   And fo my tale is tolde a.

Adewe, Sweete Harte.

ADEWE, fweete harte, adewe!
      Syth we muft parte!
   To lofe the loue of you
      It greues my harte.
Once againe come kyffe me,
Syth I fo long muft mys thee,
[My w]illinge harte fhall wyfhe thee,
   To eafe me of my fmarte.
And thoughe I nowe do leaue thee,
It wyll I not deceaue thee,
But come againe and wedde thee,
   Euen for thy iuft defarte.

Syr Launcelotte comes againe, fyr,
   So men do faye;
Tom Toffe wyll fayle to Spayne, fir,
   By Tyborne awaye.

Subtoll finne wyll haue her;
Thoughe wyttie Watte do craue her,
Yet cuttinge clowne fhall faue her,
   Vnleffe he lofe his praye.
And though ye be fo wyleye,
And fhe do loke fo hyleye,
At length fhe wyll begyle ye,
   And [ftriue] the beft ye maye.

L . . . . . is fo coye, fir,
  She . . . be folde,
W . . . . . s her ioye, fir,
  T . . . . tolde,
Ra . . . . wyll not blade it,
Jack . . . r wyll not fwade it,
The byllbowes are not made it,
   Therof ye maye be bolde.
Although ye now haue cought her,
Ye wyll repent hereafter,
For farder ye haue fought her
   Then I haue thought ye would.

Finis.

   Imprinted at London, in Flete ftrete at the
figne of the Faucon, by Wylliam Gryffith, and
are to be folde at his fhoppe in S. Dunftones
Churchyearde, 1569.

❡ *The braineles blessing of the Bull.*

> The hornes, the heads, and all,
> Light on their fquint-eyed fkonfes full,
> That boweth their knees to Ball.

The cancred curfe, that wolde confume this realme with wracke
  and ruine,
Returne to Rome with fyre and fume, to bryng the pope in
  tune !
If neither curfe nor bleffyng bare may mend thefe parties
  throwe,
I them bequeath—curft as they are—to Plutoes kyngdome
  nowe !

AS neuer worlde fo farre from orders
  rule,
  That men durft fpeake fuch fawcie
  words of kings,
Nor neuer pope fo lyke an affe or mule,
 Or dunghyll cocke, to crow and clap his winges.
 Stand backe, good dogs, the bul he leapes and
  flinges,
He bleates and bleathes as he a-baightyng were,
And fomes at mouth, lyke boare with briftled
  heare ;
A beaftlye found comes runnyng from his paunch,
He beates the ground with foote, with hip and
  haunch,
As though hell gates fhould open at his call,
And at his becke the heauens high fhould fall.

❡ O Sathans fonne ! O pope puft vp with pryde !
 What makes thee clayme the clowdes where
  God doth dwel,
When thou art knowne the glorious greedie guyde

That leades in pompe poore feelye foules to hell ?
The pumpe of fhip hath not fo fowle a fmell
As hath the fmoke and fume that flames from
    thee;
O graceles grace, O rotten hollow tree !
The branches bud, but neuer bryng forth leaues;
Thy corne is dead when reaper lookes for fheaues;
Thy golde is glaffe, and gliftereth gay a whyle,
Tyll tromperie comes, and makes the worlde to
    fmyle.

℧ Who bad thee bliffe ? O buzzarde blynd of
    fight,
    Buylt God his church vpon fuch clots of clay ?
Thou doeft blafpheme thereby the GOD of might,
    And robbeft with craft his honour cleane away.
    Curfe whome thou lift, he better thryues that day;
Bleffe whome thou wylt, and I dare gage my head,
For all thy charmes, he brynges a foole to bed.
Booke, bell and fyfe are bables fit for thofe
That gape for flyes where wafpes and hornets
    blowes;
The pardonles boxe, wherein thy reliques lye,
Doth fmell lyke fox, or fwyne fhut vp in ftye.

℧ A pope was wont to be an odious name
    Within our land, and fcrapt out of our fcroules;
And now the pope is growne fo farre paft fhame,
    That he can walke with open face in Poules.
    Go home, mad bull, to Rome, and pardon foules
That pyne away in purgatorie paynes,—
Go triumph there, where credit moft remaines.
Thy date is out in England long ago,
For Ridley gaue the bull fo great a blow,
He neuer durft apeach this land tyll now,—
In bullyng time, he met with Hardyngs cow.

Q

℃ A calfe or twayne hath here ben gotten fince,
   Whofe heades were folde of late in Butcher Row;
Come cheape calues heads, and bring in Peter pence!
   Though fome are bought, our butchers looke
        for mo,
   For Walthams calues to Tiburne needes muft go
To fucke a bull and meete a butchers axe;
The fhambles full is ftuft with prettie knacks,
As goate and lambe, and fhepe of three fcore yeare.
We haue good hope calues heads wyll not be
        deare;—
If Hardyngs cow be bulled as fhee ought,
Calues heads enough for little wyll be bought.

℃ The pope doth nought but practize mifcheif
        ftyll,
   And lets his bul runne ryot for his eafe;
But whiles his calues are drawne vp Holborne hyll,
   Both bull and cow are fafe beyond the feas.
   O that it might our holy father pleafe
To come himfelfe, and hang but halfe an hower
With fuch poore freendes as here maintaine his
        power!
I fay no more, for feare the babes awake
That holde with pope, and hang for Hardyngs fake;
Some knackes now lurkes that we fhal know ful
        playne,
When Hoballes oxe bulles Hardyngs cow agayne.

℃ I fcorne to write a vearce in any frame,
   To anfwer wordes that rayled haue fo much,
Yet baightyng oft may make a bull fo tame,
   That euery dog that comes may haue a twitch.
   I here proteft, if that my power were fuch,
By pen or fkyll to chaffe the bull at ftake,
I wolde be glad fome further fporte to make;

But fince I want the cunnyng and the arte
To baight the beaft, and play the maftiffs parte,
Let this fuffife to let you thinke in deede,
I hate the bull and all the Romifh breede.

❡ Finis.

❡ Imprinted at S. Katherins, befide the Tower
of London, ouer againft the Beare Daunce, by
Alexander Lacie.

A Ballad.

HAT lyfe is beft? The nedy is full of
woe and awe,
The welthy full of brawles and quarells
of the lawe;
To be a maryed man how much art thou beguiled,
Seeking thy reft by carking ftill for houfhold,
wif, and child!
To till it is a toyle to grace a gredy gaine,
And fuch as gotten is with drudging and with paine.
A fhrewd wyfe bringes debate,—wiue not and
neuer thriue;
Children are charge,—childlefs, the greateft lack
aliue;
Youth witlefe is and frayle, age fickly and forlorne;
Then beft it is to dye betime, or neuer to be borne.

The crie of the poore for the death of the right
Honourable Earle of Huntington.

To the tune of the Earle of Bedford.

GOD, of thy mercie remember the
          poore,
    And grant vs thy bleffings, thy plenty
          and ftore ;
For dead is LordHaftinges,—the more is our griefe;
And now vp to heauen we cry for reliefe.
    Then waile we, then weepe we, then mourne we
          ech one,
    The good Earle of Huntington from vs is gone.

To poore and to needie, to high and to low,
Lord Haftinges was friendly, all people doth know;
His gates were ftill open the ftraunger to feede,
And comfort the fuccourles alwaies in neede.
    Then waile we, &c.

The hufbandles widdow he euer did cherifh,
And fatherles infants he likewife would nourifh ;
To weake and to ficke, to lame and to blinde,
Our good Earle of Huntington euer was kinde.
    Then waile we, &c.

The naked he clothed with garments from cold,
And frankely beftowed his filuer and gold,—
His purfe was ftill open in giuing the poore,
That alwaies came flocking to Huntingtons doore.
    Then waile we, &c.

His tennants, that daylie repairde to his houſe,
Was fed with his bacon, his beefe and his ſouſe ;
Their rents were not raiſed, their fines were but
    ſmall,
And manie poore tennants paide nothing at all.
    Then waile we, &c.

Such landlordes in England we ſeldome ſhall finde,
That to their poore tennants will beare the like
    minde,—
Lord Haſtinges therefore is ioyfully crownde
With angels in heauen, where peace doth abound.
    Then waile we, &c.

His wiſedome ſo pleaſed the queene of this land,
The ſword of true juſtice ſhe put in his hand ;
Of Yorke he was Preſident made by her grace,
Her lawes to maintaine and rule in her place.
    Then waile we, &c.

Such mercifull pittie remainde in his breſt,
That all men had juſtice and none were opreſt ;
His office in vertue ſo godly he ſpent,
That prince and his countrie his loſſe may lament.
    Then waile we, &c.

And likewiſe Lord Haſtings, S. Georges true
    knight,
Did weare the goold garter of England ſo bright,—
The gift of a prince, King Edward firſt gaue,—
A gem for a ſouldier and counceller graue.
    Then waile we, &c.

His coyne was not whorded to flouriſh in pride,
His kings and his jewels and chaines to prouide ;

But gaue it to fouldiers wounded in warres,
That pike and the bullet hath lamed with fcarres.
    Then waile we, &c.

He built vp no pallace nor purchafte no towne,
But gaue it to fchollers to get him renowne,
As Oxford and Cambridge can rightly declare
How many poore fchollers maintained are there.
    Then waile we, &c.

No groues he inclofed, nor felled no woodes,
No paftures he paled to doe himfelfe good ;
To commons and countrie he liude a good friend,
And gaue to the needie what God did him fend.
    Then waile we, &c.

He likewife prouided, in time of great neede,
If England were forced with warres to proceede,
Both men and munition, with horfes of warre,
The proude foes of England at all times to fcarre.
    Then waile we, &c.

Our queene and our countrie hath caufe to com-
            plaine,
That death in his furie this noble hath flaine ;
Yet England reioyce, we reioyce without feare,
Lord Haftinges hath left a moft noble heire.
    Then waile we, &c.

A thoufand poore widdowes for Huntingtons fake,
As manie poore children their praiers will make,
That God may long profper his heire left behinde,
And graunt him old Huntingtons true noble minde.
    Then waile we, &c.

Then pray we for countrie, for prince and for peares,
That God may indew them with moſt happie yeares ;
Lord, bleſſe vs with vertue, with plentie and peace,
And manie more ſubiects like him to increaſe !
　　Then waile we, then weepe we, then mourne
　　　　we ech one,
　　Our good Earle of Huntington from vs is gone.

FINIS.

Printed at London for William Blackwall, and
　are to be ſold at his ſhoppe, nere
　　　Guild Hall gate.　1596.

⬥⬥⬥

*Joyfull Newes for true Subiectes, to God and the
　　Crowne,*

The Rebelles are cooled, their Bragges be put downe.

　Come, humble ye downe,—come, humble ye downe,
　Perforce now ſubmyt ye to the queen and the crowne.

L true Engliſh ſubiects, both moſte and
　　leſte,
　　　Geue thanks vnto God, with humble
　　　　knees downe,
That it hath pleazde him, at our requeſt,
　To vanquiſh the rebels that troubled the
　　crowne.
　　　Come, humble ye downe,—come, humble ye
　　　downe,
　　　　Perforce now ſubmit ye to the quene and the
　　　　crowne.

℄ The Weſtmerlande bull and man in the moone,
  The beare hath brought their brauerie downe;
I dare ſaye for ſorowe they are redy to ſwoone,
  That euer they ymagynde to trouble the crowne.
    Come, humble ye downe, &c.

℄ And ſir John Shorne, as fame doth reporte,
  Is hangde vp ſo hye that he cannot come downe,
Becauſe he thought it ſo good a ſporte,
  To playe the traytour againſt the crowne.
    Come, humble ye downe, &c.

℄ And becauſe he ſhould not hange alone,
  To honor his prieſthoode of holy renowne,
Sir John Swingbreeche, his felow, a rebell well
      knowen,
  They ſay, is hangde with hym for troubling the
      crowne.
    Come, humble ye downe, &c.

℄ The reſt that are fled wyll ſoone be caught,
  Though yet they lye lurkyng in countrey and
      towne;
And than they be truſde vp by and by ſtrayght,
  Except the quenes mercie that weareth the
      crowne.
    Come, humble ye downe, &c.

℄ But her Maieſtie of mercie is endued with ſtore;
  That knewe they full well that nowe are put
      downe,
Els would they not aventerd to rayſe this vprore.
  Now be they foorth commyng, as pleaſeth the
      crowne.
    Come, humble ye downe, &c.

❡ The reſt of the rebelles and traytours forſworne,
  To ſee them truſde vp, I would gage my gowne,
And ſpecially the ſect of Syr John Shorne,
  To teache them to trouble the realme and the
    crowne.
    Come, humble ye downe, &c.

❡ But that pertayneth no matter of mine ;
  Yet for my good will on me do not frowne ;—
It muſt be as pleaſeth God to aſſigne
  The hart of our quene that weareth the crowne.
    Come, humble ye downe, &c.

❡ But, thankes bee to God ! their ſpyte is donne,
  They haue ſpyt their venom, both knyght and
    clowne ;
In deede, I muſt ſaye, verye fayre haue they
    ſponne ;—
  They had better haue kept them true to the
    crowne.
    Come, humble ye downe, &c.

❡ No doubt the deuill had them bewitcht,—
  They lackt biſhop Boner, to cuniure him
    downe ;
If he had liued till now, his eares would haue icht
  For joye to heare how they trouble the crowne.
    Com, humble ye downe, &c.

❡ And ſure he would haue written in haſte
  To his holy father of hie renowne,
For helpe to ſpoyle, conſume and waſte,
  All thoſe that deſpiſed his triple crowne.
    Come, humble ye downe, &c.

And that was the meaning of thofe that began
   To roote out Chriftes doctrine, fuppreffe and
      put downe;
They haue mift their purpofe, now fhift how they
     can,—
   God hath preuented them from troubling the
     crowne.
     Com, humble ye downe, &c.

❧ If they had preuayled, then had we been wo,
   Then had ben olde wayling in countrie and
     towne;
Then fhould many a woman her hufband forgoe,
   All longe of the rebelles that troubled the
     crowne.
     Come, humble ye downe, &c.

❧ Then had ben many a fatherleffe childe,
   That fhoulde haue gon begging vp and
     downe;
Yea, many a chafte damfell fhould haue ben defilde
   By thofe popifh prieftes that troubled the
     crowne.
     Come, humble ye downe, &c.

Yea, many a good preacher fhould haue loft his
     lyfe,
   Many a lorde and lady of noble renowne;
Yea, many an infant and many a wyfe,
   By thofe cruell rebelles that troubled the
     crowne.
     Come, humble ye downe, &c.

❧ To fpoyle common wealth it was the next waye,
   Example by other realmes of renowne,—

How warre and rebellyon bred their decaye,
   And all for matters perteynynge the crowne.
      Come, humble ye downe, &c.

℃ But prayſed be God, they haue not theyr will!
   The hurt they ment other to them doth
      redowne,
In daunger both life and goods to ſpill,—
   Theſe fruiĉts do they reape for troubling the
      crowne.
      Com, humble ye downe, &c.

God ſaue the queenes maieſtie and confound hir
      foes,
   Els turne their hartes quite vpſidowne
To become true ſubieĉtes, as well as thoſe
   That faythfully and truely haue ſerued the
      crowne!
      Come, humble ye downe, &c.

℃ God graunt euery one, after his vocation,
   To remember the accompt he muſt laye downe;
And that we maye all, in this Englyſh nation,
   Be true to God, the queene and the crowne!
      Come, humble ye down,—come, humble ye
      downe,
      God graunt Queene Elizabeth longe to
      weare the crowne!

FINIS. W. Kyrkh.

℃ Imprinted at London, in Fleet ſtreete, by
   Wyllyam How for Richard Johnes.

❡ *A dittie in the worthie praise of an high
and mightie Prince.*

HEN heapes of heauie hap had fild
　　my harte right full,
　　And sorrow set forth pensiuenes, my
　　　　ioyes away to pull,
I raunged then the woods, I romde the fields
　　aboute,—
A thousand sighes I set at large, to seeke their
　　passage out;
And walkyng in a dompe, or rather in dispaire,
I cast my weeping eye aside, I saw a fielde full
　　faire;
And lokyng vpwarde than I spied a mount
　　therein,
Which Flora had, euen for her life, dect as you
　　haue not seen;
Then could I not but thinke the same some sacred
　　place,
Where god or goddes such did dwell as might
　　releue my case.
I sat me downe, for whie? Death could but stop
　　my breath,
And to a man so sorrowfull what sweter is then
　　death?
No sooner was I set, but slepe approcht mine eye,
Wherein the nymphes of Helicon appeared by
　　and by,—
And straight those sisters nine, the ground of
　　musicks arte,
My thought did striue who might preuaile to ease
　　my heauie harte.

The cunning they ſhewed there, the ſubtile notes
      they ſoung,
As were awreſt clene from my hart, my thought
      the cares they wrong.
Celeſtiall were the notes which then, amazde, I
      hearde,—
Their ditties eke were wonderfull, note ye whome
      they preferde.
As for thy bloud, quod they, right noble, we
      confeſſe,—
Thy pettigree, to long for vs, the heralds can
      expreſſe ;
But, happie, happie Duke, the ſecond chylde of
      Fame,
Which, next vnto the higheſt, ſhe doth ſo
      recoumpt the fame!
And happie Thomas ones, twiſe happie Norffolke
      toe,
Thriſe happie men that leade your liues where
      Howard hath to doe,—
Which Howards happie daies they praied God to
      encreaſe
Three times the ſpace of Natures courſe, like
      Neſtor liue in peace!
What age hath ſeen his like, ſo free of purſe and
      toung ?
Where liues a iuſter juſtice now, though rare in
      one ſo young ?
What plaint can there be tolde to his moſt godlie
      eare,
But that he kepes the other ſtyll, the blamed ſoule
      to heare?
In mekenes he more meke then is the mekeſt doue,
Yet is his ſecret wiſedome ſuch he knoweth whome
      to loue ;

In freendſhip he ſurmounts Giſippus and his Tite,
Allnobles may well note his race, and thereby take
      their lighte ;—
In peace a Salomon, in warre ſo ſtoute a prince
As raigned not tyll Hector came, nor liued neuer
      ſince,—
Then Sceuola more firme, which, for his cuntries
      turne,
His hand from arme before his foes in fierie flame
      did burne ;
He in the prideof peace delights in marciall ſhowe,—
Doe marke his turnoys vpon horſe, note well his
      vſe of bowe ;
Nay, marke him yet that ſhall note well his payne-
      fulnes,
No ſugred ſlepe can make him freend to ſluggiſh
      Idlenes.
What that becomes a prince in his good grace
      doth want?
In peace a courtier for the courte, a ſecond Mars
      in camp.
Thus ſtyll they ſoung, whoſe notes were cauſe of
      my releefe,
And I be-wrapped in a traunce had cleane forgot
      my greefe ;
And triple were my ioyes, ones cauſe my paynes
      were paſt,
And twiſe agayne, becauſe that prince amongſt vs
      here is plaſt,
I clapt my handes for ioye,—alas ! I wakt withall,
And then my muſes and their ſonges, my ioyes,
      were gone and all.
And then retournd my greefe,—I felt a further
      care,
Becauſe to ſhew what I had ſeen did paſſe my
      power ſo farre ;

And that a man vnlearnd, of arte that hath no
      ſkyll,.
Should haue a charge ſo great as this, and could
      doe it ſo yll.
Yet thus I gan to wright I knew right well that he,
Which due deſert did thus commend, ſhould ſhade
      the want in me ;
To whome I pray the Lorde to ſend like yeares
      as Noye,
In happie health and quiet ſtate, to his and all our
      ioye.

            ❡ Finis, Ber. Gar.

❡ Imprinted at London, without Alderſgate, in
      Little Britaine, by Alexander Lacy.

❡ *A newe Ballade, intituled, Agaynſt Rebel-*
lious and falſe rumours. *To the newe tune of*
the Blacke Almaine vpon Sciſſillia.

HAT rumores now are raiſed of late,
      Within this Engliſh lande,
Which is not much for to be prayſed,
      The caſe ſo harde doth ſtand.
For euery one doth talke,
There tongues contrary walke,
And ſemes to meddell of this and that,
There babling tongues ſo large doth chatte,
As fooliſhe fancye moues them ſaye,
So out there fooliſh talke they braye ;

And euery one doth befie him ftill
About the thing he hath no fkill.

℃ Some of his neighbors doth inquire
    What newes abrode there is,—
If that he any thinge doth here,
    Of thofe that dyd amiffe.
Some longeth to here tell
Of thofe that dyd rebell,
And whether they be fled or take,—
Thus ftill inquirie they do make ;
Some fayth to Scotland they be goe,
And other fayth it is not fo ;—
The rumerous deuell is now abrode,
Which makes them fo to laye on lode.

℃ Some fayth this yeare there fhal be hapte
    Much trouble in the lande ;
Of prophefies they carpe and clappe,
  · As they that haue them fkande.
Doth tell them fo abrode,
And thus they laye on lode,
And filles the peoples eares with lyes ;
Thus rumor ftill abrode he flyes,
Which makes them now in fuch a rore,
As all true hartes may well deplore.
And praye to God if that he pleafe
Thefe foolifh rumores once maye ceafe.

℃ And let vs nowe applye our tyme
    In prayer to the Lorde,
That he may ceafe this furious cryme,
    That now is blowne abrode.
And euery one to ftaye
His tongue, and nothing faye

But of the thinges he hath in hand,
And fee his befynes well be fcand,
And not to meddle of princes actes,
What they will do, nor of their factes.
If occupied well we thus abyde,
The Lorde for vs will well prouide.

℃ For furely plagues we do defarue
   Moft horrable and great,
Becaufe from God we ftill do fwarue,
   And dayly doth him frette.
And ftill prouoke his ieare,
Which glous as hotte as fyare;
His bow is now all redye bent,
Therfore in tyme let vs repent,
Leaft he for finne do vs depriue,
For warned folkes, they faye, may liue,
And warning take by other men,
Which we before our eyes haue fene.

℃ We haue hard in Fraunce the rumur there,
   That hath bene many a daye,—
There countrey fpoyled in ruth and feare,
   Vnto there cleane decaye,
With loffe of many a man,
Since firft that fturre began,
And many a noble hath bene flayne,
A duke, and eake a prince certayne,
Which weare the chiefe ftayes of that land,
Wherfore in hazarde now they ftande;
For where the chiefe are taken awaye,
The reft muft nedes runne to decaye.

℃ In what eftate doth fouldiers ftand,
   Great ruth it is to here;

That there is wrought the tirants hand,
  We nede not to declare.
Experiaunce well may fhowe
What numbers here doth flowe.
Of Flemminges fled from tirantes hand,
Which dayly commeth to this land;
Whofe harts in wrath full long hath boyld,
And eake there countrye cleane difpoyld;
Which thing may warne vs well, I faye,
Leaft that we feele the lyke decaye.

℃ The Lorde hath fuffered vs full longe,
  And fpared hath his rodde,—
What peace hath bene vs now among
  Aleuen yeares, prayfed be God!
And round about vs hath
Bene warre and cruell fayth,—
And all to caufe vs to repent,—
For we defarue worffe punnifhment
Then any of thefe landes haue done;
I feare we fhall be plagued right fone;
Thy judgement fure our God hath had,.
To plague the good ftill for the bad.

℃ Wherefore let vs with one accorde
  Fall all to faft and praye,
And pardon craue now of the Lorde,
  To kepe vs from decaye;
And leaue this murmoring fpight,
Which God doth not delight;
The Scripture playnely doth declare
The Ifralites they plagued weare,
Becaufe the murmered at there God,—
Therin we do defarue lyke rod.

With hartes deuoute now let vs praye,
To kepe this realme from all decaye.

Finis, quod Thomas Bette.

❦ Imprinted at London, in Fleteſtreat, at the
ſigne of the Faucon, by Wylliam Gryffith, and
are to be ſold at his ſhoppe in Sainct Dunſtones
Churchyarde, 1570.

❦

*The true Diſcripcion of a Childe with Ruffes,
borne in the pariſh of Micheham, in the countie
of Surrey, in the yeere of our Lord* MDLXVI.

HIS preſent yeere of our Lord MDLXVJ.
the vij. day of June, one Helene
Jermin, the wife of John Jermin,
huſbandman, dwelling in the pariſhe
of Micheham, was deliuered of a woman-childe,
named Chriſtian, beeing after this maner and
fourme following : that is to ſay, the face
comly and of a cheerful countenaunce ; the
armes and hands, leggs and feet, of right ſhape,
and the body, with all other members therunto
apperteining, wel proporcioned in due fourme and
order, ſauing that it is as it were wunderfully
clothed with ſuche a fleſhy ſkin as the like at
no time hath ben ſeene. For it hath the ſaid
fleſhy ſkin behinde like vnto a neckerchef
growing from the veines of the back vp vnto
the neck, as it were with many ruffes ſet one

after another, and beeing as it were fomthing gathered, euery ruf about an inche brode, hauing here growing on the edges of the fame, and fo with ruffes comming ouer the fhoulders and couering fome part of the armes, proceding vp vnto the nape of the neck behinde, and almofte round about the neck, like as many womens gownes be,—not cloce togither before, but that the throte beeing (with a faire white fkin) bare betweene bothe the fides of the ruffes, the faid ruffes about the neck beeing double, and as it were thick gathered, muche like vnto the ruffes that many do vfe to weare about their necks.

℄ This childe beforfaid (the day of the date vnder written) was to be feene in Glene Alley, in Suthwark, beeing aliue and x. weeks olde and iiij. dayes, not vnlikly to liue long.

℄ *An admonition vnto the Reader.*

THIS picture, preft in paper white,
  Our natures dooth declare,
Whofe fourme fo ftraunge by natures fpite
  May lerne vs to beware.

℄ By natures fpite,—what doo I faye?
  Dooth nature rule the rofte?
Nay, God it is, fay wel I may,
  By whom nature is toft.

℄ The face ful faire, the members all
  In order ftand and place;
But yet too muche by natures thrall
  Dooth woork a great difgrace.

℆ This ruffeling world, in ruffes al rolde,
  Dooth God deteſt and hate;
As we may lerne the tale wel tolde
  Of children borne of late.

℆ What meanes this childe, by natures woork
  Thus ruffed for to be?
But by theſe ruffes our natures ſpurk
  We might beholde and ſee.

℆ Her ſquares our ſquaring dooth ſet out,
  This here our heres dooth checke;
This monſtrouſe monſter, out of dout,
  Agreeth in eche reſpect.

℆ Our filthy liues in pigges are ſhewd;
  Our pride this childe dooth bere;
Our ragges and ruffes, that are ſo lewd,
  Beholde her fleſhe and here.

℆ Our beaſtes and cattel plagued are,
  All monſtrouſe in their ſhape;
And eke this childe dooth wel declare
  The pride we vſe of late.

℆ Our curled here her here dooth preche,
  Our ruffes and giſes gaie,
Our ſtraunge attire wherto we reche,
  Our fleſhe that pleſe we may.

℆ The poet telleth how Daphenes was
  Transformd into a tree;
And Io to a cow did paſſe,—
  A ſtraunge thing for to ſee.

℃ But poets tales may paſſe and go
    As trifels and vntrueth,
When ruffes of flesſhe, as I doo trowe,
    Shall moue vs vnto ruthe.

℃ Deformed are the things we were,
    Deformed is our hart;
The Lord is wroth with all this geere,—
    Repent for fere of ſmarte!

℃ Pray we the Lord our hartes to turn,
    Whileſt we haue time and ſpace,
Leſt that our ſoules in hel doo burn,
    For voiding of his grace.

℃ And thou, O England, whoſe womankinde
    In ruffes doo walke to oft,
Parſwade them ſtil to bere in minde
    This childe with ruffes ſo ſoft.

℃ In fourme as they, in nature ſo,
    A maid ſhe is indeed;—
God graunt vs grace, howeuer we go,
    For to repent with ſpeed!

FINIS, quod H. B.

℃ Imprinted at London by John Allde and
Richarde Johnes, and are to be ſolde at the long
ſhop adioining vnto S. Mildreds churche, in the
Pultrie, and at the litle ſhop adioining to the
North-weſt doore of Paules churche, anno
domini M. D. lxvi. the xx. of Auguſt.

¶ *Other thus it is, or thus it ſhoulde bee.*

THE golden world is now come agayne,
    God is knowen, beleued, loued and
      obeyed ;
    True doctryne is taught and falſe ex-
      yled cleane,
Sinne is mortified, all vice is decayed ;
Peace doeth take place, all warres be delayed ;
Youth is brought vp in learnyng vertuouſlye ;
    Commonwealth doeth flouriſh, pouertie hath
      ayde ;—
    Other thus it is, or thus it ſhoulde be.

¶ Kynges and princes doe Gods lawes aduaunce,
    Juſtice and equitie alſo they doe maintayne ;
They loue peace, they hate war and variaunce,
    Vice they ſuppreſſe, and vertue cauſe to raigne ;
    To get learning and knowledge they take great
      payne ;
They make good lawes, and ſee them kepte iuſtlie ;
    To defend their cuntries great trauel they
      ſuſtaine ;—
    Other thus it is, or thus it ſhoulde bee.

¶ Maieſtrates and officers, each one in their degree,
    Geue good enſample of obedience and liuyng ;
For the commonwealth alſo they take great ſtudie,
    They execute iuſtice iuſtlie in euery kynd of
      thyng ;
    To the poore pouertie they be good and louyng,
The wylfull they reſtrayne from their iniquitie ;

To the humble and good they be gentle and
 benigne;—
 Other thus it is, or thus it fhoulde bee.

❡ Bifhops and minifters doe themfelues apply
 Sincerelie to preach Gods holie law and gofpell,
Accordyng to their doctrine they liue vertuoufly,
 In hofpitalitie and almes deed they greatly excell;
 They geue good example for other to doe well,
They be chafte and fobre, and full of humilitie,
 They ftudie the Scriptures, all vice they doe
  expell;—
 Other thus it is, or thus it fhoulde bee.

❡ Judges that fit in iudgement, matters for to
 heare,
Be fo vncorrupte that no bribes they wyll take,
Tyll they heare both parties they ftop the one eare,
 By the lawe deliberately the cafes they debate,
 By euidence and witneffes the truth they out
  beate,
Falfehod they fetter, but right they doe fet free,
 Juft iudgement they geue, none can entreate;—
 Other thus it is, or thus it fhoulde bee.

❡ Juftices and gentlemen peace doe maintayne,
 The queenes lawes and ftatutes they fee executed,
Contention and variaunce they doe fubdue cleane,
 The oppreffour they punifh, the naughty is
  rebuked;
 The fturdy they correcte, the poore be refrefhed,
They lyue on their landes rented reafonablie,
 Matters before them be iuftly and foone ended;—
 Other thus it is, or thus it fhoulde bee.

℃ Mayours and bayliffes, and all other officers
    Of cities, boroughes, and of townes corporate,
They ſtudie ſuch decrees and ſuch godly orders,
    That the people be wel ruled; great paine they
        take
    For the commonweale; tumult and debate
They deſtroy; but they encreace godly vnitie,
    They cauſe plentie by prudence, dearth they
        abate;—
      Other thus it is, or thus it ſhoulde bee.

℃ All lawyers doe perſwade their clients to agree
    Rather then at the lawe to ſpend out their money;
Yf they wyl not, they ſearch their caſe profoundlie,
    And therein they proceed without fraude or
      delay;
    They bryng it to iudgement, or to ſome godly
      ſtay;
Yf they promiſe their clientes, they performe
      iuſtly;
    They take reaſonable fees for their paynes
      alway;—
      Other thus it is, or thus it ſhoulde bee.

℃ The commons feare God and obey the queene,
    They come to heare Gods wurd and together
      pray;
Diſobedience in no caſe is now no more ſeene,
    Contention they hate, they loue peace alway.
    Euery one is content to liue as he may,—
The rich helpe the poore, yea, and that gladly;
    The poore be content and for them doe pray;—
      Other thus it is, or thus it ſhoulde bee.

℃ Parents doe bryng vp their children very godly,
    Children obey their elders and folow their aduice;

Huſbandes loue their wiues, and they them hartely;
  Women be ſober and gentle, neither proude nor
    nice ;
  Seruants be faithful, they need no warning twice;
To vertue and learning youth geueth all their
    ſtudie ;
  Yf any fall in decay, he is holpen agayne to
    arice ;—
    Other thus it is, or thus it ſhoulde bee.

℄ All ſubiects faithfully pray for their queene,
  That God may endue her royall hart alway
With faith, feare, and loue, before him to be ſeene,
  And for her honorable counſell they humbly
    pray,
  That good lawes and ſtatutes ſet furth they
    may,
To the wealth of the realme and communaltie ;
  That the queene may rule wel, and they truly
    obey ;—
    Amen.   God graunt that ſo it may bee !

℄ Finis.

℄ Imprinted at London without Alderſgate in
  Little Brittaine, by Alexander Lacy.

A Ditty delightfull of mother Watkins ale,
A warning wel wayed, though counted a tale.

THERE was a maid this other day,
　　And fhe would needs go forth to play;
　　And as fhe walked fhe fithd and faid,
　　I am afraid to die a mayd.
　　With that, behard a lad
　　What talke this maiden had,
　　Whereof he was full glad,
　　　　And did not fpare
　　To fay, faire mayd, I pray,
　　Whether goe you to play?
　　Good fir, then did fhe fay,
　　　　What do you care?
For I will, without faile,
Mayden, giue you Watkins ale;
Watkins ale, good fir, quoth fhe,
What is that I pray you tel me?
Tis fweeter farre then fuger fine,
And pleafanter than mufkadine;

And if you pleafe, faire mayd, to ftay
A little while, with me to play,
　　　I will giue you the fame,
　　　Watkins ale cald by name,—
　　　Or els I were to blame,
　　　　In truth, faire mayd.
　　　Good fir, quoth fhe againe,
　　　Yf you will take the paine,
　　　I will it not refraine,
　　　　Nor·be difmayd.

He toke this mayden then afide,
And led her where fhe was not fpyde,
And told her many a prety tale,
And gaue her well of Watkins ale.

Good fir, quoth fhe, in fmiling fort,
What doe you call this prety fport?
Or what is this you do to me?
Tis called Watkins ale, quoth he,
 Wherein, faire mayd, you may
 Report another day,
 When you go forth to play,
  How you did fpeed.
 Indeed, good fir, quoth fhe,
 It is a prety glee,
 And well it pleafeth me,
  No doubt indeed.
Thus they fported and they playd,
This yong man and this prety mayd,
Vnder a banke whereas they lay,
Not long agoe this other day.

When he had done to her his will,
They talkt, but what it fhall not fkill;
At laft, quoth fhe, fauing your tale,
Giue me fome more of Watkins ale,
 Or elfe I will not ftay,
 For I muft needs away,—
 My mother bad me play,—
  The time is paft;
 Therfore, good fir, quoth fhe,
 If you haue done with me.
 Nay, foft, faire maid, quoth he,
  Againe at laft

Let vs talke a little while.
With that the mayd began to fmile,
And faide, good fir, full well I know,
Your ale, I fee, runs very low.

This yong man then, being fo blamd,
Did blufh as one being afhamde;
He tooke her by the midle fmall,
And gaue her more of Watkins ale; ,
 And faide, faire maid, I pray,
 When you goe forth to play,
 Remember what I fay,
  Walke not alone.
 Good fir, quoth fhe againe,
 I thanke you for your paine,
 For feare of further ftaine,
  I will be gone.
Farewell, mayden, then quoth he;
Adue, good fir, againe quoth fhe.
Thus they parted at laft,
Till thrice three months were gone and paft.

This mayden then fell very ficke,
Her maydenhead began to kicke,
Her colour waxed wan and pale
With taking much of Watkins ale.
 I wifh all maydens coy,
 That heare this prety toy,
 Wherein moft women ioy,
  How they doe fport;
 For furely Watkins ale,
 And if it be not ftale,
 Will turne them to fome bale,
  As hath report.

New ale will make their bellies bowne,
As trial by this fame is knowne;
This prouerbe hath bin taught in fchools,—
It is no iefting with edge tooles.

Thrife fcarcely changed hath the moon
Since firft this pretty tricke was done,
Which being harde of one by chance,
He made thereof a country dance;
  And, as I heard the tale,
  He cald it Watkins ale,
  Which neuer will be ftale,
   I doe beleeue;
  This dance is now in prime,
  And chiefly vfde this time,
  And lately put in rime.
   Let no man greeue
To heare this merry iefting tale,
The which is called Watkins ale;
It is not long fince it was made,—
The fineft flower will fooneft fade.

Good maydes and wiues, I pardon craue,
And lack not that which you would haue;
To blufh it is a womans grace,
And well becometh a maidens face,
  For women will refufe
  The thing that they would chufe,
  Caufe men fhould them excufe
   Of thinking ill;
  Cat will after kind,
  All winkers are not blind,—
  Faire maydes, you know my mind,
   Say what you will.

When you drinke ale beware the toaſt,
For therein lay the danger moſt.
If any heere offended be,
Then blame the author, blame not me.

FINIS.

A prettie newe Ballad, intytuled:

The Crowe ſits vpon the wall,
Pleaſe one and pleaſe all.

To the tune of, Pleaſe one and pleaſe all.

PLEASE one and pleaſe all,
  Be they great, be they ſmall,
  Be they little, be they lowe,—
  So pypeth the crowe,
Sitting vpon a wall,—
Pleaſe one and pleaſe all,
Pleaſe one and pleaſe all.

Be they white, be they black,
Haue they a ſmock on their back,
Or a kircher on their head,
Whether they ſpin ſilke or thred,
Whatſoeuer they them call,—
Pleaſe one and pleaſe all,
Pleaſe one and pleaſe all.

Be they fluttifh, be they gay,
Loue they worke, or loue they play,
Whatfoeuer be theyr cheere,
Drinke they ale, or drinke they beere,
Whether it be ftrong or fmall,—
Pleafe one and pleafe all,
Pleafe one and pleafe all.

Be they fower, be they fweete,
Be they fhrewifh, be they meeke,
Weare they filke or cloth fo good,
Veluet bonnet or French hood,
Vppon their head a cap or call,—
Pleafe one and pleafe all,
Pleafe one and pleafe all.

Be they halt, be they lame,
Be fhe lady, be fhe dame,
If that fhe doo weare a pinne,
Keepe fhe tauerne or keepe fhe inne,
Either bulke, bouth, or ftall,—
Pleafe one and pleafe all,
Pleafe one and pleafe all.

The goodwife I doo meane,
Be fhee fat or be fhe leane,
Whatfoeuer that fhe be,
This the crowe tolde me,
Sitting vppon a wall,—
Pleafe one and pleafe all,
Pleafe one and pleafe all.

If the goodwife fpeake aloft,
See that you then fpeake foft;
Whether it be good or ill,
Let her doo what fhe will;

And, to keepe yourſelfe from thrall,
Pleaſe one and pleaſe all,
Pleaſe one and pleaſe all.

If the goodwife be diſpleaſed,
All the whole houſe is diſeaſed,
And therefore, by my will,
To pleaſe her learne the ſkill,
Leaſt that ſhe ſhould alwaies brall,—
Pleaſe one and pleaſe all,
Pleaſe one and pleaſe all.

If that you bid her doo ought,
If that ſhe doo it not,
And though that you be her goodman,
You yourſelfe muſt doo it than,
Be it in kitchin or in hall,—
Pleaſe one and pleaſe all,
Pleaſe one and pleaſe all.

Let her haue her owne will,
Thus the crowe pypeth ſtill,
Whatſoeuer ſhe command
See that you doo it out of hand,
Whenſoeuer ſhe dooth call,—
Pleaſe one and pleaſe all,
Pleaſe one and pleaſe all.

Be they wanton, be they wilde,
Be they gentle, be they milde,
Be ſhee white, be ſhe browne,
Dooth ſhe ſkould or dooth ſhe frowne,
Let her doo what ſhe ſhall,—
Pleaſe one and pleaſe all,
Pleaſe one and pleaſe all.

s

Be fhe coy, be fhe proud,
Speake fhe foft or fpeake fhe loud,
Be fhe fimple, be fhe flaunt,
Dooth fhe trip or dooth fhe taunt,—
The crowe fits vpon the wall,—
Pleafe one and pleafe all,
Pleafe one and pleafe all.

Is fhe hufwife, is fhe none,
Dooth fhe drudge, dooth fhe grone,
Is fhe nimble, is fhe quicke,
Is fhe fhort, is fhe thicke,
Let her be what fhe fhall,—
Pleafe one and pleafe all,
Pleafe one and pleafe all.

Be they ritch, be they poore,
Is fhe honeft, is fhe whore,
Weare fhe cloth or veluet braue,
Dooth fhe beg or dooth fhe craue,
Weare fhe hat or filken call,—
Pleafe one and pleafe all,
Pleafe one and pleafe all.

Be fhe cruell, be fhe curft,
Come fhe laft, come fhe firft,
Be they young, be they olde,
Doo they fmile, doo they fkould,
Though they doo nought at all,—
Pleafe one and pleafe all,
Pleafe one and pleafe all.

Though it be fome crowes guife
Oftentimes to tell lyes,
Yet this crowes words dooth try
That her tale is no lye,

For thus it is and euer ſhall,—
Pleaſe one and pleaſe all,
Pleaſe one and pleaſe all.

Pleaſe one and pleaſe all,
Be they great, be they ſmall,
Be they little, be they lowe,—
So pipeth the crowe,
Sitting vpon a wall,—
Pleaſe one and pleaſe all,
Pleaſe one and pleaſe all.

Finis.   R. T.

Imprinted at London for Henry Kyrkham,
dwelling at the little north doore of Paulẻs,
at the ſigne of the Blacke Boy.

An Epitaph on the death of the Right honor-
able and vertuous Lord Henry Wriſley, the
Noble Earle of Southampton, who lieth interred
at Touchfeelde in the countie of Hamſhyre, the
30 day of Nouember, 1581, and in the 24 yeare
of our moſt drad and ſoueraigne Ladie Elizabeth,
by the grace of God, of England, Fraunce and
Ireland Queene, &c.

YOU noble peeres, refraine your courtly
        ſportes awhyle,
    Caſt on your wailefull weedes of woe,
        Dame Pleaſure doo exile.
Beholde a platforme playne of death, fit for the
        graue,
Who late inioyed a lyuing ſoule, as you this
        ſeaſon haue ;
His birth right noble was, honour beſet him
        rounde,
But Death amidſt his luſtie yeeres hath ſhrind
        him in the ground.
When time is come, he waightes, according Gods
        decree,
To conquer lyfe, reſpecting not the mightieſt in
        degree ;
Intreatie cannot ſerue, Death ſeekes no golden
        gift,
For from his reache no potentate to flye can
        make the ſhift.

The glaſſe runne forth at large, the howre fully
     ſpent,
To ſhare lifes thred a-ſunder hee by mightie
     Joue is ſent.
The Daunce of Death no king nor kayſer but
     muſt trace,
The duke, the earle, the lord and knight to him
     muſt yeeld a place;
The aged olde, the midle ſort, the luſtie youth
     in prime,
To liue on earth cannot inioy the certentie of
     time.
For as time hath no ſtaie, but fleeteth euerie
     howre,
So is the lyfe of mortall men compared to a
     flowre,
Whoſe beautie knowne to daie, to-morrow fadeth
     quight,
And vaniſheth, as though therof man neuer had
     the ſight.
So fickle is our ſtate, we fading flowres bee,
To-daie aliue, to-morrow dead, according Gods
     decree.
Of lyfe no charters giuen to any worldly
     wight,
Oh, who can ſay that he ſhall liue from morne
     vnto the night!
He that at fyrſt gaue lyfe, of lyfe will beare the
     ſway,
And when him lykes, as pleaſeth him, will take
     this lyfe away.
Sith he workes all in all, and rules as ſeemes him
     beſt,
Lets learne that earth we are, and earth to claime
     her owne is preſt;

The perfect proofe wherof apparently is feene
By this good earle, whofe lufty yeeres did florifh
 faire and greene ;
But in a moment chaunged and withered lyke
 the haie,
Bereft of lyfe and honor great, and coutched
 clofe in claie.
Yet though he fenceleffe lye, Southamtons Earle
 by name,
Yet Death in him lyes dead, no doubt, by meanes
 of noble fame ;
For whilft on earth he liu'de to vertue he was
 bent,
And after wifdomes lore to hunt he gaue his
 frank confent ;
In juftice was his ioye, and iuftly he did deale,
As they can tell that for his aide had caufe for
 to appeale ;
The widow poore oppreft he carefully did
 fhield,
And to the orphane in his right did dayly comfort
 yeeld ;
The needie poore he fed with mutton, bread, and
 beeffe,
His hand was neuer flack to giue the comfortleffe
 releefe ;
The naked back to cloth he euer ready was,
No needy poore without reward from this earles
 gates could pas ;
His houfe-keeping right good, there plentie bare
 the fway,
No honeft man forbidden was within his houfe
 to ftaie ;
His faith brought foorth fweete fruite the Lord
 God to delight,

And made him, as a feruant good, accepted in his
       fight ;
Vnto his tennauntes poore this earle was euer
       kinde,
To work their weale he carefully did alwaies
       yeeld his minde ;
Inhaunfing of his rentes did ne enlarge his ftore,
He alwaies had a care to help and aide his farmers
       pore ;
His feruauntes weale to worke no time he did
       forbeare,
To doo them good that wel deferu'd his zeale
       did ftill appeare ;
On God his hart was fet, in Chrift his hope did
       reft,
And of the mightie Lord of hoaftes this noble
       earle was bleft ;
To Prince he was moft iuft, to countrie alwaies
       true,
The fruites of loue and loyaltie in him all ftates
       might view ;
In wedlock hee obferued the vow that he had
       made,
In breach of troth through lewd luft he ne would
       feeme to wade.
Thrice happy thou, of God and man belou'de,
That euer foughtft to make a peace where difcorde
       ftriffe had mou'd ;
Though thou from vs be gone, and taken hence
       by death,
Among the fonnes of mortall men thy prayfe
       fhall liue on earth ;
For as thy lyfe was iuft, fo godly was thy ende,
Not on this world, but on fweet Chrift, thou
       alwaies didft depend ;

And as in health his name thou reuerently didſt
      praiſe,

So in his feare in ſickneſſe thou didſt ſpend thy
      lotted daies ;

This world thou heldſt as vaine, thy lyfe thou
      thoughteſt no loſſe,

In hope of heauen and heauenly bliſſe thou
      deemſt al things but dros ;

Thus houering ſtill in hope, to heauen thou tookſt
      thy flyght,

Wherewith thy Chriſt, the iuelle of ioy, thy hart
      is pight ;

And he in extreeme paine, when anguiſh did
      abounde,

To giue thee comfort from aboue was euer ready
      found.

Amidſt his mercie he, though iuſtice wrought thy
      ſmart,

Euen lyke a louing ſauiour did alwaies take thy part;

When Sathan, ſinne, and death about thee round
      were ſet,

To pray for thee moſt earneſtly he neuer did
      forget ;

And like a ſouldier iuſt by faith thou foughtſt
      the feelde,

And armſt thyſelf gainſt all thy foes, to whom
      thou woldſt not yeeld,

But ſo didſt keepe the fort that all thy foes did
      flye,

And lyke a lambe in Jeſus Chriſt preparedſt
      thyſelfe to die.

Of court thou takeſt thy leaue, thy prince thou
      bidſt farewell,

For whoſe eſtate thou praydſt to God her enemies
      to quell.

The noble peeres eche one with hart thou bidſt
      adue,
And praiedſt that they to glad her hart may
      loyaltie enſue.
Of all thy louing friendes thou takeſt a fynall
      leaue,
And vnto God moſt conſtantly for comfort thou
      doeſt cleaue.
Thy noble children thou right louingly doeſt .
      bleſſe,
To ſeruants all thou giueſt adue, they may thee
      not poſſeſſe,
From them thou doeſt prepare thy paſſage ſtraight
      to make,
And vnto Chriſt with cheareful voice thy ſoule
      thou doeſt betake,
Who, with outſtretched armes, receiues it to his
      grace,
And with his ſaintes in glorie great appointes the
      happye place.
Thy freendes thy loſſe lament, thy children waile
      and weepe
To ſee their father and their freend in clay in-
      cloſed deepe.
Thy ſeruants ſtreme foorth teares, they wring
      their wofull handes
To ſee that all to ſoone of lyfe death hath de-
      ſolued the bandes.
His tennants all doo mourne, their ſmoking ſobs
      abounde,
And to the ſkies the needie poore their pitious
      plaints reſounde ;
Their foſter freend from them by death they ſay
      is hent,
Whoſe want in court and towne eche-where both
      old and yong lament.

But teares are fpent in vaine; though they fuppofe
    him dead,
He liues in heauen where Jefus Chrift with glory
    crownes his head.
And thus, right noble earle, thy laft adue receiue,
To thine auaile behinde thee thou good name
    and fame doeft leaue,
Which fo fhall conquer Death that Death in thee
    fhall die,
And moue the fonnes of mortall men to heaue
    thy praife to fkie.

Omnis caro fenum, quod John Phillip.

A Ballad reioyfinge the fodaine fall,
Of Rebels that thought to deuower vs all.

REIOYCE with me, ye Chriftians all,
    To God geue laude and prayfe,
    The rebels ftoute haue now the fall,
    Their force and ftrength decayes.

Which hoped, through their traitrous traine,
    Their prince and natiue foyle
To put by their deuifes vaine
    Vnto a deadly foile.

And with their armies ftoute in feilde
    Againft their prince did rife,
And thought by force of fpeare and fheilde
    To win their enterprife.

It was the Erle of Weftmerland
   That thought himfelfe fo fure,
By the aide of his rebellious bande,
   His countrie to deuoure.

The Erle eke of Northumberland
   His traitorous parte did take,
With other rebels of this lande,
   For Aue Maries fake.

Saying they fought for no debate,
   Nor nothing els did meane,
But would this realme weare in the ftate
   That it before hath ben.

What is that ftate, I would faine know,
   That they would haue againe?
The popifh maffe it is, I trowe,
   With her abufes vaine,—

As by their doings may apeare,
   In comming through ech towne;
The Bibles they did rent and teare,
   Like traytours to the crowne.

And traytours vnto God, likewife,
   By right we may them call,
That do his lawes and worde defpife,
   Their country, queene and all.

The lawes that fhe eftablifhed
   According to Gods word,
They feeke to haue abolifhed
   By force of warre and fword,

Forgetting cleane their loyaltie
  That to their prince they owe,
Their faith, and eke fidelitie,
  That they to hir fhould fhow.

And rather feeke to helpe the Pope
  His honour loft to winne,
In whom they put their faith and hope
  To pardon al their finne ;

That if they fhould their natiue land,
  Their queene and God denie,
They fhould haue pardon at his hand
  For their iniquitie.

Therfore with thofe that loue the Pope
  They did their ftrength employ,
And therby fteadfaftly did hope
  Gods flocke cleane to deftroy.

And then fet vp within this land,
  In euery churche and towne,
Their idols on roodeloftes to ftand,
  Like gods of greate renowne.

Their aulters and tradicions olde,
  With painted ftocke and ftone,
Pardons and maffes to be folde,
  With Keryeleyfon.

Friers fhoulde weare their olde graye gownes
  And maides to fhrift fhould com,
Then prieftes fhould finge with fhauen crownes,
  Dominus vobifcum.

All thefe and fuch-like vaneties
  Should then beare all the fway,
And Gods word through fuch fantafies
  Should cleane be layd away.

But like as God did them defpife
  Which were in Moyfes dayes,
That did a calfe of gold deuife
  As God, to giue him prayfe;

And for the fame idolatry,
  In one day with the fword
Did thre and twenty thoufand dye,
  That did neglect his worde.

The children eke of Ifraell,
  In Ezechias time,
He made among their foes to dwell,
  That did committe that crime.

But when that Ezechias praied
  To God to helpe his owne,
The Lorde forthwith did fend them aide,
  Their foes weare ouerthrowne.

A hundred thoufande eightie fiue,
  By Gods aungelles weare flaine,
And none of them were left aliue
  That toke his name in vaine.

Senacherib alfo, the kinge
  Then of the Affirians,
As he his God was honouring,
  Was flaine by his two fonnes.

Like as he did thofe rebels ftill,
  Which did his flocke purfewe,
From time to time, of his free will,
  By force of warre fubdewe.

As Hollifernus and the reft
  He put them ftill to flight,
That had his little flocke oppreft
  In prefence of his fighte.

So hath he now thefe rebels all,
  Through their vngodly trade,
Caft downe into the pit to fall
  That they for others made.

To whom ftill daily let vs praye,
  Our noble queene to fende
A profperous raigne, both night and day,
  From her foes to defende

Her and her counfaile, realme and all,
  During her noble life,
And that ill hap may them befall
  That feeke for warre and ftrife.

Finis.

Imprinted at London, in Fleete ftreete, by William
  How, for Henry Kirkham, and are to be
  folde at his fhop at the middle north doore of
  Paules Churche.

Notes.

PAGE 1, line 2. *As Donſtable waye.* "As plain as Dunſtable road. It is applied to things plain and ſimple, without welt or guard to adorn them, as alſo to matters eaſie and obvious to be found, without any difficulty or direction," Bedfordſhire Proverbs in Fuller's Worthies. Howell gives the proverb in a ſlightly different form,— "as plain as Dunſtable high-way." The author of the Cobler of Canterburie, 1608, ſpeaks of the "clownes plaine Dunſtable dogrell."

Page 1, line 4. *Syr Thomas Plomtrie. Sir* is here the title of a prieſt, anſwering to the Latin *dominus.* This clergyman took a conſpicuous part in the rebellion, and was amongſt thoſe executed at Durham early in the year 1570. "The 4. and 5. of January did ſuffer at Durham to the number of three ſcore and ſix, conſtables and other, among whom an alderman of the towne named Struthar, and a prieſt called Parſon Plomtree, were the moſt notable," Stow's Annales, ed. 1615, p. 664.

Page 2, line 13. *Northumberland.* The Earl fell into the hands of outlaws on the Borders, and was treated with great indignity. He was ſubſequently betrayed, and confined in the caſtle of Loch Leven. See Sir C. Sharp's Memorials, 1841, p. 323. Weſtmoreland made his eſcape to Flanders, and ſpent the remainder of his life on the Continent, dying, at a very advanced age, in November, 1601. He concealed himſelf in Scotland for a time immediately after the rebellion, and Elderton, in another ballad, preferved in the library of the Society of Antiquaries, fays of the two earls,—

> And to Saint Androwe be they gone,
> With very harde fhyfte, to make theare moane,
> And fom of theare ladies lefte behinde.

Page 2, line 16. *No more is not Norton.* Several members of this family were concerned in the rebellion, but the perfon here alluded to was Richard Norton, of Norton Conyers, generally called " old Norton," a very confpicuous leader in the movement. On the flight of the rebels, a fpy, named Conftable, endeavoured to perfuade him to put himfelf under his protection in England until a pardon could be obtained; but he wifely declined. He fled into Flanders, and received a penfion from the King of Spain. The period of his death is uncertain. There is a portrait of him ftill preferved at Grantley Hall. " The countenance," obferves Sir C. Sharp, " is florid; the hair grey, but the flight beard on the chin and upper lip is of a fandy colour; his eyes are fmall and grey; the contour is pleafing, and the general expreffion is grave, but not ftern,—vigilant, wary, and contemplative," Sharp's Memorials, p. 277.

Page 2, line 24. *Gentyll John Shorne.* This was the name of a Kentifh faint, whofe fhrine was much vifited by pilgrims in the early part of the fixteenth century. Latimer, in one of his fermons, fays he prefers not to " fpeak of the popifh pilgrimage, which we were wont to ufe in times paft, in running hither and thither to Mafter John Shorne or to our Lady of Walfingham." The bones of Shorne were originally depofited at Canterbury, where his fhrine remained, but it would appear from MS. Afhmole 1125, f. 107, that they were removed in 1478, probably to Windfor, where there was a chapel confecrated to him. The name of John Shorne afterwards became to be ufed as a generic term for a Roman Catholic prieft.

Page 6, line 4. *Aftonyed.* " Troubled in minde, *aftonied*, made fore afeard," Baret's Alvearie, 1580.

Page 5, line 7. *By Thomas Colwell.* " Receved of Thomas Colwell, for his lycenfe for the pryntinge of a ballett intituled a newe wel a daye, as playne, m^r. papefte, as Dunftable waye, iiij.*d.*," Regifters of the Stationers' Company, 1569-70. A tune called *Well-a-day* is frequently mentioned. See Chappell's Popular Mufic, p. 175.

Page 5, line 11. *The Black Almayne.* A tune often referred to, for inftance in a Handeful of Pleafant Delites, 1584, in Collier's Old Ballads, p. 53, &c. The tune itfelf is unknown.

Page 6, line 1. *I-wys.* Certainly; truly. This old Anglo-Saxon adverb was now beginning to be corrupted into the pronoun and verb, *I wis*, I know.

Page 8, line 25. *The upper end of Fleet lane.* Moft of the pieces which iffued from the prefs of Richard Jones are dated from St. Paul's. This was one of his early publications, mentioning a refidence not heretofore noticed. He was living at St. Paul's in the following year, 1573.

Page 9, line 2. *Gar.* Literally, make. The late Mr. Bright poffeffed an early MS. mifcellany, in which there was a copy of this ballad, fubfcribed,—" Fynis, quod Jhon Heywood." This ballad was licenfed to Alde, as a ballad " agaynfte detrection," in 1561-2.

Page 9, line 8. *And all thofe.* So in the original, but it appears from the MS. copy that *and* is an error for *on.*

Page 10, line 5. *Skaine.* A kind of fcimitar. Hall, in his Chronicle, 1548, fpeaks of " a band of Iryfhmen armed in mayle with dartes and *fkaynes*, after the manner of their countrey." Palfgrave, how-ever, in 1530, explains *fkeyne*, " a knyfe," a word frequently fynonymous with dagger.

Page 10, line 22. *Bothe.* All, Bright MS.

Page 11, line 31. *Heere.* Cleere, MS. Bright. In the next page, line 2, for *it is*, we here, MS. ibid.

Page 12, line 17. *Me to enfue.* Meete to efchewe, MS. Bright.

Page 12, line 29. *Wo by.* Wo be, MS. Bright.

·T

This and the previous ftanza are tranfpofed in the
MS. In the next page, line 8, the manufcript
reads :—

> To make them glowe,
> 　As grace by grace may ftay.

Page 13, line 1. *To fleke.* "I flecke, I quenche
a fyre; whan you flecke a hoote fyre with water,
it maketh a noyfe lyke thunder," Palfgrave, 1530.

Page 14, line 3. *New lufty gallant.* The favourite
tune of the Lufty Gallant is frequently alluded to, but
Mr. Chappell confiders that the prefent ballad was
intended for another air, becaufe there are feven lines
in each ftanza. See his Popular Mufic of the Olden
Time, vol. i. p. 91. Breton, in his Workes of a
Young Wyt, 1577, mentions a dance tune called the
Old Lufty Gallant. An early notice of the tune
occurs in MS. Afhmole 48, f. 112.

The prefent ballad was printed in the year 1569, as
appears from the following entry in the books of the
Stationers' Company,—"Receved of Thomas Colwell
for his lycenfe for pryntinge of a ballett intituled the
prayfe of my lady marques, iiij.*d.*" *Marques,* marchionefs. Shakefpeare makes Henry the Eighth fpeak
of the "lady marquis Dorfet," act v. fc. 2. In the
original ballad there are five woodcuts, in a line at the
top of the fheet. The fourth, which reprefents a
fage holding up the forefinger of the left hand, is alfo
found, with the addition of three ftars, in the title-
page of Larke's Boke of Wifdome, 1565.

Page 16, line 9. *Finis quod W. Elderton.* Drayton,
in his Elegies, fpeaking of his beginning to read the
Claffics as a boy, fays,—

> I fcorn'd your ballet then, though it were done
> And had for *Finis,* William Elderton.

Page 16, line 14. *The Prifoners' Petition.* This
title is not in the original, which is printed on a flip of
paper meafuring 5 by 3½ inches, and appears to be a

hand-bill fent round to the wealthy inhabitants of the City.

Page 16, line 19. *The hole of Wood-ſtreet Counter.* There is no doubt that the beſt portion of Wood-ſtreet Counter was very far from being an agreeable place of reſidence, but *the hole*, as it was called, was the very worſt part of the priſon.

Put. Well, wee cannot impute it to any lacke of good-will in your worſhip,—you did but as another would haue done ; twas our hard fortunes to miſſe the purchaſe, but if ere wee clutch him againe, the Counter ſhall charme him.

Rauen. The *hole* ſhall rotte him.

> *The Puritaine, or the Widdow of Watling-ſtreete,* ed. 1607, fig. F.

> Next from the ſtocks, *the Hole*, and Little-eaſe,
> Sad places, which kind nature do diſpleaſe.
> *The Walks of Hogsdon,* 4to. 1657.

On the eaſt ſide of this ſtreet (Wood Street) is one of the priſon houſes pertayning to th'e ſhiriffes of London, and is called the Compter in Wood-ſtreet, which was prepared to be a priſon houſe in the yere 1555, and, on the Eue of S. Michaell the Archangell, the priſoners that lay in the Compter in Bred-ſtreete were remoued to this Compter in Wood-ſtreete.— *Stow's Survay of London,* ed. 1603, p. 298.

Page 17, line 14. *Ballad of Patient Griſſell.* This is the earlieſt copy known of a ballad which was frequently reprinted. There are numerous variations in the later editions, few, however, of which are of much importance. The ſtory was introduced to Engliſh readers by Chaucer, who derived the incidents from Boccaccio ; and in the ſixteenth century it was extremely popular in this country, becoming the ſubjeȼt of plays, chap-books, and ballads. See notices of theſe collecȼted in the Shakeſpeare Society's reprint of the comedy of Patient Griſſil, 1841. The preſent ballad forms the larger portion of a little chap-book of the ſeventeenth century entitled, " The Pleaſant and

Sweet Hiſtory of Patient Griſſell, ſhewing how ſhe, from a poore mans daughter, came to be a great lady in France, being a patterne to all vertuous women. Tranſlated out of Italian. London: Printed by E. P. for John Wright, dwelling in Giltſpur Street at the ſigne of the Bible," n.d. The poem is here introduced by the following epiſode,—" In the countrey of Saluſa, which lyeth neere Italy and France, there lived a noble and wealthy prince named Gualter, Marqueſſe and Lord of Saluſa, a man of ſuch vertues that the world did ring of; beloved of his ſubjects for his good parts, that, before his dayes nor ſince, was very few the like for his continuall care of his ſubjects good, and they, in their dutifulneſſe, ſought to out-ſtrip him in love. From his youth his onely exerciſe was hunting, wherein he tooke ſuch delight, that nothing was more pleaſing unto him; withall the ſubjects loyalty to this worthy prince, in their carefulneſſe that ſuch excellent vertues ſhould not faile for want of iſſue, intreated him by humble petition to marry, that from his loynes their children might enjoy the like happineſſe. This ſpeech thus ſpoke to the prince drave ſuch love and affection into his mind, that moſt graciouſly he made them anſwer that when it ſhould pleaſe God that hee ſhould ſee one that he could love, hee moſt willingly would fulfill their good and honeſt requeſt. Withall this anſwer gave them ſuch content, that they earneſtly prayed to ſee that day."

Page 17, line 15. *The Brides Good-morrow.* The ballad of the Bride's Good-Morrow, " to a pleaſant new tune," is in the Roxburghe Collection, i. 15, " Printed by the Aſſignes of Thomas Symcocke," but the ballad itſelf is older than the period of that printer. It commences thus,—

> The night is paſſed, and joyfull day appeareth,
> Moſt cleare on every ſide;
> With pleaſant muſick we therefore ſalute you,—
> Good morrow, Miſtris Bride.

The exclamation, " Good morrow, Miſtreſs Bride," is found, obſerves Mr. Collier, " as a quotation, in more than one play of the time of Shakefpeare, with other allufions to this ballad." The tune itfelf has not been found under this title. Did Shakefpeare have the ballad in his recollection when he makes Petruchio fay,—

> But what a fool am I, to chat with you,
> When I fhould bid good-morrow to my bride,
> And feal the title with a lovely kifs?

Page 19, line 16. *Malift.* Maliced; envied.

Page 21, line 6. *Alone.* " All alone,'" chap-book ed.

Page 21, line 21. *Biffe and pureft pall.* Bifs and pall were filk and cloth of expenfive and fine textures. They are frequently mentioned in the old Englifh romances as figns of the wealth of their poffeffors. " That grete cite that was clothed with *biffe* and pur-pur, and overgyld with gold and prefious ftonys," Wimbleton's Sermon, 1388. " And on hym were the purpull palle," MS. Afhmole 61.

Page 22, line 25. *All and fome.* That is, every-body—

> We are betrayd, and y-nome,
> Horfe and harnefs, lords, *all and fome.*
> *The Romance of Richard Coer de Lion,* 2284.

Page 23, line 2. *Brauery.* That is, rich apparel. " Lionello he haftes him home, and futes him in his braverye," Tarlton's Newes out of Purgatorie, 1590.

Page 23, line 4. *As he.* " At his," later verfion. And, in the next line, "I will afk of thee." The chap-book verfion, at the conclufion of the ballad, adds the following,—" The lords and gentlemen, be-ing aftonifhed, looked one upon another, and feeing no remedy, but that the noble Marqueffe had an unremoveable love upon her, befought her to pardon them of their envy towards her, and to take them into her favour, which fhe, with a modeft behaviour, pro-mifed to doe. The noble Marqueffe, feeing all in peace, ordained a great and fumptuous feaft, where patient Griffel fate miftreffe of the feaft; the Marqueſſe on her right hand, on her left her aged father, old Janicola; her two children betweene them both, the lords and gentlemen doing them ſervice. This feaſt continued fourteene dayes, to the comfort of the commons. When this ſolemne feaſt was ended, the Marqueſſe, to ſhew his love to his Griſſell, made her father one of his counſel, and governour of his palace, where for many yeeres he lived in the love of the whole court. The noble Marqueſſe and his faire Griſſell lived almoſt thirty yeeres, ſaw their children's children, and then dyed, beloved and bewayled of their ſubjects."

Page 24, line 1. *Ballade of a Lover.* This ballad was originally printed by Colwell in 1563, as appears from the Regiſters of the Stationers' Company,— "receved of Thomas Colwell for his lycenſe for pryntinge of a ballett intituled the lover extollynge hys ladyes, iiij.*d.*" In the original, the firſt eight lines are ſet to muſic. "The tune," obſerves Mr. Chappell, "is worthleſs as muſic, and, I ſuſpect, very incorrectly printed. It ſeems a mere claptrap jumble to take in the countryman."

Page 24, line 3. *Damon aud Pithias.* "This," obſerves Mr. Chappell, "is probably a tune from the very old drama of Damon and Pithias."

Page 25, line 6. *Woulde.* "Wolude," original.

Page 27, line 1. *A monſtrous childe.* It is a curious fact that the woodcut of this child, and of ſome other monſters deſcribed in the preſent collection, ſhould be copied by hand on the margins of the regiſter-book of Wills in the Prerogative Court of Canterbury for the year 1562, headed by the following note, here copied exactly as it ſtands in the original,—*Prodigia quæ-dam contra ſolitum naturæ curſum nata et in lucem ædit: anno Domini* 1562. In addition to thoſe found in theſe broadſides may be mentioned drawings of a caterpillar and of a dog with a band round its neck. "Item, ther was (a) pyge brothe to London in May with ij alff bodys, behyng with viij fette, that mony pepull dyd ſe ytt; and after cam a ſyne and token of a monſtorous chyld that was borne be-fyd Colchefter at a town callyd (*blank*)," Machyn's Diary, 1562, ed. J. G. Nichols, p. 281.

Page 27, line 16. *Braſt*. Burſt. "Braſt in the middes, or in ſundre," Huloet's Dictionarie, 1572.

Page 28, line 4. *Beholde a calfe*. "In Aprell was browth to London a pyde calff with a great ruffe about ys neke, a token of grett ruff that bowth men and women," Machyn's Diary, 1562, ed. J. G. Nichols, p. 280.

Page 28, line 24. *Linne*. Ceaſe. "He never *linns*, he gives it not over, he is alwaies doing," Terence in Engliſh, 1614.

Page 29, line 6. *A ſcape*. So Shakeſpeare, in King John, ſpeaks of a "ſcape of nature."

Page 30, line 16. *Lady, Lady*. A favourite burden to a ſong, as in that of the Conſtancy of Suſanna, quoted by Shakeſpeare in Twelfth Night. Compare a ſong in the old interlude of the Trial of Treaſure, 1567,—

> Thou paſſeſt Venus far away,
>   Lady, lady ;
> Love thee I will both night and day,
>   My dere lady !

Page 31, line 2. *Forked cap*. The mitre.

Page 31, line 12. *And famiſhed him till lyfe was donne.* The author does not here follow the ordinary popular belief of the time, which was afterwards adopted by Shakeſpeare. According to Stow, who quotes an in-edited MS. by Sir John Forteſcue as his authority, the king "was impriſoned in Pomfrait Caſtle, where xv. dayes and nightes they vexed him with continuall hunger, thirſt and cold, and finally bereft him of his life with ſuch a kind of death as never before that time was knowen in England." The Percies, in the manifeſto which they iſſued againſt Henry the Fourth the day before the battle of Shrewſbury, expreſsly charge him with the reſponſibility of this crime.

Page 32, line 7. *Trentalles*. "Trentals or trigin-tals were a number of maſſes, to the tale of thirty, ſaid on the fame account, according to a certain order inftituted by Saint Gregory," Ayliffe's Parergon.

Page 33, line 1. *The Pope in his fury.* This ballad was licenfed to Kirkham, or Kyrham, as it is written in the regifter, in 1570-1, " his lycenfe for pryntinge of a ballett, the Pope in greate fury doth." So the words of the entry conclude.

Page 33, line 2. *To a letter the which to Rome is late come.* This perhaps refers and is a fuppofed reply to another ballad, by Stephen Peele, now in the Miller Collection, " to the Tune of Row well ye Mariners," which is headed,—

> A Letter to Rome, to declare to the Pope,
> John Felton, his freend, is hang'd in a rope;
> And farther, aright his Grace to enforme,
> He dyed a Papift, and feemed not to turne.

The fame day (4 Auguft, 1571) was arraigned at Guildhal of London Iohn Felton, for hanging a bull at the gate of the Bifhop of London's palace, and alfo two young men for coyning and clipping of coine, who all were found guilty of high treafon, and had judgement to be drawne, hanged and quartered.—*Stowe's Annales*, ed. 1615, p. 666. The eight of Auguft, John Felton was drawne from Newgate into Paules Church-yeard, and there hanged on a gallowes new fet up that morning before the Bifhoppes palace gate, and being cut downe aliue, he was bowelled and quartered.—*Ibid.*, p. 667.

Page 34, line 2. *To-to.* Exceedingly. " *Too-too*, ufed abfolutely for very well or good," Ray's Englifh Words, ed. 1674, p. 49.

Page 34, line 14. *Senceyng.* That is, incenfing. " And whan thei comen there, thei taken enfenfe and other aromatyk thinges of noble fmelle, and *fenfen* the ydole, as we wolde don here Goddes precyoufe body," Maundevile's Travels, p. 174, ed. 1839.

Page 34, line 16. *Mell.* That is, to meddle with. " Hence, ye profane; *mell* not with holy things," Hall's Satires.

Page 35, line 21. *The Nortons' bones.* Two of

this family, Thomas and his nephew Chriftopher Norton, were executed for their implication in the Northern rebellion, at Tyburn, in May, 1570. Their heads were fet upon London Bridge, and their quarters upon the various gates. There was a little poem by Sampfon Davie on them printed the fame year. " Receved of Wylliam Pekerynge for his lycenfe for pryntinge of the ende and confeffion of Thomas Norton and Chriftofer Norton, rebelles in Yorkefhyre, which dyed the xxvij. of Maye, 1570," Stationers' Regifters.

Page 36, line 7. *Frump*. That is, mock. "*Mocquer*, to mock, flowt, frump, fcoffe, deride," Cotgrave. " To frump, *illudo*," Coles.

Page 36, line 20. *Queen Elizabeth*. Thefe lines under a portrait form together a fingularly curious broadfide. In the State Paper Office is an undated draft of a proclamation, in the handwriting of Cecil, prohibiting all " payntors, pryntors, and gravors " from drawing Queen Elizabeth's picture, until " fome conning perfon mete therefor fhall make a naturall reprefentation of Her Majefty's perfon, favour, or grace," as a pattern for other perfons to copy. This proclamation was moft likely never publifhed, as it is not mentioned in Humfrey Difon's lift of the proclamations of Queen Elizabeth. The " pycture of quene Elyzabeth" was entered to Gyles Godhed on the books of the Stationers' Company, 1562-3.

Page 37, line 11. *Ane new Ballet*. The date of this ballad fixes it to the period of the author's efcape from Paris at the time of the St. Bartholomew maffacre.

Page 37, line 15. *Tykit*. Tied, bound ?

Page 37, line 16. *At Baftianes brydell*. The allufion here is to Queen Mary's leaving Darnley, on the night of his murder, to attend a ball at Holyrood, on the occafion of the marriage of one of her attendants named Baftian. The intention of the author of the ballad is obvioufly to eftablifh a parallel between the murder of Darnley and the maffacre at Paris.

Page 37, line 19. *Wyte of this cummer.* That is, blame of this trouble or vexation. "Delivir us fra all dangears and perrellis of fire and wattir, of fyirflauchtis and thundir, of hungar and derth, feditioun and battel, of pleyis and *cummar*, feiknes and peftilence," Hamiltoun's Catechifme, ap. Jamiefon.

Page 37, line 22. *Conuoyit.* By artful contrivance, deceitfully.

Page 38, line 4. *Farlie.* Wonder.

Page 38, line 6. *Ganzelon.* Ganelon, the celebrated traitor of the romances of Charlemagne, the perfon who was bribed into betraying the French army to the King of the Saracens. He was executed at Aix-la-Chapelle by order of Charlemagne.

Page 38, line 12. *Be doand ane quhyle.* Go on for a time.

Page 38, line. 14. *Ding.* To overcome.

Page 38, line 18: *Wapis.* That is, cafts or throws. So, in Ramfay's poems,—

> Get Johnny's hand in haly band,
> Syne *wap* ye'r wealth together.

Page 38, line 21. *The feryne.* That is, the fyren. *Ouirfylit,* circumvented.

Page 38, line 24. *Volatill.* Bird. "Make we man to oure ymage and liknefle, and be he fovereyn to the fifchis of the fee, and to the *volatils* of hevene," Bible, MS. Bodl. "Volatile, wyld fowle," Prompt. Parv.

Page 39, line 6. *Burreo.* Executioner. Bourreau, Fr.

Page 39, line 8. *Sane.* That is, the river Seine. *Huking,* confidering, regarding.

Page 39, line 13. *Thy faces was four.* Thy fauce was four, taftelefs, or infipid.

Page 40, line 8. *Tythance.* Tidings.

Page 41, line 3. *Graith.* Accoutrements.

Page 41, line 9. *Calk.* That is, chalk (to mark with). Mark their doors with chalk.

Page 41, line 18. *Go fay.* So in the original.

Can thefe words be erroneoufly printed for *affay?*
In the next line *thie* in the original, clearly a mifprint for *this.*

Page 42, line 1. *The Bryber Gehefie.* "Receved
of Thomas Colwell, for his lycenfe for pryntinge of a
ballett intituled of bryber Jehefye, taken out of the
vth chapter of the iiijth Bokes of Kynges, iiij.*d*," Stationers' Regifters, 1566-7. The reference, in the
modern tranflations of the Bible, is to the Second
Book of Kings.

Page 42, line 3. *To the tune of Kynge Salomon.* It
appears, from the Newe Enterlude of Vice, conteyninge
the Hiftorye of Horeftes, 1567, that this is the fame
tune as "Lady, lady." The ftage-direction is,—
"Enter Egiftus and Clytemneftra, finginge this fonge
to the tune of King Salomon;" and then follows the
fong, commencing,—

> And was it not a worthy fight
> Of Venus childe, Kinge Priames fonne,
> To fteale from Grece a ladye bryght,
> For whom the wares of Troye begon,
> Naught fearinge daunger that might faull,
> Lady, ladie!
> From Grece to Troye he went withall,
> My deare lady!

It appears, from the regifters of the Stationers' Company, that Tyfdale had a licenfe in 1561-2 for printing
"a new ballett after the tune of Kynge Salomon."

Page 45, line 6. *The fhape of ii monfters.* This
broadfide is probably that mentioned in the following
entry in the Stationers' Regifters, 1561-2,—"Receved
of John Alde for his lycenfe for pryntinge of a
picture of a monfterus pygge, iiij.*d.*" It is alfo
alluded to in another ballad. See p. 64. There are
engravings of two "monftrous pigs" in the original
broadfide, but only one is defcribed in the text.

Page 49, line 3. *Feinzeit.* That is, feigned. The
word *cruellus*, in the next line, is invented for the fake
of the rhyme. This ballad evidently belongs to the
earlier part of the year 1581, before James Earl of

Morton was brought to trial, and executed on the following day.

Page 49, line 17. *Dowkand.* That is, diving.

Page 50, line 8. *Volt.* Face; countenance.

Page 50, line 9. *Ingyne.* Capacity; ability.

Page 51, line 8. *Potteris.* "Porteris," original. The claffical allufions in this ballad are too trite to require annotation.

Page 51, line 13. *Landwart.* That is, country. It is hardly neceffary to fay that *pleuch*, here and in other places, ftands for *plough*.

Page 51, line 19. *Ane tit.* A quick pull; a hafty turn of the wheel.

Page 51, line 26. *Subumbragit.* Overfhadowed.

Page 52, line 3. *Git.* The laft letter of this word in the original appears, on clofe examination, to be an imperfect *f*, not a *t*. Read *gif*, if.

Page 52, line 11. *Litils.* So in the original, but probably a mifprint for *litill*.

Page 52, line 16. *Law.* To lower or humble.

Page 52, line 29. *Danter.* Conqueror; fubduer. Under the firm government of Morton, the Border diftricts, which had become the fcene of great lawleffnefs, were reduced into order. " He was very wyfe, and a guid juftitiar in adminiftration. His fyve yeirs war eftimed to be als happie and peaceable as euer Scotland faw. The name of a Papift durft nocht be hard of; ther was na theiff nor oppreffour that durft kythe."—Melvill's Diary, 1577.

Page 53, line 21. *Franke.* So in the original, but it may poffibly be an error for *fracke*, active, diligent. So in a poem cited by Jamiefon,—

> He wald not lat the Papifts caufe ga bak,
> Gif it were juft, bot wald be for him *frak*.

Page 54, line 10. *Pleit.* Maintained; debated.

Page 54, line 13. *Eith.* That is, eafy.

Page 54, line 21. *Dowie.* Dull; melancholy.

Page 55, line 9. *Eluottis.* So in the original. It may be right, and a mere fpecimen of cacography, but more probably a mifprint for *Elyottis*.

Page 55, line 12. *Labeis.* Jamiefon has, " *Lebbie*, the lap or fore-fkirt of a man's coat, S. B. Loth."

Page 55, line 25. *Glaikrie.* Idle wantonnefs.

Page 56, line 3. *Detreitis.* So in the original, obvioufly intended for *decreitis.* In the previous line, *decore*, that is, decorate.

Page 56, line 7. *Sempill.* Can it be that the author is here quibbling upon his own name?

Page 56, line 10. *Robert Lekprewicke.* This printer was at Edinburgh from about the year 1561 until 1570. In 1571, he is found at Stirling, and in 1572 at St. Andrew's. See p. 41. In 1573, he had re-turned to Edinburgh.

Page 56, line 12. *The Plagues of Northomberland.* " Receved of Thomas Colwell, for his lycenfe for pryntinge of a ballett intituled, Plaiges of Northum-berlande, iiij.*d*," Regifters of the Stationers' Company, 1569-70. At the top of this broadfide is a row of five woodcuts.

Page 56, line 13. *Appelles.* This tune is referred to in Googe's Eglogs, 1563, in the Handeful of Pleafant Delites, 1584, and in the Crown Garland of Golden Rofes, 1659. A " ballett intituled Kynge Pollicrate, to the tune of Apelles," was entered to Colwell in the Stationers' Regifters, 1565-6.

Page 56, line 14. *When that the Moone, in Northom-berland.* The Silver Crefcent is a well-known creft or badge of the Northumberland family. It was probably brought home from fome of the Crufades againft the Saracens. In an ancient pedigree in verfe, finely illuminated on a roll of vellum, and written in the reign of Henry VII, we have this fabulous account given of its original. The author begins with ac-counting for the name of Gernon or Algernon, often borne by the Percies; who, he fays, were

Gernons fyrft named Brutys bloude of Troy :
Which valliantly fyghtynge in the land of Persè
At pointe terrible ayance the mifcreants on nyght,
An hevynly myftery was fchewyd hym, old bookys reherfe ;
In hys fcheld did fchyne a *Mone* veryfying her lyght,

Which to all the ooſte yave a perfytte fyght,
To vaynquys his enemys, and to deth them perſue :
And therefore the Perſès the Creſſant doth renew.
From a Note by Biſhop Percy.

Page 56, line 24. *With horſe and armes.* "I have
certaine advertyſement that all reteyners and huſehold
ſervants appertening the Erle of Weſtmorland, with
the moſte part of all others his tennants, beyng
furniſhed with armour and weapon, of his lordſhip of
Raby, in their warlike apparel, repared to Branſepeth
yeſterday and this nyght paſt, and all the reſt of his
tennants ar by his lordſhip's officers commandyt to ſet
forthe upon one hour's warning," Letter of Sir George
Bowes to the Duke of Suſſex, 7 November, 1569.

Page 57, line 1. *Pyght.* That is, placed, fixed.
Redyght, to reſtore, (Lat.)

Page 57, line 27. *Bellinge.* That is, bellowing.
" Bellynge of nete," Prompt. Parv. " Becking,
belling, ducking, yelling, was their whole religio,"
Anſwere to a Romiſh Rime, 1602.

Page 60, line 4. *In Somer time.* This is the ſame
tune which is mentioned in a ballad in the Pepys'
Collection, " The Rimer's New Trimming, to the
tune of *In Sommer time*," which commences as
follows,—

> A rimer of late in a barber's ſhop
> Sate by for a trimming to take his lot ;
> Being minded with mirth, until his turn came
> To drive away time he thus began.

Page 61, line 20. *Fat.* A vat or brewing-tub.
" Fatte, a veſſel, *quevue*," Palſgrave, 1530. " A vate
or fat, *labrum*," Rider's Dictionarie, ed. 1617.

Page 63, line 17. *A monſterous Chylde.* In 1564-5,
there was entered on the books of the Stationers'
Company,—" Receved of William Greffeth, for his
lycenſe for pryntinge of a pycture of a chylde borne in
the Ile of Wyghte, with a cluſter of grapes about ys
navell, iiij.*d.*" Notwithſtanding the variation in this
deſcription, there can be little doubt that this entry

refers to the broadside printed in the text. If so, the ingenious compiler of the narrative altered the character of the "cluster" between the date of entry and the period of issue.

Page 65, line 23. *Vnparfett.* An unusual form of the word. Huloet has, "unperfecte, *imperfectus*," ed. 1572; and *unparfited*, for *unperfected*, occurs in Surrey's Songs and Sonnets, 1557. In the next line, the word *porte*, by a singular licence, appears to be used for *report*.

Page 66, line 3. *Confortor.* A genuine old form of the word, derived from the Anglo-Norman.

Page 66, line 12. *The Marchants Daughter.* This is the earliest copy of this ballad known to exist. William Blackwall, its printer, dwelt "over against Guildhall Gate," but very few productions from his press are known to exist. See another specimen at p. 231. He is alluded to by the author of the Declaration of the true Causes, 1592, as the printer "of obscure and trifling matters." This ballad was extremely popular. The fiddler in Fletcher's Monsieur Thomas, 1639, mentions it as one of the songs he is best versed in. A later copy, a few of the stanzas being omitted, is preserved in the Roxburghe collection.

Page 66, line 13. *Bristow.* The usual old way of spelling the name of the town of Bristol.

Page 66, line 14. *The Maydens Joy.* This tune is referred to in Anthony Wood's collection of ballads at Oxford, in Old Ballads, 1729, vol. iii. p. 201, &c.

Page 67, line 12. *Fine.* "Then," ed. Roxburghe.
Page 67, line 18. *Waste.* "Waile," ed. Roxburghe.
Page 68, line 7. *She.* "He," in the original.
Page 68, line 8. *Though naked.* Even as lately as the sixteenth century, the use of night linen was far from being universal. "To bed he goes, and Jemy ever used to lye naked, as is the use of a number, amongst which number she knew Jemy was one," Armin's Nest of Ninnies, 1608. Hence arose the expression, *naked bed*, of which Shakespeare has made such a pretty use,—

Who fees his true love in her naked bed,
    Teaching the fheets a whiter hue than white.

Page 71, line 23. *Joyfull.* " Mortall," ed. Roxburghe.

Page 72, line 7. *Trauell.* " Triall," ed. Roxburghe.

Page 72, line 14. *Al her iorneys.* " Her forrow,"
ed. Roxburghe.

Page 72, line 20. *On her perills.* " Of her
forrowes," ed. Roxburghe. The next ftanza is omitted in this later copy.

Page 73, line 10. *Euer.* This fhould be *evermore,*
as required by the rhyme, and as it ftands in the Roxburghe copy.

Page 73, line 18. *Eyes.* " Eys" in the original.

Page 73, line 24. *Such grieuous.* The fpace for
the word following thefe is alfo left blank in the original.
" Such grievous *doome,*" ed. Roxburghe. In the next
line, *ladies* is a mifprint in the original for *laddes.*

Page 74, line 28. *And of a paffing pure life.* " And
paffing pure of life," ed. Roxburghe.

Page 75, line 18. *Feareful.* " Freareful" in the
original.

Page 78, line 8. *To the tune of Labandalafhotte.*
This tune is the fame as " I waile in woe, I plunge in
pain." See the Handeful of Pleafant Delites, 1584,
and Ritfon's Ancient Songs, p. 151. The tune is referred to for " A fong of King Edgar, fhewing how he
was deceived of his Love." That ballad commences,—

Whenas King Edgar did govern this land,
    Adown, adown, down, down, down ;
And in the ftrength of his years he did ftand,
    Call him down-a, &c.

Mrs. Quickly fings this burden in the Merry Wives
of Windfor, act i. fc. 4, and Ophelia fang one of her
fnatches to the tune of Labandalafhotte. " You muft
fing, *Down-a-down, an you call him a-down-a,*" Hamlet,
act iv. fc. 5. " *Filibuftacchina,* the burden of a countrie fong, as we fay, hay doune a doune douna,"

Florio's Worlde of Wordes, 1598, p. 131. The fame
tune is clearly referred to in the Ballad againſt Slander
and Detraction, p. 9; and Rhodes, in his Anſwere to
a Romiſh Rime, 4to. 1602, ſays,—" I found it ſet to
no certaine tune, but becauſe it goeth moſt neere to the
olde tune of *Labandalaſhot*, therefore I have made that
all may be ſung to that tune, if neede be."

Page 79, line 5. *Marketſted*. A market-place.
" And their beſt archers plac'd the market-ſted about,"
Drayton's Polyolbion.

Page 79, line 30. *Ance*. That is, once, in the
ſenſe of, once for all. " Once, twenty-four ducattes
he coſt me," Gaſcoigne's Suppoſes.

Page 80, line 22. *Nicholas Colman of Norwich.* A
new name in the hiſtory of Engliſh publiſhing. The
ballads were printed for him in London.

Page 81, line 1. *A proper newe ſonet.* It is probably this ballad, not the preceding one, which is
thus entered in the Stationers' Regiſters for 1586,—
" Nicholas Colman, received of him for printinge a
ballad of the lamentation of Beckles, a market towne
of Suffolke, on St. Andrewes day laſte paſte, beinge
burnt with fier, to the number of lxxx. houſe, and
loſſe of xx. m. *li.*" Contributions in aid of the
ſufferers from this fire were raiſed throughout the
counties of Norfolk and Suffolk. Blomefield mentions a ſum of money as having been collected in the
pariſh of Harpham " for the burning of Beccles."
In the book of the Mayor's Court at Norwich is
this entry,—" William Fleming, preacher of Beccles,
raiſed in Court of Mr. Mayor, £30.10.8, which
was collected in this city towards the re-edifying of
Beccles Church, which was lately burnt," Suckling's
Suffolk, vol. i. p. 12.

Page 81, line 8. *To Wilſon's Tune.* This tune
does not appear to be known. In the library of the
Society of Antiquaries is, A proper newe Ballad declaring
the ſubſtaunce of all the late pretended Treaſons againſt
the Queenes Majeſtie, 1586, *To Wilſon's new Tune.*

Page 83, line 11. *The church and temple by this*

fyre. " The roof, feats, and woodwork of the church were confumed, though the walls and the ftonework of the windows efcaped deftruction. The lower part of the fteeple remains blackened with fmoke in a very remarkable degree to the prefent day," Suckling's Hiftory and Antiquities of the County of Suffolk, vol. i. p. 12. The parifh regifters were, probably, deftroyed, the prefent books commencing in the year 1586.

Page 85, line 1. *Franklins Farewell.* James Franklin was the apothecary whofe poverty or whofe will confented to furnifh the poifons, according to order, in the Overbury murders. See his Trial in Cobbett's State Trials, vol. ii. col. 947. According to his own account, he bought the poifons at the entreaty of the Countefs and Mrs. Turner, protefting his ignorance of what they intended to do with them. See further particulars in Amos's Great Oyer of Poifoning, 1846. In the library of the Society of Antiquaries is a broadfide, entitled,—" James Franklin, a Kentifhman of Maidftone, his owne Arraignment, Confeffion, Condemnation, and Judgment of Himfelfe, whilft hee lay Prifoner in the Kings Bench for the Poifoning of Sir Thomas Overbury. He was executed the 9 of· December, 1615."

Page 88, line 1. *The xxv. orders of Fooles.* " Receved of Henry Kyrham, for his lycenfe for the pryntinge of a ballett, intituled the xx. orders of fooles, iiij.*d*," Regifters of the Stationers' Company, 1569-70.

Page 88, line 4. *A quarterne.* That is, a quarter (of a hundred). Maundevile fpeaks of the moon being in " the feconde quarteroun," Travels, p. 301.

Page 88, line 19. *Or els a fox-tayle.* One of the diftinguifhing badges of a fool. " I fhall prove him fuch a noddy before I leave him, that all the world will deeme him worthy to weare in his forehead a coxcombe for his foolifhnefs, and on his back a fox tayle for his badge," The Pope's Funerall, 1605.

Page 89, line 17. *Wood.* That is, mad. " Phœbus

grows ftark *wood* for love and fancie to Daphne,"
Countefs of Pembroke's Ivy-Church, 1591. "The
name Woden fignifies fierce or furious; and in like
fenfe we ftill retain it, faying, when one is in a great
rage, that he is *wood*, or taketh on as if he were *wood*,"
Verftegan's Reftitution of Decayed Intelligence, 1605.
"Woode or madde, *fureux*," Palfgrave.

Page 91, line 1.   *Foole.*   "Feele" in the original.

Page 92, line 23.   *Apayd.*   Satisfied; pleafed.   "In
herte I wolde be wele apayede," MS. Lincoln.   "I
am well apayed, *je fuis bien content*," Palfgrave, 1530.

Page 95, line 12.   *Or els to Lolers tower toft.*   "At
eyther corner of this weft end (of St. Paul's) is alfo
of auncient building a ftrong tower of ftone, made
for bell towers, the one of them, to wit, next to the
pallace is at this prefent to the vfe of the fame
pallace; the other, towardes the fouth, is called the
Lowlardes Tower, and hath beene ufed as the
Bifhoppes prifon, for fuch as were detected for
opinions in religion contrary to the faith of the
church," Stow's Survay of London, ed. 1603, p.
372.

Page 95, line 16.   *To fwage.*   "I fwage, I abate
the fwellyng of a thyng " Palfgrave, 1530.   "Swage,
or to mitigate or appeafe, *complacare*," Huloet's Dictionarie, 1572.

> But wicked wrath had fome fo farre enraged,
> As by no meanes their malice could be fwaged. .
> *Gafcoigne's Works*, 4to. 1587.

Page 96, line 9.   *A forayne.*   That is, a foreigner.
(Fr.)

Page 96, line 29.   *Threape.*   That is, obftinately
maintained.   "I threpe a mater upon one, I beare
one in hande that he hath doone or faide a thing
amyffe; this terme is alfo farre northren; he wolde
threpe upon me that I have his penne," Palfgrave,
1530.

Page 98, line 1.   *A Ballad.*   This is probably the
earlieft, as it undoubtedly is the moft curious, of
the Englifh verfions of a notion which fubfequently

became familiar as the Five Alls. As late as the reign
of George the Third, there was iſſued a ſatirical print
by Kay in five compartments, the firſt of which repre-
ſented a clergyman in his deſk, with the inſcription,
"I pray for all;" the ſecond a barriſter, "I plead for
all;" the third a farmer, "I maintain all;" the fourth
a ſoldier, "I fight for all;" the fifth his Satanic ma-
jeſty, "I take all." There are ſeveral old epigrams,
each line ending with the word *all.* See copies of two
in Larwood and Hotten's Hiſtory of Signboards, p.
452. Inns called the *Four Alls* are ſtill well-known;
but the ſign appears to be gradually going out of
faſhion.

Page 101, line 1. *A godly Ballad.* This ballad is
printed on the back of a waſte ſheet of an old alma-
nac, one ſide only having been printed of the latter,
which was a Prognoſtication for the year then following, 1567. Each month is illuſtrated by a ſmall woodcut.

"Receved of John Alde for his lycenſe for pryntinge of a ballett intituled declarynge by the Scriptures
the plages that have inſued of whoredom, iiij.*d,*" Stationers' Regiſters, 1566-7.

Page 101, line 5. *Leſt in.* "Leſt if" in the original. Perhaps the correƈt reading may be, *left in.*

Page 101, line 15. *The woorm.* That is, the ſerpent. The uſe of the word in this ſenſe is very common in early Engliſh.

Page 101, line 21. *The harmes.* "Thy harmes" in
the original.

Page 105, line 8. *Tantara.* This odd word was
uſually employed to ſignify the noiſe made by a drum.
So, in the old ballad of the Winning of Cales,—

> Long the proud Spaniards had vaunted to conquer us,
>   Threatning our country with fyer and ſword;
> Often preparing their navy moſt ſumptuous
>   With as great plenty as Spain could afford.
>   Dub a dub, dub a dub, thus ſtrike their drums:
>   *Tantara, tantara,* the Engliſhman comes.

It was alſo, however, the name of a tune. A ſong

called Gibfon's Tantara is given in the Handeful of
Pleafant Delites, 1584. In the Miller collection is a
ballad, dated 1590, " to the tune of the new Tantara."
The uncouth orthography ufed by the writer of this
ballad, and the allufion to Bewdley ale, indicate a provincial origin. Such words as *blofe*, blows, *Rafe*,
Ralph, *fincke*, cinque, *gofe*, goes, hardly require expla-
nation.

Page 106, line 2. *Upon the molde.* Upon the ground
or earth. This was a favourite expreffion in the old
Englifh romances. " Moold or foyle of erthe, *folum*,"
Prompt. Parv.

Page 106, line 14. *Plaie.* " Plate" in the original.

Page 106, line 28. *To bafte.* That is, to beat.
" To baft, beat, *fufte cædere*," Coles. *Baftian*, a
cudgel. " *Baculus*, a bafton, a ftaffe," Nomenclator,
1585. *Bumbde*, ftruck, beat. The verb *to bum*, to
beat, is ftill in ufe in the North. *Vnguentum Bakaline*,
ointment for the back.

Page 107, line 19. *He fpurres his cutte.* That is,
his horfe. " Am I their cutt? muft Jack march with
bag and baggage," Play of Sir Thomas More. " But
mafter, 'pray ye, let me ride upon Cut," Sir John
Oldcaftle.

> He's buy me a white cut forth for to ride,
> And ile goe feeke him throw the world that is fo wide.
> *The Two Noble Kinfmen*, 1634, p. 42.

Page 108, line 8. *Her life.* " His life" in the
original.

Page 110, line 17. *Bedftaffe.* A wooden pin in the
fide of the bedftead for holding in the bed-clothes.
" Hofteffe, lend vs another bedftaffe here quickly,"
Every Man in his Humour, ed. 1601, fig. C. 4.

Page 111, line 12. *Did laugh a-good.* In good
earneft. " The world laughed *a-good* at thefe jefts,"
Armin's Neft of Ninnies, 1608. " This mery aunfwer
made them all laughe a-good," North's Plutarch.

Page 112, line 1. *Defcription of a monftrous pig.*
" Receved of Garrad Dewes, for his lycenfe for

pryntinge of a pycture of a monsterus pygge at Hamsted,"
Registers of the Company of Stationers, 1562. There
are two views of the pig in the original broadside.

Page 112, line 19. *Flean.* That is, flayed.

Page 113, line 15. *The tune of Lightie Loue.* This
tune, which is constantly alluded to by our early
writers, and twice by Shakespeare, will be found in
Chappell's Popular Music of the Olden Time, p. 224.
The words of the original song have not been dis-
covered. " Hee'l dance the morris twenty mile an
houre, and gallops to the tune of *Light a' love*," Two
Noble Kinsmen, 1634, p. 77. The earliest notice of
the tune yet met with occurs in Proctor's Gorgious
Gallery of Gallant Inventions, 1578, in which " the
louer exhorteth his lady to be constant, to the tune of,
Attend thee, go play thee." It commences,—-

> Not light of loue, lady,
> Though fancy doo prick thee.

Page 114, line 1. *Nicyngs and ticings.* Pretty
follies and allurements. *Tysing* for *enticing* occurs in
Aminta, 1628.

Page 114, line 6. *Shouer.* Perhaps for *shiver*,
tremble.

Page 114, line 10. *Glose.* Dissimulation; falsehood.

> Tell me, Gobrias, dost thou simplie thinke
> That this discourse is naught but naked truth,
> Or else some forged or dissembled *glose.*
> *The Warres of Cyrus, King of Persia,* 1594.

Page 114, line 15. *And you twincke.* " Twynkyne
wythe the eye, *conniveo*," Prompt. Parv.

> Some turne the whites up, some looke to the foote;
> Some winke, some twinke, some blinke, &c.
> *Lane's Tom Tel-Troths Message,* 1600.

Page 115, line 18. *Bearyng your louers in hande.*
To bear in hand, that is, to persuade to a false
conclusion. " I beare in hande, I threp upon a man
that he hath done a dede or make hym byleve so,"
Palsgrave, 1530.

Page 118, line 1. *Sapartons Alarum.* There was licenſed to Colwell, in 1569-70, " a ballett intituled my gentle John Saperton," who may be the ſame perſon with the author of the preſent ballad.

Page 119, line 14. *What thoe?* What then? This expreſſion alſo occurs in Shakeſpeare. See Henry the Fifth, aƈt ii. ſc. 1.

Page 120, line 5. *The barded horſe.* The horſe equipped with military trappings or ornaments. "Their horſes were barded for feare of arrowe ſhotte," Palſgrave, 1530. " At all alarmes he was the firſt man armed, and that at all points, and his horſe ever barded," Comine's Hiſtory, 1596. The word is ſometimes written *barbed.*

Page 120, line 30. *Vnder the Lotterie houſe.* The Lottery Houſe was ſituated for many years near the weſtern gate of St. Paul's Cathedral. It is deſcribed by Stow as " an houſe of timber and boord." See his Annales, ed. 1615, p. 719.

Page 122, line 13. *A let.* That is, a hindrance. " Let, *impedimentum*," Huloet's Diƈtionarie, 1572. " Let, impediment, hinderaunce," Baret's Alvearie, 1580.

Page 122, line 27. *Stroy.* That is, deſtroy. " Some they ſtroye and ſome they brenne," MS. Cantab. " Stroyed in diſhonour," Antony and Cleopatra, aƈt iii. ſc. 9.

> Diſſolving all her circles and her knots,
> And *ſtroying* all her figures and her lots.
> *Harington's Orlando Furioſo,* 1591.

P. 123, line 19. *The Groome-porters lawes at Mawe.* The Groom-porter was an officer of the royal houſe-hold, whoſe chief buſineſs it was to provide cards and dice, and to decide all diſputes reſpeƈting games of chance. Mawe was a favourite old game at cards, and is frequently alluded to. Braithwait obſerves that " in games at cards, the maw requires a quicke conceit or preſent pregnancy," which implies that it was a game of unuſual difficulty. All the games at cards played by our anceſtors were, however, more difficult and complicated than thofe in vogue at the prefent day.

Page 123, line 27. *Vied cardes.* Cards which have been betted upon. So, in Hall's Satires,—

> More than who *vies* his pence to fee fome tricke
> Of ftrange Morocco's dumb arithmeticke.

Page 125, line 12. *Sodome and Gomorra.* Kyrkham had a licenfe, in 1570-1, " for pryntinge of a ballett of Sodom and Gomore."

Page 127, line 21. *Shryked.* " I fhrike, I kry out, as one dothe that is fodaynly afrayde, *je me efcrie*," Palfgrave, 1530.

Page 129, line 18. *A mery balade.* Alexander Lacy, the printer of this ballad, appears to have either died or retired from bufinefs about the year 1571.

Page 130, line 7. *Neither mocke nor mow.* " I mowe with the mouthe, I mocke one; he ufeth fo moche to mocke and mowe, that he disfygureth his face," Palfgrave, 1530. *Loute*, in the next line, has a fimilar meaning, perhaps to contemn. " Lowted and forfaken of theym by whom in tyme he myght have bene ayded and relieved," Hall's Chronicle. This is alfo probably the meaning of the term in a paffage in the Firft Part of Henry the Sixth, act iv. fc. 3.

Page 130, line 19. *Houfe-kepers.* Perfons who keep at home. Shakefpeare ufes the term in the fame fenfe in the play of Coriolanus.

Page 131, line 2. *To hyll.* That is, to cover. " You muft hyll you wel nowe anyghtes, the wether is colde," Palfgrave, 1530.

Page 131, line 8. *Sad.* That is, ferious. The ufe of the term in this fenfe was very common.

Page 132, line 26. *The iob.* The peck or ftroke. " Jobbyn wythe the bylle, byllen or jobbyn as bryddys," Prompt. Parv.

Page 133, line 1. *The Othe of euerie Freeman.* A woodcut of the City arms is at the top of this broad-fide. Hugh Singleton, the printer, appears to have ftarted in bufinefs about the year 1562. He died in 1592 or 1593. A later copy of this oath is given in Stow's Survey of London, ed. 1633, p. 689.

Page 133, line 7. *Obeyſant.* Submiſſive. " That were obeiſſant to his heſte," Gower.

Page 134, line 10. *Neybourhed, loue, &c.* "Receved of Rychard Lante for his lycenſe for pryntinge of a ballett intituled, how neyghborhed, love, and tru dealinge ys gonne, iiij*d*.," Regiſters of the Stationers' Company, 1561.

Page 136, line 16. *Percialneſſe.* Partiality.

Page 138, line 14. *Philoſophers learnynges.* There is a row of five woodcuts at the top of this ſheet. The firſt one is alſo introduced by Colwell into Larke's Boke of Wiſdome, ed. 1565, fig. B. i. Colwell had a licenſe " for pryntinge of a ballett intituled the philoſifor lernynges" in 1568-9.

Page 138, line 17. *Que paſſa.* A dance, properly called *Qui paſſa*, but ſometimes ſpelt *quipaſcie* or *kypaſcie.* There is a ſong " to the tune of Kypaſcie" in the Handeful of Pleaſant Delites, 1584.

Page 139, line 5. *Surance.* Warrant; ſecurity; aſſurance. " Now give ſome ſurance that thou art Revenge," Titus Andronicus, act v. ſc. 2.

Page 140, line 3. *Corzye.* Diſtreſs; inconvenience. " To have a great hurt or domage, which we call a corſey to the herte," Eliote's Dictionarie, 1559.

Page 140, line 10. *Exuperate.* Surmount. (Lat.)

Page 141, line 11. *It is olde ſyr John.* The title of *ſir* was formerly the deſignation of a Bachelor of Arts, and, in conſequence, the Engliſh clergy were diſtinguiſhed by this title affixed to their Chriſtian names. Hence Shakeſpeare introduces Sir Hugh, Sir Topas, &c. " Within the limits of myne own memory, all readers in chapels were called *ſirs*," Machell's MSS., temp. Car. II.

Page 141, line 18. *A graye.* A badger. " Grey, beeſt, *taxus*," Prompt. Parv. " Graye, a beeſt, *taxe*," Palſgrave, 1530. " Graye, bagger, brocke, a beaſt," Huloet's Dictionarie, 1572.

Page 142, line 24. *The ſwap of the ſwalowe.* The

flang expreffions in this and fome other of thefe ballads can only be conjecturally explained.. Can this
mean, the blow of the drunkard?

Page 143, line 8. *To bewite.* To hinder.

Page 143, line 11. *Mome.* A blockhead. " *Ca-
parrone*, a pugge, an ape, a munkie, a babuine, a gull,
a ninnie, a mome, a fot," Florio's Worlde of Wordes,
1598. " She will make a mome of thee, if fhee get the
upper hand once," Withals' Dictionarie, ed. 1608,
p. 460.

> And pluck up thy hart, thou faint-harted *mome;*
> As long as I lyve, thou fhalt take no harme.
> *The Conflict of Confcience, by N. Woodes,* 1581.

> And yet, to fpeake the veritie, I roame not farre from home;
> My yeeres be not expyred yet that bound me for a *mome.*
> *The Caftell of Courtefie, by James Yates,* 1582.

Page 143, line 12. *Talle.* Valiant; warlike. " He
is as tall a man as any in Illyria," Twelfth Night.

Page 145, line 1. *Marueilous ftraunge Fifhe.* This
is one of the earlieft broadfides relating to " ftrange
fifhes" known to exift, and is a modeft account
in comparifon with that given by Stowe of a fifh taken
near Ramfgate in 1574, one of the eyes of which,
" being taken out of his head, was more then fix
horfes in a cart could draw; a man ftoode upright
in the place from whence the eye was taken;" Annales, ed. 1615, p. 677. The fondnefs of the public
for exaggerated accounts of fuch things is pleafantly
ridiculed by Shakefpeare,—" Here's another ballad, Of
a fifh, that appeared upon the coaft, on Wednefday the
fourfcore of April, forty thoufand fathom above water,
and fung this ballad againft the hard hearts of maids."
I am not acquainted with any very early ballad refpect-
ing a fifh, but in the Miller collection is a broadfide,
" The Difcription of a rare or rather moft monftrous
fifhe, taken on the Eaft Coft of Holland the xvii. of
Nouember, anno 1566," at the conclufion of which
are fome verfes commencing thus,—

> As thou this formed fifhe doeft fee
>   I-chaunged from his ftate,
> So many men in eche degree
>   From kynd degenerate;
> To monfters men are turned now,
>   Difguifed in their raye,
> For in theyr fonde inuentions new
>   They kepe no meane ne ftaye.

Page 145, line 14. *Scooles.* Shoals. "Into the town of Rochell, they fay, God hath fent a *fkull* of fifh for their relief," MS. Harl. 388.

Page 146, line 15. *Daye fertayne.* The comma here fhould be placed after the word *daye*. In the 15th line of this page the laft word in the line is, in the original, mifprinted *ferteintaintie.*

Page 146, line 17. *The Kinges Head in new Fifh-ftreat.* A celebrated tavern for the "faft" men of the time of Elizabeth, noted for its wines. "Ha' your diet-drinke ever in bottles ready, which muft come from the Kings-head," Ben Jonfon's Magnetick Lady, ed. 1640, p. 37. "The King's-head in New Fifh-ftreet, where royfters do range," Newes from Bartholomew Fayre.

Page 147, line 12. *The fantafies.* This poem and the three following are printed together in double columns on one page of a large broadfide. This firft one is alfo found amongft the "Songes and Sonnettes of Uncertain Auctours," in Tottel's Mifcellany, 1557, there headed, "Of the mutabilitie of the world." Lacy, in 1565-6, had a licenfe "for prynting of a ballett intituled a fonge of Appelles, with another dytty;" and Griffith, in the fame year, "for prynting of a ballett intituled of Apelles and Pygmalyne, to the tune of the fyrft Apelles." Lacy, however, alfoin the fame year, had a licenfe "for pryntinge of a ballett intituled the Fantifes of a trubbled mans hed;" fo that the firft poem in the prefent broadfide may have been iffued feparately.

Page 147, line 17. *A fea of wofull forrowes.* "Or to take arms againft a fea of troubles," Hamlet.

Page 148, line 10. *And is.* "As is," ed. 1557.

Page 148, line 17. *Payne.* "Gaine," ed. 1557, which has alſo *runne* for *rome* in the next line but one.

Page 149, line 12. *Of euyll tounges.* This is alſo printed in Tottel's Miſcellany, 1557, the preſent copy giving the name of the author, which was unknown to the compiler of that work.

Page 150, line 5. *Ye make great hatred.* In ed. 1557 this ſtanza commences thus,—

> Ye make great warre, where peace hath been of long;
> Ye bring rich realmes to ruine and decay.

Page 151, line 24. *Coucht.* Laid; placed. This term was ſpecially applied to artiſtic work.

> Alle of palle werke fyne,
> *Cowchide* with newyne.—*MS. Lincoln.*

Page 152, line 2. *A worlde it was to ſee.* That is, it was worth a world to ſee, it was wonderful to ſee. "It is a worlde to ſe him lowte and knele," Palſgrave, 1530. "It is a worlde to ſee what a wit wickedneſſe hath," Racſter's Booke of the Seven Planets, 1598.

> It is a worlde to ſee eache feate diſplaying wiſe,
> Of Venus nimphes, of curtizans, whom folly doth diſguiſe.
> *Grange's Golden Aphroditis,* 1577.

> But, Lord, it is a world to ſee how fooliſh fickle youth
> Accompts the ſchoole a purgatorie, a place of paine and ruth.
> *The Chariot of Chaſtitie, by James Yates,* 1582.

Page 154, line 7. *Roiſters.* Rioters.

> If he not reeke what ruffian *roiſters* take his part,
> He weeldes unwiſely then the mace of Mars in hand.
> *Mirrour for Magiſtrates,* ap. Nares.

Page 154, line 12. *Crake.* "I crake, I boſte, *je me vante;* whan he is well whyttelled, he wyll crake goodly of his manhode," Palſgrave, 1530. "Cracke or to bragge foolyſhely, *exultare,*" Huloet's Dictionarie, 1572.

Page 154, line 29. *Gage.* A pledge or pawn. "He

that taketh a gage for a furetie of payment," Baret's Alvearie, 1580.

Page 156, line 2. *Holborne Hill.* Holborn Hill was always the road through which criminals, taken from Newgate to be hung at Tyburn, were conducted. There are innumerable references to this in our old writers.

Page 156, line 17. *Capichini.* So in the original. "Behold yet a new fwarm of locufts, the order of the Capuchins, and of thofe fhamelefs companions which attribute unto themfelves the name of the companie of Jefus, which are within thefe forty years crawled out of the bottomlefs pit," Sermon publifhed in 1587.

Page 157, line 3. *Lies.* "Lie" in the original.

Page 157, line 8. *The faire Widow of Watling ftreet.* This ballad has no connection with the play fo called. It was entered in the Stationers' Regifters by Richard Jones in Auguft, 1597, as "two ballads, being the firft and fecond partes of the Widowe of Watling Street." No copy printed by Jones is known to exift, the prefent, iffued by Pavier, being the earlieft edition yet difcovered. There is a later copy in the Roxburghe collection "printed for Fr. Cowles."

Page 157, line 12. *To the tune of Bragandary.* In Anthony Wood's collection of ballads at Oxford is one entitled, "A Defcription of a ftrange and mira-culous fifh caft upon the fands in the meads, in the hundred of Worwell in the county Palatine of Chefter or Chefheire; to the tune of Braganary."

Page 158, line 25. *For-why.* Becaufe.

Page 162, line 6. *Fauor.* Countenance. "He was a youth of fine favour and fhape," Bacon's Hiftory of Henry the Seventh.

Page 162, line 20. *A fort.* A company. "What care I for waking a forte of clubbifh loutes," Enter-lude of Jacob and Efau, 1568. "A fort of country fellows," Tale of a Tub. "Ye fhall be flain, all the fort of you," Pfalms.

Page 162, line 23. *Witneffes.* "Witneffe" in the original, and fo alfo in the Roxburghe copy.

Page 163, line 9. *And how it fell.* " And how it befell, they two mark'd it well," Roxburghe ed.

Page 163, line 19. *As the fcufe.* " An excufe," ed. Roxburghe. This is fimply a modernization. *Scufe* for *excufe* occurs in Shakefpeare.

Page 163, line 23. *You maflers.* " My mafters," Roxburghe ed.

Page 164, line 6. *Quod the widdow.* " Quoth the young man," Roxburghe ed.

Page 164, line 11. *He.* " She" in the original, corrected in the Roxburghe copy.

Page 164, line 18. *To fpeake fo.* The word *fo*, wanting in the original, is fupplied by conjecture. The Roxburghe copy reads *ill.*

Page 165, line 4. *Stamberd.* Stammered. " Stamber, or to ftutte, *titubo*," Huloet's Dictionarie, 1572. " Playes on thoughts, as girls with beads, when their maffe they ftamber," Armin's Neft of Ninnies, 1608.

Page 165, line 15. *To loofe, at the leaft.* Thefe two lines are thus given in the Roxburghe edition,—

> For forfeit even all the goods he poffeft,
> To loofe both his eares, and banifht fo reft.

Page 166, line 15. *Almightie God I pray.* This and the next article are printed on one broadfide page. The initial letters of the lines in the prefent poem read, when placed together,—" *Tempvs edax rervm*, Time bryngethe al thynges to an ende, qvod Chriftopher Wilfon."

Page 167, line 6. *Xpe.* Chrifte.

Page 169, line 15. *Reduce.* Bring back (Lat.) " The mornynge, forfakyng the golden bed of Titan, reduced the defyred day," Hiftory of Lucres and Eurialus, 1560.

Page 173, line 17. *Trone.* " Trone or feate royall, *thronus*; trone-fitter, or he that fytteth in Maieftye, *altitronus*," Huloet's Dictionarie, 1572.

Page 174, line 15. *Pepper is blacke.* There was a dance-tune fo called. " When his wench or frifkin was footing it aloft on the greene, with foote out and foote in, and as bufie as might be at Rogero, Bafilino, Turkelony, all the flowers of the broom, *Pepper is black*," &c., Nafh's Have With You to Saffron-Walden, 1596. The tune is found in the Dancing Mafter, 1650. See it in Chappell's Popular Mufic, p. 121.

Page 175, line 15. *Baggage.* Refufe. " Scum off the green baggage from it, and it will be a water," Lupton's Thoufand Notable Things.

Page 178, line 8. *An Epitaph.* The name of the Lord Mayor was Avenon, not Avenet, as here given. The death of this eftimable lady in July was, fingularly enough, followed by the widower's marriage on October 22nd in the fame year. " 1570, Oct. 22, was married Sir Alexander Avenon, Lord Mayor, and miftrefs Blunden, widow, by a licenfe, within his own houfe," Regifter of Allhallows, Bread Street, ap. Malcolm, ii. 12. The epitaph upon this lady is recorded in Stow's Survay of London, ed. 1618, p. 496. His firft wife, the lady commemorated in the ballad, was Elizabeth, daughter of John Slow of King's Norton. See a pedigree in MS. Harl. 1096.

Page 178, line 18. *Fine.* End. This word is now only ufed in the expreffion, *in fine.*

Page 179, line 10. *Schortchyng.* The *r* is probably inferted by miftake in this word, which feems to be merely a form of *fcotching.*

Page 179, line 14. *Could not want.* That is, could not do without. " I myffe, I wante a thyng that I feke for," Palfgrave, 1530. " *De cela je ne puis paffer,* I can by no meanes want it, I cannot bee without it," Cotgrave.

> And he is one that cannot wanted be,
> But ftill God keepe him farre enough from me.
> *Workes of Taylor, the Water-Poet,* 1630, ii. 134.

Page 181, line 18. *Keyfar.* An old term for an emperor, confidered by fome to be a corruption of Cæfar. " Es there any kyde knyghte, kayfere or other," Morte Arthure, MS. Lincoln. " Mighty kings and kefars into thraldom brought," Spenfer.

" To be kaiſer or kyng of the kyngdom of Juda,"
Piers Ploughman.

Page 182, line 10. *A famous dittie.* " The 12. of
Nouember the queenes maieſtie, returning after her
progreſſe, came to her manor of S. James, where the
citizens of London, to the number of 200, the graueſt
ſort in coats of veluet and chaines of gould, on horſe-
back, and 1000 of the companies on foote, hauing with
them 1000 men with torches ready there to giue light
on euery ſide, for that the night drew on, receiued and
welcomed her."—*Stow's Annales,* p. 700.

Page 182, line 14. *Wigmores Galliard.* This tune
is given in Chappell's Popular Muſic of the Olden
Time, p. 242, from William Ballet's MS. Lute-Book.
It is frequently alluded to by our early writers.
" This will make my maſter leap out of the bed for
joy, and dance Wigmore's Galliard in his ſhirt about
his chamber," Middleton's Five Gallants.

Page 186, line 13. *A meruaylous ſtraunge deformed
Swyne.* This and other marvels of the time are
thus alluded to in a letter from Biſhop Jewell to
H. Bullinger, written in Auguſt, 1562,—" Incredibilis
fuit hoc anno toto apud nos cœli atque aeris
intemperies. Nec ſol, nec luna, nec hyems, nec ver,
nec æſtas, nec autumnus, ſatisfecit officium ſuum. Ita
effatim et pene ſine intermiſſione pluvit, quaſi facere jam
aliud cœlum non queat. Ex hac contagione nata ſunt
monſtra : infantes fœdum in modum deformatis
corporibus, alii prorſus ſine capitibus, alii capitibus
alienis ; alii trunci ſine brachiis, ſine tibiis, ſine
cruribus ; alii oſſibus ſolis cohærentes, prorſus ſine
ullis carnibus, quales fere imagines mortis pingi ſolent.
Similia alia complura nata ſunt e porcis, ex equabus, e
vaccis, e gallinis. Meſſis hoc tempore apud nos
anguſtius quidem provenit, ita tamen ut non poſſimus
multum conqueri."

Page 187, line 8. *Tallents.* Talons. This form
of the word was very common, and the occaſion of
many a quibble. " Are you the kite, Beaufort?
Where's your talents ?" Firſt Part of the Contention,
1600.

Page 188, line 17. *White-faſte.* That is, white-faced.

Page 190, line 8. *Love deſerveth Love.* This, and the four pieces which follow, are not printed, but accompany the ballads in contemporary manuſcript.

Page 190, line 19. *He beares her gloue.* The glove of a lady, worn in a helmet as a favour, was conſidered a very honourable token, and much of the wearer's ſucceſs was ſuppoſed to be derived from the virtue of the lady. See Nares, in v.

Page 191, line 2. *Tell me, ſweete girle.* There is another MS. of this ballad in MS. Aſhmole 781, beginning, "Tell mee, ſweete *harte*," fol. 145.

Page 192, line 9. *Croſs-row.* The alphabet, ſaid to be ſo called from the croſs prefixed to it in the early horn-book.

> Thine eies taught me the alphabet of love,
> To kon my croſs-rowe ere I learn'd to ſpell.
> *Drayton's Idea.*

Page 194, line 8. *A monſtrous Child.* "Receved of John Sampſon, for his lycenſe for the pryntinge of a monſterus chylde which was bornne at Maydeſtone, iiij.*d*," Regiſters of the Stationers' Company, 1568-9. This entry is not inconſiſtent with the imprint, Sampſon frequently ſtyling himſelf Awdeley, which was, in faƈt, his *alias*. The original is embelliſhed with two hideous wood-engravings, ſhowing the front and back of the child.

Page 194, line 22. *Played the naughty packe.* "A whore, queane, punke, drab, flurt, ſtrumpet, harlot, cockatrice, *naughty pack*, light huſwife, common hackney," Cotgrave.

Page 195, line 3. *Libardes.* "Libarde, *leopardus*," Huloet's Diƈtionarie, 1572. "Hee is a moſt excellent turner, and wil turne you waſſel-bowles and poſſet-cuppes, carv'd with libberdes faces and lyons heades, with ſpoutes in their mouthes to let out the poſſet-ale moſt artificially," Sir Gyles Gooſecappe, 1606.

Page 197, line 16. *To the tune of Fortune.* This favourite old tune is given in Queen Elizabeth's Virginal Book, and in various other mufical compilations. See a long account of it in Chappell's Popular Mufic, p. 162.

Page 198, line 9. *Shute.* Robert Shute was a Juftice of the Queen's Bench from the year 1586 until his death in 1590. See Fofs's Judges of England, vol. v. p. 541.

Page 201, line 1. *A difcription of a monftrous Chylde.* "The iiij day of June ther was a chyld browth to the cowrte in a boxe, of a ftrange fegur, with a longe ftrynge commyng from the navyll,—browth from Chechefter," Machyn's Diary, 1562, ed. J. G. Nichols, p. 284. Francis Godliff had a licenfe, in 1562, for "the py&ure of a monftrus chylde which was bourne at Chechefter." See Herbert's Ames, p. 1325.

Page 202, line 11. *Our.* The original has *it*, and the alteration may be unneceffary. When it was made, it was not recolle&ed that *it* occafionally ftands for *yet.* "And *it*, God knowes what may befall," Marriage of Wit and Wifdome, 1579.

Page 202, line 15. *A lame.* A lamb. "Lam or loom, yonge fcheep, *agnus*," Prompt. Parv. "*Agnus*, a lame; *agna*, a new lame," Nominale MS.

Page 203, line 2. *The calues and pygges fo ftraunge.* "This yeare (1562) in England were manie monftruous births. In March, a mare brought foorth a foale with one bodie and two heads, and, as it were, a long taile growing out betweene the two heads. Alfo a fow farrowed a pig with foure legs like to the armes of a manchild with armes and fingers, &c. In Aprill, a fow farrowed a pig with two bodies, eight feet, and but one head. Manie calves and lambs were monftruous, fome with collars of fkin growing about their necks like to the double ruffes of fhirts and neckerchers then ufed. The foure and twentith of Maie, a manchild was borne at Chichefter in Suffex, the head, armes and legs whereof were like to an anatomie, the breaft and bellie monftruous big, from the navill as it

were a long ſtring hanging; about the necke a great
collar of fleſh and ſkin growing like the ruffe of a ſhirt
or neckercher comming up. above the eares, pleited
and folded, &c." Holinſhed's Chronicles, ed. 1587,
vol. 3, p. 1195. Cf. Stow's Annales, ed. 1615,
p. 647.

Page 206, line 7. *Diſgeſt.* A common form of
digeſt. "I have ſet you downe one or two examples
to try how ye can *diſgeſt* the maner of the deviſe,"
Puttenham.

Page 206, line 27. *Take.* "Toke" in the original.

Page 207, line 28. *Meſſe.* Entertainment. The
term is generally applied to a party of four. "And
you are the fourth, to make up the meſſe," Wapull's
Tyde Taryeth no Man, 1576. "The meſſe of
conſtables were ſhrunke to three," Taylor's Workes,
fol. Lond. 1630.

Page 208, line 2. *Lidgate, Wager, Barclay and
Bale.* There was a William Wager, the author of
the comedy called, The Longer thou Liueſt the more
Foole thou Art, n. d. Another comedy by him, entitled, 'Tis Good ſleeping in a Whole Skin, was amongſt
the number of plays deſtroyed by Warburton's ſervant,
and Winſtanley aſcribes the play of the Trial of
Chivalry to the ſame writer. The perſon alluded to
in the text may, however, be Lewis Wager, the
author of "A new Enterlude, never before this tyme
imprinted, entreating of the Life and Repentaunce
of Marie Magdalene," 1567. The other writers
alluded to in the text are too well known to require
a note.

Page 211, line 1. *Fynſbery fylde.* Open fields
outſide Moorgate. They were uſed for archery meet-
ings, and, at a period later than the probable date of
this ballad, they were the favourite reſort of the
citizens for walking. It would appear, from the
ſatirical remarks of the writer, that Finſbury Fields
were, at this early period, infeſted with thieves. There
is a long and intereſting account of the hiſtory of this
ſpot in Stow's Survey of London, ed. 1633, p. 475.

Page 211, line 3. *A nylde.* A needle. "Like pricking neelds, or points of fwords," Lucan's Pharfalia by Sir A. Gorges, 1614.

Page 211, line 20. *I pas not moche.* I care not much. "To paffe (care), *moror;* I pafs not for it, *quid mea;* I paffe not for his help, *ejus operam nihil moror*," Coles.

Page 214, line 9. *Cornelis Woltrop.* No printer of this name is mentioned by Ames or Herbert.

Page 214, line 11. *As pleafant a dittie.* This popular ballad is printed in Robert Jones's Firft Booke of Songs and Ayres, 1601, with the mufic. In Marfton's Dutch Courtezan, 1605, Francifchina, who is the Dutch courtezan, fings in broken Englifh,—

> Mine mettre fing non oder fong,
> But ftill complaine me doe her wrong,
> For me did but kiffe her,
> For me did but kis her,
> And fo let her go!

That its popularity extended to Holland is proved by the Dutch words to the tune printed in Starter's Boertigheden, 4to. Amft. 1634. It is alfo quoted more than once by Shirley.

Page 214, line 14. *I do.* "I did," ed. Jones, 1601; and in the next line, *was* for *is.*

Page 215, line 2. *As teehe.* This jocular term was ufed to fignify the noife made in laughing. "Ye tee-heeing pixy," Exmoor Scolding.

Page 215, line 10. *Was this any harme.* "This was no harme," ed. Jones, 1601. In the next line, that printed copy reads,—"But fhee, alas, is angrie ftill;" and, after this ftanza, there is only the following one, correfponding to the laft verfe in our copy,—

> Yet fure her lookes bewraies content,
> And cunningly her brales are meant;
> As louers vfe to play and fport,
> When time and leifure is too-too fhort.

Page 219, line 17. *In a breef.* We now fay, in brief. The form of the phrafe, as it occurs in the text, is very unufual.

Page 220, line 5. *At randon*. A common old form, and the more correct, (Fr.)

> Oh yes, it may, thou haſt no eyes to ſee,
> But hatefully *at randon* doeſt thou hit.
> *Venus and Adonis*, ed. 1593, fig. F. 4, v°.

Page 221, line 1. *Good Fellowes*. This and the next ballad are on one broadſide page. There appears to have been an earlier edition, for Griffith had a licenſe, in 1567-8, "for the pryntinge of a ballett intituled, Good felowes muſte go learne to daunce, &c."

Page 221, line 5. *A brall*. "*Branſle*, a brawle, or daunce, wherein many men and women, holding by the hands, ſometimes in a ring, and otherwhiles at length, moue all together," Cotgrave's Dictionarie, ed. 1611.

Page 221, line 6. *The tryxt*. That is, the neateſt. "Tricke, gallaunt and trymme, *cultus*, *eligans*; tricke, gallaunt or trimme wench," Huloet's Dictionarie, ed. 1572.

Page 221, line 16. *Slyper faſte*. Faſtened in a ſlippery manner. "Slypper, *gliſſant*," Palſgrave, 1530.

Page 221, line 23. *In bauderycke wyſe*. That is, in the manner of a belt. It appears to have been a technical term applied to bells. "Payd to goodman Godden, for makinge the buckelle to the baldrike, and truſſinge up the belle, ij.*s.* viij.*d*," MS. Accounts, Stratford-on-Avon, 1592.

Page 221, line 25. *A ſhurte after the Moryce guyſe.* Alluding, perhaps, to the ſtreamers worn by Morris-dancers on their ſleeves, which fluttered in the wind, ſpecimens of which are ſeen in the celebrated Tollett window.

Page 221, line 27. *A wyſſler*. Wiſlers were per-ſons who went before a leading perſonage in a pro-ceſſion to clear the way. They were furniſhed with wands, and formerly were an eſſential part of every proceſſion of any magnitude. "Paſſing the gate,

wifflers, fuch officers as were appointed by the mayor
to make me way through the throng of the people
which preft fo mightily upon me, with great labour I
got thorow that narrow preaze into the open market-
place," Kemp's Nine Daies Wonder, 1600.

Page 222, line 5. *It fkylles not.* It matters not.
" It fkills not greatly who impugns our doom," Second
Part of Henry the Sixth, act iii. fc. 1.

Page 222, line 10. *Or at Cotfolde.* The allufion
to dancing on the Cotfwold hills may here probably
refer to the fhepherds' feftivals in that locality alluded
to by Drayton. The Cotfwold games were not
inftituted until a later period.

Page 223, line 2. *Wyttie Watte.* Wat was an
old name for a hare, and hence ufed for a wily
perfon. The more ufual expreffion was Wily Wat.
Cuttinge, fwaggering. " Wherefore have I fuch a
companie of cutting knaves to waite upon me ? "
Hiftorie of Friar Bacon.

Page 223, line 6. *Hyleye.* That is, highly.

Page 223, line 15. *The byllbowes are not made it.*
That is, not made yet. The bilboes were a fpecies of
ftocks ufed for the punifhment of failors. " The pore
feloe was put into the *bilboes,* he being the firft upon
whom any punyfhment was fhewd," MS. Journal of a
Sea Voyage, temp. Eliz.

Page 224, line 1. *The braineles bleffing of the Bull.*
Lacy had a licenfe in 1570 " for pryntinge of a ballett
intituled the brayneles bleffynge of the bull."

" The 25. of May in the morning was found hanging
at the Bifhop of Londons palace gate, in Paules Churchyard, a Bull which lately had beene fent from Rome
containing diuerfe horrible treafons againft the Queenes
maiefty, for the which one Iohn Felton was fhortly
after apprehended, and committed to the Tower of
London."—*Stow's Annales,* ed. 1615, p. 666.

This ballad is equalled in fiercenefs, and is well
illuftrated, by an exceedingly curious contemporary
tract entitled, " A Difclofing of the great Bull, and
certain calues that he hath gotten, and fpecially the

Monſter Bull that roared at my Lord Byſhops gate,"
n. d.

Page 224, line 14. *Bleathes.* Bellows? This
word may poſſibly be connected with the provincial
term *blether*, to make a great noiſe. "The ſelfe ſame
monſter Bull is he that lately roared out at the Biſhops
Palace gate, in the greateſt citie of England, horrible
blaſphemies agaynſt God, and villanous diſhonors
agaynſt the nobleſt queene in the world, Elizabeth,
the lawfull Queene of England ; he ſtamped and
ſcraped on the ground, flong duſt of ſpitefull ſpeches
and vaine curſes about him, puſhed with his hornes
at her noble counſellors and true ſubiectes, and for pure
anger all to berayed the place where he ſtoode," A
Diſcloſing of the great Bull, n. d.

Page 225, line 10. *Clots.* "Clodde or to clotte
lande, *occo*," Huloet's Dictionarie, ed. 1572. "No
clot in clay," Legen. Cathol., p. 2.

Page 225, line 14. *Gage my head.* A common
jocular form of a wager. So Biron exclaims,—

> I'll lay my head to any good man's hat,
> Theſe oaths and laws will prove an idle ſcorn.

Page 225, line 16. *Syſe.* "Syſe, waxe candell,
bougee," Palſgrave, 1530. In the ſolemn form of
excommunication, the bell was tolled, the book of
offices for the purpoſe uſed, and three candles
extinguiſhed, with certain ceremonies. See further in
Nares, in v. *Bell, Book, and Candle.*

Page 225, line 30. *Hardyngs cow.* "Since he
(the bull) came ouer ſo lately diſguiſed, he hath light
upon certaine ranke kyen, who I thinke by their long
forbearing are become the luſtier, that is, treaſon,
ſuperſtition, rebellion and ſuch other, and with them
he hath ſo beſtirred him that, by the helpe of maiſter
Doctor Harding, Sanders, and other, ſome there, ſome
here, iolly cowkeepers and herdemen of Popiſh clergie,
which ſent and brought him ouer, and brake open for
him the ſeuerall hedges and fenſes of true religion,
obedience, allegeance, fayth, and honeſtie, he hath be-

gotten a marueilous number of calues in fewe yeares,"
A Difclofing of the great Bull, n. d.

Page 226, line 2. *Butcher Row*. There was
a place fo called near the Strand, " from the butchers'
fhambles on the fouth fide," Strype, iv. 118, ap.
Cunningham.

Page 226, line 5. *Walthams calues*. In allufion
to the old proverb about Waltham's calf, which ran
nine miles to fuck a bull. " Some running and
gadding calues, wifer than Walthams calfe that ranne
nine miles to fucke a bull, for thefe runne aboue nine
hundred miles," A Difclofing of the great Bull, n. d.

Page 226, line 26. *A twitch*. A touch. So we
have *twiche-box*, a touch-box, in the play of Damon and
Pithias.

Page 227, line 10. *What lyfe is beft*. This is in
manufcript and figned by the initials I. G. in a
monogram. It is fimilar in chara&ter and evidently by
the fame writer as the poem already printed at p. 192,
but it is on a feparate paper, and apparently another
effay.

Page 228, line 1. *The crie of the poore*. Henry,
the third Earl of Huntingdon, married Catherine,
daughter to John Dudley, Duke of Northumberland,
and dying at York in December, 1595, in the fixty-
firft year of his age, was buried at Afhby-de-la-Zouch
with great folemnity. The expenfes of his funeral
amounted to nearly £1400. The corpfe was embalmed
at an expenfe of £28 ; liveries to fixty poor men, £60;
in alms to the poor of divers parifhes, £26 13s. 4d. The
wood-engraving which illuftrates the original ballad was
probably intended for fome other fimilar fcene, and may
have been previoufly ufed for another purpofe. Certain
it is, at leaft, that the Earl died inteftate, adminiftration
to his effe&ts having been granted in June, 1596, to
his brother George, who fucceeded to the title. See
the Adminiftrations in the Court of Probate, London,
3 June, 1596. The Earl, whofe death is here la-
mented by one to whom he had probably been a kind
patron, was diftinguifhed by his piety and goodnefs.

There are letters of his to the Bifhop of Chefter, ftill
extant, in which he fpeaks of his ftrenuous endeavours
to obtain good preachers for the people.

Page 229, line 2. *Soufe.* " I fouce meate, I laye
it in fome tarte thynge, as they do brawne or fuche
lyke," Palfgrave, 1530.

Page 229, line 13. *Of Yorke he was Prefident made
by her grace.* " Henry Earle of Huntingdon was made
Prefident of the Councell in the North. This Prefi-
dentfhip, which is now full of honour, hath from a
poore beginning grown up in fhort time to this great-
neffe," Camden's Annales of 1574, ed. 1635, p. 179.

Page 232, line 1. *The Weftmerlande bull.* So, in
the ballad of the Rifing in the North,—

> Lord Weftmorland his ancyent raifde,
> The Dun Bull he rays'd on hye.

" The fupporters of the Nevilles, Earls of Weftmoreland, were Two Bulls Argent, ducally collar'd Gold,
armed Or, &c. In another ballad his banner is thus
defcribed,—

> Sett me up my faire dun bull,
> With gilden hornes, hee beares all foe hye."

Note by Bifhop Percy.

Page 232, line 13. *Sir John Swingbreeche.* The
Proteftants of this time were fond of giving jocular
names to priefts. So, in a contemporary manufcript,
we have the names of Sir John Lack-Latin, Sir John
Mumble-Matins, and Sir John Smell-fmoke.

Page 232, line 17. *Though yet they lye lurkyng.*
" What a fond and folifhe ende thefe rebells have
made of their traiterous rebellion. They alwais fled
afore us after we cam firft within xij. myles of them,
and we folowed after them as faft as we might, without reft ; neverthelefs you fee how they bee efcaped,
which they might eafily do in this waft and defolat
country," Sadler to Cecil, State Papers.

Page 232, line 21. *But her Maieftie of mercie is endued with ftore.* So, in a rare poem, An Aunfwere to
the Proclamation of the Rebels in the North, 1569, —

> If lenity may make men rife,
>   Or meekneffe gender yre,
> If cold may caufe the coles to burne,
>   Or water kindell fire;
> If adamant may thruft away
>   The iron or the fteel,
> Or fhining fun the naked man
>   May caufe the colde to feele;
> Then may our Queene Elizabeth
>   Be thought to be the caufe,
> Why thefe rebels do go about
>   The breaking of hir lawes.

Page 234, line 7. *Olde.* A common augmentative. "On Sunday at maffe, there was olde ringing of bels," Tarlton's Newes out of Purgatorie, 1590. "We fhall have old fwearing," Merchant of Venice, act iv. fc. 2.

Page 234, line 21. *Next.* Nigheft; neareft. "Home, home, the next way," Winter's Tale, act iii. fc. 3.

Page 235, line 10. *Vpfidowne.* Upfide-down.

> Thus es this worlde torned upfodowne,
> Tyll many mans dampnacyowne.—*Hampole.*

"Tornyng upfodowne, *fubvercion*," Palfgrave, 1530.

Page 236, line 1. *A dittie.* This ballad in honour of Thomas Howard, the fourth Duke of Norfolk, was probably written about the year 1561, when the Duke was ftill young, but yet had diftinguifhed himfelf as a fuccefsful commander, two facts which are mentioned by the writer.

Page 237, line 6. *Thy pettigree.* "Petygrewe, *genealogie*," Palfgrave, 1530. "Petigrewe, petigree, or geneologie, *ftemma*," Huloet's Dictionarie, 1572.

Page 238, line 1. *Gifippus and his Tite.* An allufion to the well-known ftory of Titus and Gifippus, related in the Decameron, x. 8. In 1562 appeared a poem by Edward Lewicke entitled, "The moft wonderfull and pleafaunt Hiftory of Titus and Gifippus, whereby is fully declared the figure of perfect frendfhyp."

Page 238, line 8. *Turnoys.* "*Torno*, a turne, a twirle," Florio's Worlde of Wordes, 1598.

Page 239, line 5. *As Noye.* "A Noye" in the original, *Noye* being of courfe an old form of *Noah*.

Page 239, line 10. *A newe Ballade.* The allufion to the uncertain fate of the rebels fixes the date of the compofition of this ballad to the earlier part of the year 1570.

Page 241, line 11. *leare.* That is, ire.

Page 242, line 14. *Aleuen.* Eleven. "Aleuen widdowes and nine maides," Merchant of Venice, ed. 1623.

Page 242, line 20. *Plagued.* "Plagud" in the original.

Page 242, line 24. *And.* "Ond" in the original.

Page 243, line 8. *The true Difcripcion.* There was a ballad at a later period on a fimilar odd birth, which was licenfed in 1586-7, as "a newe ballad intituled Stowp gallant, concerning a child borne with great ruffes." In the original copy of the broadfide here printed, each fide of the leaf is filled with exactly the fame matter. There are two hideous woodcuts reprefenting the front and back of the child.

Page 245, line 7. *Spurk.* That is, fpirt.

Page 251, line 1. *Mother Watkins ale.* This ballad is mentioned in a letter with the fignature of T. N. to his good friend A. M. [Anthony Munday], prefixed to the latter's tranflation of "Gerileon of England," 1592,—"I fhould hardly be perfwaded, that anie profeffor of fo excellent a fcience (as printing) would be fo impudent to print fuch ribauldrie as *Watkin's Ale*, the Carman's Whiftle, and fundrie fuch other." The tune is preferved in Queen Elizabeth's Virginal Book in the Fitzwilliam Mufeum, Cambridge. See the mufic in Chappell's Popular Mufic of the Olden Time, p. 137. It has been ftated in print that the mufic, without the words, has been difcovered among the papers of Dr. Pepufch. This ftatement, however, is a filly and mifchievous fabrication.

Page 251, line 4. *Needs.* "Nœds" in the original. *Sithd*, in the next line, fighed.

Page 251, line 7. *Behard.* Beheard, i. e., heard.

Page 251, line 20. *Muſkadine.* A kind of ſweet wine, frequently alluded to by our early writers. Cotgrave, in v. *Muſcadet,* ſpeaks of "a cyder which, made of a verie ſmall and ſweet apple, reſembles muſcadine in colour, taſt, and ſmell."

Page 254, line 1. *Bowne.* That is, ſwell. The term is ſtill in uſe in the provinces. Palſgrave has *bowlne,* 1530.

Page 254, line 29. *Cat will after kind.* A common old proverbial ſaying, immortalized by Touchſtone,—

> If the cat will after kind,
> So, be ſure, will Roſalind.

" Cat after kinde, ſaith the proverbe, ſwete milke wil lap," Enterlude of Jacob and Eſau, 1568.

" What is hatcht by a hen will ſcrape like a hen, and cat after kinde will either hunt or ſcratch, and you are an ill bird ſo fowly to defile your neſt."— *Florio's Second Frutes,* 1591.

" An evill bird layeth an ill egge, the cat will after her kinde, and ill tree cannot bring foorth good fruit, the young cub groweth craftie like the damme."—*Arraignment of Lewd, Idle, Froward, and Unconſtant Women,* 1617, p. 44.

Page 255, line 7. *The Crowe ſits vpon the wall.* Entered on the Regiſters of the Stationers' Company in 1591-2, " xviij. die Januarii, 1591, Henry Kirkham entred for his copie under Mr. Watkin's hande a ballad intituled the Crowe ſhee ſittes upon the wall; pleaſe one and pleaſe all." This ballad is of great intereſt, being the only copy known of the one referred to by Malvolio,—"But what of that, if it pleaſe the eye of one, it is with me as the very true ſonnet is,—Pleaſe one, and pleaſe all."

Page 255, line 19. *Their.* This word is here, and alſo in line 12 of the next page, miſprinted *her* in the original copy of the ballad. *Kircher,* kerchief.

Page 256, line 19. *Bulke.* A ſort of board or ledge outſide a houſe upon which articles were expoſed for fale. "*Balcone*, a bulke, a ftall of a fhop," Florio's Worlde of Wordes, 1598.

Page 258, line 3. *Be fhe flaunt.* That is, be fhe fine or fafhionable. Shakefpeare ufes the fubftantive *flaunts*, fineries, in the Winter's Tale, act iv. fc. 3. "The one a flaunting fellow, ufeth to wear a fcarlet cloak over a crimfon fattin fuit," Gee's Foot out of the Snare, 1624.

Page 260, line 2. *Lord Henry Wrifley.* The fecond Earl, born 30 November, 1546. See Efc. 4 Edw. VI., ii. 78. He was a devoted adherent of Mary Queen of Scots, an attachment which occafioned his being imprifoned in the Tower in 1572. Camden affigns the date of his death to the year 1583. See his Annales, ed. 1635, p. 255. This, however, is undoubtedly an error, for he died at the early age of thirty-five, on October 4th, 1581, as appears from the inquifition taken after his deceafe (Efc. 24 Eliz., i. 46). The date of the month, as given in the title of the ballad, is therefore erroneous. By his will, he directs his body to be interred in the Chapel of Tichfield Church, bequeathing fufficient money to his executors to renovate the faid chapel, which was to be divided by iron grating from the reft of the church. He alfo bequeaths the fum of £200 to the poor. Warton's account of Tichfield is interefting and curious,—"I vifited Tichfield-houfe, Aug. 19, 1786, and made the following obfervations on what is now remaining there. The abbey of Tichfield being granted to the firft Earl, Thomas, in 1538, he converted it into a family manfion, yet with many additions and alterations: we enter, to the fouth, through a fuperb tower, or Gothic portico, of ftone, having four large angular turrets. Of the monaftic chapel only two or three low arches remain, with the moor-ftone pilafters. The greater part of what may properly be called the houfe, forming a quadrangle, was pulled down about forty years ago. But the refectory, or hall of the abbey, ftill remains complete, with its original raftered roof of good workmanfhip: it is embattelled; and has three Gothic

windows on each fide, with an oreille or oriel window.
It is entered by a portico which feems to have been
added by the new proprietor at the diffolution; by
whom alfo the royal arms *painted*, with the portcullis
and H. R. (Henricus Rex), were undoubtedly placed
over the high-table.   At the other end is a mufic-
gallery.   Underneath is the cellar of the monaftery,
a well-wrought crypt of chalk-built arches; the ribs
and·interfe&ions in a good ftyle.   In a long cove-ceiled
room, with fmall parallel femicircular arches, are the
arms of King Charles the Firft on tapeftry; he was
prote&ed here in his flight from Hampton-court.
Two or three Gothic-fhaped windows, perhaps of the
abbey, in a part of the houfe now inhabited by a fteward
and other fervants.   In thefe and other windows fome
beautiful fhields of painted glafs are preferved; parti-
cularly one of Henry the Eighth impaling Lady Jane
Seymour, who were married at Maxwell, twenty miles
off, and who feem from thence to have paid a vifit at
this place to Lord Southampton.   Here are fome fine
old wreathed chimneys in brick.   In an angle of the
dilapidated buildings, to the weft of the grand entrance
or tower, is an elegant fhaft of a pilafter of polifhed
ftone, with the fpringing of an arch which muft have
taken a bold and lofty fweep : thefe are fymptoms of
fome confiderable room or office of the monaftery."

Page 263, line 4.   *Ne.*   That is, not.
Page 266, line 6.   *Moue.*   "More" in the original.
Page·267, line 19.   *The Bibles they did rent and teare.*
"Rent," that is, rend.   "While with his fingers he
his haire doth rent," Legend of Orpheus and Eury-
dice, 1597.

"Chriftians I can not terme you that haue defaced
the Communion of Chriftians, and in deftroying the
booke of Chryftes moft holy Teftament, renounced
your parts by his Teftament bequethed unto you."—
*Norton, To the Queene's Maiefties poore deceiued Subie&s
of the Northe Contrey*, 1569.

"The earles have beene at Durefme, with ther force
in armor, to perfwade the people to take ther partes,

and some of ther company have throwen downe the comunion table, and torne the Holy Bible in pieces, so as it appereth directly they intende to make religion ther grownd."—*Letter from the Council of the North to the Queen*, November 15th, 1569.

FINIS.

CHISWICK PRESS:—PRINTED BY WHITTINGHAM AND WILKINS,
TOOKS COURT, CHANCERY LANE.